and the
Soul

The Doctor *and the* Soul

From Psychotherapy to Logotherapy

by Viktor E. Frankl, M.D., Ph.D.

Translated from the German by Richard and Clara Winston

Third, expanded edition, with a new preface,
an updated bibliography and an
added chapter written in English by the author

Vintage Books
A Division of Random House
New York

Second Vintage Books Edition, October 1986

Library of Congress Cataloging in Publication Data

Frankl, Viktor Emil.
    The doctor and the soul.
    Translation of Ärztliche Seelsorge.
    Bibliography: p.
    1. Logotherapy. 2. Psychoanalysis.
3. Existentialism. I. Title. [DNLM:
1. Psychotherapy. wm 420 F831a]
RC489.L6F675413   1986   616.89'14   85-40681
ISBN 0-394-74317-2   (pbk.)

Manufactured in the United States of America
C 9 8 7 6 5 4 3 2 1

To the Memory of Tilly

Contents

Preface to the Third Edition

This new—revised and enlarged—edition of *The Doctor and the Soul* is the fifty-seventh that has been published in nine languages (in addition to the German original and the English edition, there are Spanish, Italian, Japanese, Finnish, Dutch, Danish, and Portuguese versions). Let me, therefore, say a few words regarding the story behind the book—a story that has often been obscured by the misconceptions of the mass media whose representatives never weary of proclaiming that Viktor Frankl came out of Auschwitz with a brand-new psychotherapeutic system he had developed in the concentration camp. The very opposite is true: I *entered* the camp with a full-length book manuscript (hidden under the lining of my overcoat) which was indeed an outline of the basic concepts of logotherapy. I had worked on it up to the last moment and hoped to save it during my period of imprisonment. I could not anticipate that it would be taken away from me immediately and, of course, destroyed. Under the circumstances, I felt like a father who was not spared watching his children murdered before his eyes. The book was, in fact, my spiritual child who I'd hoped would survive even if I did not do so myself.

To be sure, the concentration camps I went through did in fact serve as a testing ground that confirmed one of the main tenets of logotherapy, the theory that the basic meaning orientation of an individual—or, as I am used to calling it, the "will to meaning"—has actual survival value. Under comparable circumstances, those inmates who were oriented toward the future, whether it was a task to complete in the future, or a beloved person to be reunited with, were most likely to survive the horrors of the camps (I say "camps" because the same lessons can be learned from the psychiatric literature on American soldiers kept in Japanese, North-Korean, and North-Vietnamese Prisoner of War camps).

Certainly this is true in my own "case"—my strong desire to rewrite my lost manuscript surely contributed to the chances of my survival. When, a few months before my liberation from my last concentration camp, I was suffering from typhus and, as a physician, knew that a vascular collapse during sleep was the principal danger, I tried hard to keep myself awake by scribbling shorthand notes on the back of small scraps of paper that a comrade had stolen for me, together with the stub of a pencil. Later these notes proved to be very helpful when I started reconstructing the manuscript.

Naturally, the new version was enriched by my personal experiences in the four camps where I was imprisoned for nearly three years. Just look at the chapter dealing with "Psychology of the Concentration Camp." This chapter had really begun *before* I was given the scraps of paper and pencil: In another book of mine, *Man's Search for Meaning,* I describe its genesis:

Almost in tears from pain (I had terrible sores on my feet from wearing torn shoes), I limped a few kilometers with our long column of men from the camp to our work site. Very cold, bitter winds struck us. I kept thinking of the endless little problems of our miserable life. . . . I became disgusted with a state of affairs which compelled me, daily and hourly, to think of only such trivial things. I forced my thoughts to turn to another subject. Suddenly I saw myself standing on the platform of a well-lit, warm and pleasant lecture room. In front of me sat an attentive audience on comfortable upholstered seats. I was giving a lecture on the psychology of the concentration camp! All that oppressed me at that moment became objective, seen and described from a remote viewpoint of science. By this method I succeeded somehow in rising above the situation, above the sufferings of the moment, and I observed them as if they were already of the past.

By the end of the same year in which all this happened, the manuscript of this book—including the new chapter "On the Psychology of the Concentration Camp"—was completed. And I will never forget the sense of deep reward that I experienced when I went to my publisher in Vienna with the manuscript whose first version I had carried to Auschwitz. I felt like the man in the psalm:

he that goeth forth weeping, bearing precious seed, shall doubtless come again with rejoicing, bringing his sheaves with him.

The first printing of the book sold out within three days. But it still took nine years before an English translation was published, even though a commission appointed by the U.S. government to find European books that ought to be translated into English and issue them with its financial support selected *The Doctor and the Soul* as the only Austrian book published immediately after World War II worthy of this recommendation.

Frankly speaking, I do not like the title of the American edition. In English, terms such as "soul" and "spirit" are loaded with so many distinctly religious connotations (unlike the corresponding German words *Seele* and *Geist*) that, at least in the eyes of the scientifically minded psychiatrist and/or psychologist, the title more often than not works as a deterrent—suggesting inspirational reading based on a mixture of psychiatry and religion. The truth is that almost no one else has so sharply delineated the demarcation line between the two fields as I am often credited with having done. As an M.D., I have to see to it that logotherapy is applicable to each and every patient, including the irreligious, and that it is usable in the hands of each and every psychiatrist, including the agnostic. Nevertheless logotherapy sees in religion an important ingredient of human existence; religion, that is, in the widest possible sense of the word, namely, religion as an expression of "man's search for *ultimate* meaning." Yet logotherapy—by its very name a meaning-centered psychotherapy—views even man's orientation toward *ultimate* meaning as a *human* phenomenon rather than anything divine.[1]

The fact remains that logotherapy is a supplement rather than a substitute for psychotherapy. And it is not intended to serve

---

[1] When the American Psychiatric Association honored me by conferring upon me the 1985 Oskar Pfister Award, my "Oskar Pfister Lecture," was an attempt to elaborate and finally clarify the pertinent problematics. Audiocassettes (L 19-186-85) of the lecture are available from Audio Transcripts, 610 Madison Street, Alexandria, VA 22314.

as a substitute for religion. By its very nature, it is concerned with what we logotherapists call "noögenic" neuroses, in the first place. However, according to the result of empirical research, the percentage of noögenic neuroses does not exceed twenty percent.[2] In other words, we do not overrate our own findings, although we may sometimes leave the impression of being one-sided. But, taking this for granted, let me ask the question, if there isn't—along with a sound eclecticism—a sound one-sidedness? Wasn't it the great, and first, existentialist Sören Kierkegaard who admonished us by saying that he who has to offer a corrective should be one-sided—*boldly* one-sided—because such one-sidedness is not only his right but also his duty.

We must remain aware of the fact that as long as absolute truth is not accessible to us (and it will never be), relative truths have to function as mutual correctives. Approaching the one truth from various sides, sometimes even in opposite directions, we cannot attain it, but we may at least encircle it.

V. E. F.

Vienna
November 1985

---

[2] Thus far, ten statistical studies—based on the ten logotherapeutic tests now available—have been published on the subject.

Introduction*

A well-known psychiatrist once remarked that Western humanity has turned from the priest to the doctor. Another psychiatrist complains that nowadays too many patients come to the medical man with problems which should really be put to a priest.

Patients are constantly coming to us with problems such as, what is the meaning of their lives. It is not that we doctors attempt to carry philosophy over into medicine, although we are often accused of doing so; the patients themselves bring us philosophical problems. The individual doctor, confronted with such problems, may well be driven into a corner. But medicine, and psychiatry in particular, has thereby been compelled to cope with a new field.

The doctor can still make things easy for himself if he wishes. He can, for instance, take refuge in psychology by pretend-

---

* An abridgment and revision of a paper read, by special invitation, before the Royal Society of Medicine, Section of Psychiatry, in London, on June 15, 1954.

ing that the spiritual distress of a human being who is looking for a meaning to his existence is nothing but a pathological symptom.

Man lives in three dimensions: the somatic, the mental, and the spiritual. The spiritual dimension cannot be ignored, for it is what makes us human. To be concerned about the meaning of life is not necessarily a sign of disease or of neurosis. It may be; but then again, spiritual agony may have very little connection with a disease of the psyche. The proper diagnosis can be made only by someone who can see the spiritual side of man.

Psychoanalysis speaks of the *pleasure principle,* individual psychology of *status drive.* The pleasure principle might be termed the *will-to-pleasure;* the status drive is equivalent to the *will-to-power.* But where do we hear of that which most deeply inspires man; where is the innate desire to give as much meaning as possible to one's life, to actualize as many values as possible—what I should like to call the *will-to-meaning?*

This will-to-meaning is the most human phenomenon of all, since an animal certainly never worries about the meaning of its existence. Yet psychotherapy would turn this will-to-meaning into a human frailty, a neurotic complex. A therapist who ignores man's spiritual side, and is thus forced to ignore the will-to-meaning, is giving away one of his most valuable assets. For it is to this will that a psychotherapist should appeal. Again and again we have seen that an appeal to continue life, to survive the most unfavorable conditions, can be made only when such survival appears to have a meaning. That meaning must be specific and personal, a meaning which can be realized by this one person alone. For we must never forget that every man is unique in the universe.

I remember my dilemma in a concentration camp when faced with a man and a woman who were close to suicide; both had told me that they expected nothing more from life. I asked both my fellow prisoners whether the question was really what we expected from life. Was it not, rather, what life was expecting from us? I suggested that life was awaiting something from them. In fact the woman was being awaited by her child abroad, and the man had a series of books which he had begun to write and publish but had not yet finished.

A goal can be a goal of life, however, only if it has a meaning. Now, I am prepared for the argument that psychotherapy belongs to the realm of science and is not concerned with values; but I believe there is no such thing as psychotherapy unconcerned with values, only one that is blind to values. A psychotherapy which not only recognizes man's spirit, but actually starts from it may be termed *logotherapy*. In this connection, *logos* is intended to signify "the spiritual" and, beyond that, "the meaning."*

It is, of course, not the aim of logotherapy to take the place of existing psychotherapy, but only to complement it, thus forming a picture of man in his wholeness—which includes the spiritual dimension. Such a therapy directed toward the human spirit will be indicated in cases where a patient turns to a doctor for help in his spiritual distress, not because of actual disease. It is possible, of course, to speak of neuroses even in such cases—neuroses in the widest sense of the term. In this sense despair over the meaning of lif may be called an *existential neurosis* as opposed to *clinical neurosis*. Just as sexual frustration may—at least according to psychoanalysis—lead to neuroses, it is conceivable that frustration of the will-to-meaning may also lead to neurosis. I call this frustration *existential frustration*.

---

* It must be kept in mind, however, that within the frame of logotherapy "spiritual" does not have a religious connotation but refers to the specifically human dimension.

When existential frustration results in neurotic symptomatology, we are dealing with a new type of neurosis which we call noögenic neurosis. To substantiate this concept, Crumbaugh and Maholick, directors of an American research center, devised their PIL (Purpose In Life) Test and tried it on 1200 subjects. "The results," they said in a paper published in the *Journal of Clinical Psychology,* "consistently support Frankl's hypothesis that a new type of neurosis—which he terms noögenic neurosis—is present in the clinics alongside the conventional forms. There is evidence," these authors conclude, "that we are in truth dealing with a new syndrome." As to its frequency of occurrence, I refer to statistical research conducted by Werner in London, Langen and Volhard in Tübingen, Prill in Würzburg, and Niebauer in Vienna. They estimate that about 20 per cent of neuroses are noögenic in nature and origin.

In these cases logotherapy is a specific therapy; in other cases it is a non-specific therapy. That is to say, there are cases in which ordinary psychotherapy must be applied and yet a complete cure can be effected only by logotherapy. There are also cases in which it is not a therapy at all, but something else which we term *medical ministry.* As such, it is to be used not only by the neurologist or the psychiatrist, but by every doctor. The surgeon, for example, needs to minister to his patient when he is faced with an inoperable case, or when he must cripple the patient for life by amputating a limb. The orthopedic surgeon faces similar spiritual problems; so does the dermatologist who deals with disfigured cases, the general practitioner who must treat permanent invalids.

In all such cases there is much more at stake than psychotherapy has hitherto attempted to deal with. Psychotherapy has been concerned with men's capacity to work and to enjoy life; medical ministry is concerned with the capacity to suffer. We are faced here with an interesting problem: what are the possibilities for giving life meaning, for realizing values? There are several answers. Men can give meaning to their lives by realizing what I call *creative values*, by achieving tasks. But they can also give meaning to their lives by realizing *experiential values*, by experiencing the Good, the True, and the Beautiful, or by knowing one single human being in all his uniqueness. And to experience one human being as unique means to love him.

But even a man who finds himself in the greatest distress, in which neither activity nor creativity can bring values to life, nor experience give meaning to it—even such a man can still give his life a meaning by the way he faces his fate, his distress. By taking his unavoidable suffering upon himself he may yet realize values.

Thus, life has a meaning to the last breath. For the possibility of realizing values by the very attitude with which we face our unchangeable suffering—this possibility exists to the very last moment. I call such values *attitudinal values*. The right kind of suffering—facing your fate without flinching—is the highest achievement that has been granted to man.

I should like to illustrate my point by the following case. A nurse in my department suffered from a tumor which proved to be inoperable. In her despair the nurse asked me to visit her. Our conversation revealed that the cause of her despair was not so much her illness in itself as her incapacity to work. She had loved her profession above all else, and now she could no longer follow it. What should I say? Her situation was really hopeless; nevertheless, I tried to explain to her that to work eight or ten hours per day is no great thing—many people can do that. But to be as eager to work as she was, and so incapable of work, and yet not to despair —that would be an achievement few could attain. And then I asked her: "Are you not being unfair to all those thousands of sick people to whom you have dedicated your life; are you not being unfair to act now as if the life of an incurable invalid were without meaning? If you behave as if the meaning of our life consisted in being able to work so many hours a day, you take away from all sick people the right to live and the justification for their existence."

It goes without saying that the realization of attitudinal values, the achievement of meaning through suffering, can take place only when the suffering is unavoidable and inescapable.

It may well be asked whether such an approach still belongs to the realm of medicine. Certainly medical science is necessary if we wish to save a life by amputating a leg. But how can medical science prevent the patient from committing suicide either before or after the amputation? The great psychiatrist Dubois once said so rightly: "Of course one can manage without all that and still be a doctor, but in that case one should realize that the only thing that makes us different from a veterinarian is the clientele."

And how easy it sometimes is for a doctor to provide consolation. A colleague, an aged general practitioner, turned to me because he could not come to terms with the loss of his wife, who had died two years before. His marriage had been very happy, and he was now extremely depressed. I asked him quite simply: "Tell me what would have happened if you had died first and your wife had survived you?" "That would have been terrible," he said. "How my wife would have suffered!" "Well, you see," I answered, "your wife has been spared that, and it was you who spared her, though of course you must now pay by surviving and mourning her." In that very moment his mourning had been given a meaning—the meaning of a sacrifice.

I have said that *man should not ask what he may expect from life, but should rather understand that life expects something from him.* It may also be put this way: in the last resort, man should not ask "What is the meaning of my life?" but should realize that he himself is being questioned. Life is putting its problems to him, and it is up to him to respond to these questions by being responsible; he can only answer to life by answering *for his life.*

Life is a task. The religious man differs from the apparently irreligious man only by experiencing his existence not simply as a task, but as a mission. This means that he is also aware of the taskmaster, the source of his mission. For thousands of years that source has been called God.

Medical ministry does not aspire to be a substitute for the proper cure of souls which is practiced by the minister or priest. What is the relation between psychotherapy and religion? In my view, the answer is simple: the goal of psychotherapy is to heal the soul, to make it healthy; the aim of religion is something essentially different—to save the soul. But the side-effect of religion is an eminently psychohygienic one. Religion provides man with a spiritual anchor, with a feeling of security such as he can find nowhere else. But, to our surprise, psychotherapy can produce an analogous, unintended side-effect. For although the psychotherapist is not concerned with helping his patient to achieve a capacity for faith, in certain felicitous cases the patient regains his capacity for faith.

Such a result can never be the aim of psychotherapy from the start, and a doctor will always have to beware of forcing his philosophy upon the patient. There must be no transference (or, rather, countertransference) of a personal philosophy, of a personal concept of values, to the patient. The logotherapist must be careful to see that the patient does not shift his responsibilities onto the doctor. Logotherapy is ultimately education toward responsibility; the patient must push forward independently toward the concrete meaning of his own existence.

Anxiety is usually called the disease of our time; we speak of the Age of Anxiety. But previous centuries probably had much more reason for anxiety than ours. It is also doubtful whether the relative incidence of anxiety neurosis has increased. The collective neurosis, insofar as this term has validity, is characterized by four symptoms, which I shall briefly describe.

First, there is the planless, day-to-day attitude toward life. Contemporary man is used to living from one day to the next. He learned to do so in the last world war, and since then this attitude has not been modified. People lived in this way because they were waiting for the end of the war; meanwhile, further planning made no sense. Today the average man says: "Why should I act, why should I plan? Sooner or later the atom bomb will come and wipe out everything." And thus he slides into the attitude of: *"Après moi, la bombe atomique!"* This anticipation of atomic warfare is as dangerous as any other anticipatory anxiety, since, like all fear, it tends to make its fears come true.

The second symptom is the fatalist attitude toward life. This, again, is a product of the last world war. Man was pushed. He let himself drift. The day-to-day man considers planned action unnecessary; the fatalist considers it impossible. He feels himself to be the helpless result of outer circumstances or inner conditions.

The third symptom is collective thinking. Man would like to submerge himself in the masses. Actually, he is only drowned in the masses; he abandons himself as a free and responsible being.

The fourth symptom is fanaticism. While the collectivist

ignores his own personality, the fanatic ignores that of the other man, the man who thinks differently. Only his own opinion is valid. In reality, his opinions are those of the group and he does not really have them; his opinions have him.

A moral conflict, a conflict of conscience, can lead to an existential neurosis. And as long as a man is capable of conflict of conscience, he will be immune to fanaticism and to collective neurosis in general; conversely, a man who suffers from collective neurosis will overcome it if he is enabled once more to hear the voice of conscience and to suffer from it. Existential neurosis will then cure the collective neurosis! Some years ago I spoke on this subject at a congress. Colleagues who lived under a totalitarian regime came to me after the lecture and said: "We know this phenomenon very well; we call it 'functionary's disease.' A certain number of Party functionaries are ultimately driven into a nervous breakdown by the increasing burden on their conscience, and they are then cured of their political fanaticism."

Fanaticism crystallizes in the form of slogans which produce a chain reaction. This psychological chain reaction is even more dangerous than the physical one which takes place in the atom bomb. For the latter could never be employed were it not preceded by the psychological chain reactions of slogans.

We may thus speak of the pathological spirit of our time as a mental epidemic. And we might add that somatic epidemics are typical consequences of war, while mental epidemics are potential originators of war. In tests carried out by my associates with non-neurotic patients, only one was completely free of all the four symptoms of collective neurosis, whereas fifty per cent of them displayed at least three of the four symptoms.

Ultimately, all these four symptoms can be traced back to man's fear of responsibility and his escape from freedom. Yet responsibility and freedom comprise the spiritual domain of man. Contemporary man, however, has become weary of all that is spiritual, and this weariness is perhaps the essence of that nihilism which has so often been mentioned and so rarely been defined. It will have to be counteracted by collective psychotherapy. It is true that Freud once declared in conversation: "Humanity has always known that it possesses a spirit; it was my task to show that it has instincts as well." But I myself feel that humanity has demonstrated *ad nauseam* in recent years that it has instincts, drives. Today it appears more important to remind man that he has a spirit, that he is a spiritual being. Psychotherapy should remember this, particularly when dealing with collective neurosis.

Every school of psychotherapy has a concept of man, although this concept is not always held consciously. It is up to us to make it conscious. We who have learned so much from Freud need scarcely point out how dangerous the unconscious can become. We must make explicit the implicit concept of man in psychotherapy. For a psychotherapist's concept of man, under certain circumstances, can reinforce the patient's neurosis, can be wholly nihilistic.

Three factors characterize human existence as such: man's spirituality, his freedom, his responsibility.

The spirituality of man is a thing-in-itself. It cannot be explained by something not spiritual; it is irreducible. It may be conditioned by something without being caused by it. Normal bodily functions affect the unfolding of the spiritual life, but they do not cause it or produce it. To illustrate: some years ago a witty gentleman inserted the following advertisement in *The Times:* "Unemployed. Brilliant mind offers its services completely free; the survival of the body must be provided for by adequate salary."

Freedom means freedom in the face of three things: (1) the instincts; (2) inherited disposition; and (3) environment. Certainly man has instincts, but these instincts do not have him. We have nothing against instincts, nor against a man's accepting them. But we hold that such acceptance must also presuppose the possibility of rejection. In other words, there must have been freedom of decision. We are concerned above all with man's freedom to accept or reject his instincts.

As for inheritance, research on heredity has shown how high is the degree of human freedom in the face of predisposition. For example, twins may build different lives on the basis of identical predispositions. Of a pair of identical twins, one became a cunning criminal, while his brother became an equally cunning criminologist. Both were born with cunning, but this trait in itself implies no values, neither vice nor virtue.

As for environment, we know that it does not make man, but that everything depends on what man makes of it, on his attitude toward it. Freud once said: "Try and subject a number of very strongly differentiated human beings to the same amount of starvation. With the increase of the imperative need for food, all individual differences will be blotted out, and, in their place, we shall see the uniform expression of the one unsatisfied instinct." But in the concentration camps we witnessed the contrary; we saw how, faced with the identical situation, one man degenerated while another attained virtual saintliness. Robert J. Lifton, writing in the *American Journal of Psychiatry* about American soldiers in North Korean prisoner-of-war camps, comments: "There were examples among them both of altruistic behavior as well as the most primitive forms of struggle for survival."

Thus, man is by no means merely a product of heredity and environment. There is a third element: decision. Man ultimately decides for himself! And, in the end, education must be education toward the ability to decide.

Psychotherapy also must appeal to the capacity for decision, to freedom of attitude. Thus, it must appeal not only to what we have called man's will-to-meaning, but also to the freedom of man's will.

This will cannot simply be derived from the instincts. And so we come to the third factor—after the spirituality and the freedom of man: his responsibility. To whom is man responsible? First of all, to his conscience. But conscience is again an irreducible thing-in-itself. One day I was sitting in a restaurant with an internationally famous psychoanalyst. He had just delivered a lecture, which we were discussing. He denied that such a thing as conscience existed at all, and asked me to tell him what this conscience was. I answered briefly: "Conscience is what has made you give us such a splendid lecture tonight." Whereupon he lost his temper and screamed at me: "That isn't true—I did not deliver this lecture for my conscience, but to please my narcissism!"

But today modern psychoanalysts have come to the conclusion that "true morality cannot be based on the concept of a superego" (F. A. Weiss).

Freud once said: "Man is not only often much more immoral than he believes, but also often much more moral than he thinks." I should like to add that he is often much more religious than he suspects. These days people see more in man's morality than an introjected father-image, and more in his religion than a projected father-image. To consider religion a general obsessional neurosis of humanity is already old-fashioned.

We must not make the alternative mistake of looking upon religion as something emerging from the realm of the id, thus tracing it back again to instinctual drives. Even the followers of Jung have not avoided this error. They reduce religion to the collective unconscious or to archetypes. I was once asked after a lecture whether I did not admit that there were such things as religious archetypes. Was it not remarkable that all primitive peoples ultimately reached an identical concept of God—which would seem to point to a God-archetype? I asked my questioner whether there was such a thing as a Four-archetype. He did not understand immediately, and so I said: "Look here, all people discover independently that two and two make four. Perhaps we do not need an archetype for an explanation; perhaps two and two really do make four. And perhaps we do not need a divine archetype to explain human religion either. Perhaps God really does exist!"

If we derive the ego from the id and the super-ego from the id plus the ego, what we achieve is not a correct picture of man, but a caricature of man. The results sound like a tall story by Baron Munchhausen, with the ego pulling itself out of the bog of the id by its own super-ego bootstraps.

If we present a man with a concept of man which is not true, we may well corrupt him. When we present man as an automaton of reflexes, as a mind-machine, as a bundle of instincts, as a pawn of drives and reactions, as a mere product of instinct, heredity, and environment, we feed the nihilism to which modern man is, in any case, prone.

I became acquainted with the last stage of that corruption in my second concentration camp, Auschwitz. The gas chambers of Auschwitz were the ultimate consequence of the theory that man is nothing but the product of heredity and environment—or, as the Nazi liked to say, of "Blood and Soil." I am absolutely convinced that the gas chambers of Auschwitz, Treblinka, and Maidanek were ultimately prepared not in some Ministry or other in Berlin, but rather at the desks and in the lecture halls of nihilistic scientists and philosophers.

I

From
Psychotherapy
to
Logotherapy

I   From Psychotherapy to Logotherapy

We cannot discuss psychotherapy without taking for our starting-points psychoanalysis and individual psychology, the two great psychotherapeutic systems created by Freud and Adler respectively. The history of psychotherapy cannot be dealt with apart from their work, which is in the best sense of the word "historic"— but historic also in the sense that Freud and Adler already belong to history, later developments having left them far behind. So, though it may often be necessary to go beyond the premises of psychoanalysis or individual psychology, we find ourselves again and again drawn back to the doctrines of these two schools. Stekel put the matter very aptly when he remarked, clarifying his position on Freud, that a dwarf standing upon the shoulders of a giant can see farther than the giant himself.*

Since our purpose is to transcend the limits of all previous

---

* After all, though a person may admire Hippocrates or Paracelsus, he is not required to follow their prescriptions or methods of surgery.

psychotherapy, we must first make it clear that such limits exist, determine what they are, and establish the need for going further.

Freud compares the essential achievement of psychoanalysis with the draining of the Zuider Zee. Just as the engineers endeavor to win fertile soil where once the waters rolled, so psychoanalysis strives to conquer new territory for the "ego" from the dark domain of the "id." That is to say, consciousness shall replace the unconscious; material previously thrust into the unconscious shall be redeemed by the overcoming of "repressions." Psychoanalysis is therefore concerned with undoing the consequences of repression—reversing, that is, the processes of making psychic material unconscious. The concept of repression is of central importance within the psychoanalytic scheme. The chief task of analytic therapy is to wrest repressed experiences from the unconscious, to reinstate them in consciousness and so magnify the power of the ego.

Individual psychology sees the matter somewhat differently. The key concept of this scheme is that of "arrangement"—which plays a part analogous to that assigned by Freud to repression. Arrangement is the process by which the neurotic seeks to clear himself of guilt. Instead of relegating something to the unconscious, he seeks to relieve himself of responsibility. The symptom, as it were, assumes the responsibility which the patient therefore need no longer bear. Individual psychology thus holds that symptoms represent an effort by the patient to justify himself to society or (an alibi) to clear himself in his own eyes. The aim of individual-psychological therapy is to make the neurotic person accept responsibility for his symptoms, include them within his personal sphere of responsibility, and thus strengthen the ego.

Psychoanalysis, then, regards neurosis as a limitation upon the ego qua consciousness; individual psychology regards it as a limitation upon the ego qua sense of responsibility. Both theories may be criticized for the narrowness of their field of vision—the one putting all emphasis on consciousness, the other on responsibleness. When we look upon human life without the blinkers of preconception, we must conclude that both consciousness and responsibleness play the basic roles in the drama of existence. One might in fact state it as a basic theorem that *being human means being conscious and being responsible*. Both psychoanalysis and individual psychology err in that each sees only one aspect of human existence—whereas the two aspects must be taken jointly to yield a true picture of man. These two schools would appear to be diametrically opposed to each other; but closer examination reveals that they are complementary, that there is a link of logical necessity between them.*

---

* In their one-sidedness psychoanalysis and individual psychology both focus attention on one side of man. But the intimate bond between consciousness and responsibility is recognized by language. French and English, for example, employ words with a common root to express "consciousness" and "conscience"—the latter being a concept closely akin to that of "responsibility." The closeness of the words suggests the closeness in actuality.

Consciousness and responsibility join to form an entity; together they make up the wholeness of the human being. This can be explained ontologically. To start with, we must point out that "to be" always means in essence "to be different." We only discover certain aspects of reality by extracting them, as it were, and isolating them from the massive flow of what is. Only when one aspect of reality is counterposed to something different does either come into being. Anything real, that is, requires as a precondition the reality of something other than itself. "To be" equals "to be different"—that is, "to be different from something"; relationship is supremely important. Actually, only the relationship "exists." We might therefore state it this way: all that is has its being only with reference to something else.

Differences in states of being, however, can be simultaneous, or can follow one another. Consciousness assumes simultaneity of

*1 From Psychotherapy   5
    to Logotherapy*

However, psychoanalysis and individual psychology are opposed not only in their picture of the general nature of man. They are opposed also in the picture each draws of the nature of psychic illness. And here, too, the opposites complement one another. Pan-sexualism recognizes only the sexual content of psychic strivings. To be sure, it interprets sexuality in the broadest sense, as libido. But this concept is carried so far, is in fact so strained, that libido finally comes to be equated with psychic energy in general. Such generalization ends in meaninglessness. We find a similar tendency in the history of philosophical thought: in solipsism. Here, too, a single concept, that of the psychic, is stretched so far that ultimately it includes everything. The concept, however, has been stripped of meaning because the boundary between psychic and physical has been wiped out. To say that everything is illusion, appearance, idea, is meaningless—for with the elimination of truth, reality, and object, the antithetical concepts also disappear.

When pan-sexualism arbitrarily restricts psychic reality to sexuality, it deliberately limits its insight into the nature of psychic strivings. Individual psychology commits its own kind of error in that its psychopathological scheme is narrower. For it does not admit the genuineness of psychic strivings, but instead insists on

---

subject and object—"being different" in the spatial dimension, that is. Responsibility, on the other hand, presupposes a succession of different states, separation of a future from a present state of being. This is "being different" in the time dimension, a "becoming different." The will, as the bearer of responsibility, strives to convert the one state into the other. The identity of the twin notions "consciousness" and "responsibility" grows out of this first sub-division of being (since "to be" equals "to be different") into the two dimensions of simultaneity and succession. Of the two possible views of man which are based on this ontological situation, psycho-analysis and individual psychology each avail themselves of only one.

viewing them (where they take the form of neurotic symptoms) as mere means to an end—either as "arrangement" or as excuse. Individual psychology, unlike pan-sexualism, recognizes psychic factors other than sexuality, such as the will to power, status drive, or "social interest." But in spite of its greater scope, it does an injustice to the richness and variety of psychic reality by its refusal to admit that psychic phenomena and neurotic manifestations have a meaning in themselves. Psychoanalysis does not fall into this error. Although postulating the existence of a "secondary disease motif" (sometimes called the "neurotic gains"), psychoanalysis never forgets that the neurotic symptoms are primary, that they are the genuine and direct expression of psychic strivings before they are used or "misused" as means to a neurotic end.

Once more, then, we see psychoanalysis and individual psychology, each in its one-sided position, necessarily complementing one another. Each is right about the side of reality that it sees; but only both sides together can produce a rounded picture of the psychic life. To our mind the situation is this: pan-sexualism to the contrary, psychic strivings can revolve about other than sexual matters; individual psychology to the contrary, neurotic symptoms are not only means to an end, but are also (primarily, at least) a direct expression of the most variegated psychic strivings.

This becomes especially important where culture and art are examined in terms of psychopathology. For example, psychoanalysts have repeatedly asserted that the basis for artistic creation or religious experience is repressed sexuality. This is not so. But equally wrong is the claim of a good many individual psychologists that all such experience or creation represents nothing genuine, nothing original, is rather only a means to an end—whether that end be escape from society, evasion of life, or similar negative tendencies. Such interpretations as these only distort the image of man; the subject of study for these psychologists is not man, but a caricature of man. Scheler has quite rightly pointed out, in an irreverent footnote, that individual psychology fits only a particular type of human being: the careerist. Perhaps we need not go so far in our criticism; we believe nevertheless that individual psychology, finding status drives everywhere and under all conditions, has over-looked the fact that something like a striving for moral status exists; that a great many men can be activated by a more fundamental ambition than plain ordinary ambition; that there is a striving which, so to say, will not be content with earthly honors, but which longs for something far, far more, for an immortalizing of the self in some durable form.

The expression depth-psychology is much in favor today. But we must ask ourselves whether it is not high time to examine human existence, even within psychotherapy, in all its many-layered extent; to look not only for its depths, but for its heights as well. To do so we would have deliberately to reach out not only beyond the sphere of the physical, but also beyond that of the psychic, and take in the realm of what we shall in this book call the spiritual aspects of man. By that term—*Geist* in German—we mean the core or nucleus of the personality.

Hitherto psychotherapy has given too little attention to the spiritual reality of man. For the aim of the psychotherapist should be to bring out the ultimate possibilities of the patient, to realize his latent values—remembering the aphorism of Goethe, which might well be adopted as the maxim of psychotherapy: "If we take people as they are, we make them worse. If we treat them as if they were what they ought to be, we help them to become what they are capable of becoming."

Aside from their views of man and their interpretations of psychic disease, it is evident that psychoanalysis and individual psychology also differ in the aims they set themselves. Here, however, we are not dealing with pure antitheses, but with successive stages—and we believe that the final stage has not yet been reached.

Let us consider the philosophical goals which, consciously or unconsciously, rarely admitted but implicitly present, underlie psychoanalysis. What, ultimately, does psychoanalysis hope to accomplish in its treatment of neurotics? Its alleged goal is to help bring about a compromise between the demands of the unconscious on the one hand and the requirements of reality on the other. It attempts to adjust the individual with his private drives to the outer world, to reconcile him to reality. This "reality principle" frequently decrees that certain drives be totally renounced.

In contrast, the goal of individual psychology goes deeper. Beyond mere adjustment, it demands of the patient a courageous reshaping of reality; to the id's "must" it opposes the ego's "will." But we must now ask ourselves whether these goals are all there are; whether a break-through into another dimension may not be permissible, or even requisite in order to yield a true picture of the total psycho-physico-spiritual entity which is man. Only then shall we be in a position to help the suffering human person entrusted to us, and trusting us, to achieve his own wholeness—and health.

As we see it, this final requirement is fulfillment. Between the reshaping of the outer life and the inner fulfillment of the individual, there is a fundamental difference. If to shape life is a geometrical magnitude, then to fulfill life is a vector magnitude. It has direction, it is directed toward the value-potentialities of each individual human person. And the realization of those value-potentialities is what life is all about.

To make these distinctions clear by an example, let us imagine a young person who has grown up in poverty-stricken circumstances. Instead of being content with the narrowness and deprivations of these circumstances, and adjusting to them, let us assume that he imposes his personal will upon the outer world and so "reshapes" his life that he can, say, further his education and enter a profession. Assume further that he follows his aptitudes and inclinations, studies medicine and becomes a physician. A tempting offer is made to him of a lucrative post which will also provide him with a fashionable private practice. Here is the way to secure mastery over his life and win an outwardly rich existence. But suppose also that this young man's talent lies in a special branch of his profession, which branch he will have to give up if he takes the good post that is being offered to him. Such a choice would ensure him a successful life, but would deny him inner fulfillment. He might be prosperous and indeed enviable—might own a substantial home, drive an expensive car, and afford all kinds of luxuries. But when he devoted some thought to the question, this person would know that somehow his life had gone awry. Encountering another man who, renouncing wealth and all its pleasures, had remained faithful to his true vocation, our young man would have to confess to himself, in Hebbel's words: "The man I am greets mournfully the man I might have been."

On the other hand we can also very well imagine our young man passing up a splendid worldly career, doing without the things it would offer, and dedicating himself to his chosen field—and in so doing finding the meaning of his life. His inner fulfillment would come from accomplishing precisely what he, and perhaps only he, could do best. From this point of view a humble country doctor who is firmly rooted in his locality may seem a greater man than many of his successful metropolitan colleagues. Similarly, the theoretician in a remote outpost of science may nevertheless be doing more heroic service than many of the more active figures who stand "in the midst of life," allegedly carrying on the battle against death. For on the battle fronts where science carries on the struggle against the unknown, the theoretician may be performing a unique and irreplaceable service, small though his sector of the front may be. And in the uniqueness of this personal achievement no one can supplant him. He has found his place and filled it—and thereby he has fulfilled himself.

By pure deduction, then, we may say that we have discovered a blank area in the science of psychotherapy, an empty space which awaits filling. For we have shown that psychotherapy as it has hitherto been conceived needs to be supplemented by a procedure which operates, as it were, beyond the fields of the Œdipus complex and the inferiority complex. Or, to put the matter more generally: beyond all affect-dynamics. What is still missing is a form of psychotherapy which gets underneath affect-dynamics, which sees beneath the psychic malaise of the neurotic his spiritual struggles. What we are concerned with is *a psychotherapy in spiritual terms.*

Psychotherapy was born when the attempt was first made to look behind physical symptoms for their psychic causes—to discover, in other words, their psychogenesis. Now, however, a further step must be taken: we must look beyond psychogenesis, past the affect-dynamics of neurosis, in order to see the distress of the human spirit—and to try to alleviate this distress. We are well aware that in so doing the doctor assumes a position fraught with intricate problems, for it then becomes necessary for the doctor to take a stand on the question of values. The moment the doctor commits himself to such a "psychotherapy in spiritual terms" his own philosophy necessarily comes to the fore—whereas previously his outlook remained hidden behind his role as doctor. Previously the only obvious philosophical tenet that entered into the doctor's work was the tacit affirmation of the value of health. This tenet as the ultimate guiding principle of medicine is, however, always taken as self-evident. The doctor need only refer to the mandate given him by society. He has been installed in his office, after all, precisely for the preservation of health.

The type of psychotherapy we have postulated—psychotherapy extended to include in psychic treatment the spiritual element—contains hidden difficulties and dangers. We shall have occasion to deal with these later, in particular with the danger of the doctor's imposing his personal philosophy upon the patient. It is a crucial question, and one on which the entire structure of our new psychotherapy hinges. As long as the question remains open, we cannot carry our new psychotherapy beyond the realm of theory. To prove that it is necessary is not enough; we must also prove that it is practicable. We must show good reason for the introduction of the spiritual (and not only the psychic) element into medical treatment. And if our criticism of "orthodox" psychotherapy is to be completely scrupulous, we must show the place that value-judgments would occupy within psychotherapy. But this part of our task is reserved for the final chapter of this book. We have already pointed to the presence of a value-judgment in all medical treatment—namely, the moral tenet implicit in the affirmation of health. Let us now turn to the why and how of such value-judgments and deal not with the need for them, but with the down-to-earth, everyday occasions when we feel their need with special force.

Practice in fact reinforces our previous deductive conclusion that there is a real lack of psychotherapy in spiritual terms. The psychotherapist is daily and hourly, in the regular course of his practice, and in consultation with each individual patient, confronted with philosophical questions. In the face of these, all the equipment with which he has been provided by "pure" psychotherapy proves to be inadequate.

Every psychotherapist knows how often in the course of his psychiatric work the question of the meaning of life comes up. It helps us little to know that the patient's feeling of futility and philosophical despair has developed psychologically in this or that fashion. No matter that we may be able to disclose the inferiority feelings which were the psychic origin of his spiritual distress; no matter that we may "trace" the patient's pessimistic view of life back to certain complexes, and even convince him that his pessimism springs from these and these alone—in reality we are only talking around the patient's problem. We do not strike to the heart of it, any more than does a doctor who, completely eschewing any psychotherapeutic approach, contents himself with physical treatment or prescription of tranquilizers.* How wise, by contrast, is the classic dictum: physic the mind, and the body will need no physics.

Our point is that all such medical approaches, in the face of the patient's philosophical conflicts, amount to talking at cross-purposes with the patient under the pretense of being scientific.

What is needed here is to meet the patient squarely. We must not dodge the discussion, but enter into it sincerely. We must attack these questions on their own terms, at face value. Our patient has a right to demand that the ideas he advances be treated on the philosophical level. In dealing with his arguments we must honestly enter into these problems and renounce the temptation to go outside them, to argue from premises drawn from biology or perhaps sociology. A philosophical question cannot be dealt with by turning the discussion toward the pathological roots from which the question stemmed, or by hinting at the morbid consequences of philosophical pondering. That is only evasion. If only for the sake of

---

* What is said here is true only of the treatment of spiritual distress; it would not, of course, be applicable to treatment of any psychogenic or somatogenic disorders.

philosophical fairness, we ought to fight with the same weapons. A doctor should not prescribe a tranquilizer cure for the despair of a man who is grappling with spiritual problems. Rather, with the tools of a "psychotherapy in spiritual terms" he will attempt to give the patient spiritual support, to provide him with some spiritual anchorage.

This is especially appropriate in our dealings with a typically "neurotic" world-view. Suppose the patient's world-view should turn out to be a valid one. In that case we would be committing a serious error in opposing it, for we must never leap to the conclusion that a neurotic's world-view is necessarily wrong simply because it is neurotic. However, it may happen that the patient is wrong in his world-view. In that case, correcting it calls for non-psychotherapeutic methods. We may put it this way: if the patient is right, psychotherapy is unnecessary, as a valid world-view requires no correcting on our part. On the other hand, if the patient is wrong, psychotherapy is impossible—a distorted world-view cannot be set straight by psychotherapy. Consequently, in the face of all spiritual problems, psychotherapy in its old form proves to be inadequate. Not only is it inadequate, but not competent—in the sense that these problems do not fall within its province. As we have seen, psychotherapy has insufficient resources to deal with the totality of psychic reality. On top of this insufficiency there is its incompetence to deal with spiritual reality as a thing in its own right. Not only is it exceeding its authority in dealing with the individual's world-view as a "neurotic" phenomenon; it is going too far altogether when it constructs theories of the pathological origin of all world-views. A philosophical structure is not just the product of the diseased psyche of its creator. We have no right to conclude from the psychic illness of a person who has produced a particular world-view that his philosophy is therefore not valid.

We must still refute it. Only after we have done so can we go on to deal with the "psychogenesis" of his "ideology," and to try to understand it in terms of his personal biography. Consequently, there is no room for a psychopathology or psychotherapy of world-views. The most there can be is a psychopathology or psychotherapy of the viewer, the living person from whose head the view in question issued. And it is self-evident that no such psychopathology can ever pass judgment on the validity or invalidity of a world-view (cf. Allers). It is not empowered to make statements in regard to a particular philosophical question; its comments must be limited to the personality of the philosophizer. The standards with which psychopathology works, "health—sickness," are in every case relevant only to the human being, never to his productions. That we make a psychopathological statement about a person does not, therefore, exonerate us from the need to come to grips philosophically with his world-view and to examine it for its rightness or wrongness. We repeat: the psychic health or illness of the holder of a world-view has no bearing on the correctness or incorrectness of that view. Two times two equals four even if a paranoiac makes the statement. Our evaluation of ideas does not depend on the psychic origins of those ideas.

What the whole problem comes down to is the fallacy of psychologism, for such we must call the pseudo-scientific procedure which presumes to analyze every act for its psychic origin, and on that basis to decree whether its content is valid or invalid. Such an attempt is doomed to failure from the start. It is philosophical dilettantism to rule out, for example, the existence of a divine being on the ground that the idea of God arose out of primitive man's fear of powerful natural forces. It is equally false to judge the worth of a work of art by the fact that the artist created it in, say, a psychotic phase of his life. Individual or social misuse should not

1 From Psychotherapy
to Logotherapy

be allowed to overcast our view of the work in itself. It is throwing out the baby with the bathwater to repudiate the validity and the value of an artistic creation or religious experience simply because these may be used by an individual for his own neurotic purposes, or by a culture for its own decadent ends. Such a critical method is reminiscent of the man who, confronted with a stork, exclaimed: "Why, I thought storks didn't exist." Because the stork has a "secondary" use as the bearer of babies in the nursery myth, shall we therefore assume that the bird itself is a fable?

All this is not to deny that ideas are still conditioned psychologically, biologically, and sociologically. "Conditioned" but not "caused." Wälder has rightly pointed out that all such conditioning of ideas and cultural phenomena may well be a source of error, may well produce wrong slants and exaggerations here and there, but does not account for the essential content. Nor can it be adduced as explanation for the intellectual achievement behind those ideas and phenomena. (Every such attempted "explanation" confuses the field of expression of a person with the field of representation of a thing.) And in regard to the formation of the individual's image of the world, Scheler has demonstrated that characterological differences enter into it only insofar as they influence his choice; they cannot form the content of that vision. Hence Scheler calls the conditioning elements "elective" and not "constitutive." They can serve as a basis for our understanding why the individual in question happens to have his personal way of viewing the world, but they can never "explain" what part of the world's abundance is set forth in this individual, though perhaps narrow, vision. The particularity of all perspective, the fragmentary nature of all images of the world, after all presupposes the objectivity of the world. We know of the presence of sources of error and conditioning factors in astronomical observation—the fact is expressed in the astronomers' well-known "personal equation." Nevertheless, nobody doubts that in spite of such subjective factors something like Sirius really exists. Similarly, a verdict upon a given world-view in terms of the psychological (or psychopathological) structure of the person who holds that view is neither intrinsic nor fruitful. Only an objective approach, directed toward the inner truth of the world-view, has any point.

We would certainly not be entitled to brand something as "true" because it was "healthy" or, vice versa, something as "false" because it was "sick."

If only for exploratory purposes, therefore, we must continue to maintain that psychotherapy as such is exceeding its scope in dealing with philosophical questions since, as we have shown, the special categories of psychopathology—namely "health" and "sickness"—have no bearing on the truth or validity of ideas. Once psychotherapy ventures a judgment in this regard, it instantly falls into the error of psychologism. If, therefore, we want to combat the psychologistic deviations of existing psychotherapy and put a stop to their dangerous invasions, it is necessary to supplement psychotherapy by a new procedure. In the field of philosophy, psychologism has been overcome by the critical methods of phenomenology; in the field of psychotherapy, psychologism must now be overcome by a method which we shall call *logotherapy*. To this logotherapy would be assigned the task we have described as "psychotherapy in spiritual terms." Logotherapy must *supplement* psychotherapy; that is, it must fill the void whose existence we have mentioned. By the use of logotherapy we are equipped to deal with philosophical questions within their own frame of reference, and can embark on objective discussion of the spiritual distress of human beings suffering from psychic disturbances.

Logotherapy cannot and in the nature of things is not intended to replace psychotherapy, but to supplement it (and even this only in special cases). *De facto* its aims are not new and its approach has been tried, usually unwittingly. However, we are here examining the possibility of applying logotherapy *de jure*, and striving to determine in which cases and to what extent it is desirable. For the purposes of clarification we must attack the question methodically, and first of all separate the logotherapeutic from the psychotherapeutic factors. This is done for the sake of analysis, but in so doing we must never forget that in psychiatric practice both factors have a living connection with one another; they merge, as it were, in working with the patient. In the end the concerns of psychotherapy and logotherapy—namely, the psychic and the spiritual aspects of man—are indissolubly joined.

In principle, however, the fact remains that the spiritual and the psychic aspects of man must be considered apart; both represent realms essentially different. The error of psychologism consists in arbitrarily veering from the one plane to the other. Psychologism leads to shifting the grounds of the argument. To avoid this in the field of psychotherapeutic treatment, and so finally to purge psychotherapy of psychologism, is the intention and the real business of logotherapy.

Here, at the conclusion of this chapter, we will not refrain from turning psychologism against itself, using it as a weapon against itself and defeating it with its own arms. Reversing the tip of the lance, we will apply psychologism to itself by examining its own psychogenesis—that is, the motives which underlie it. What is its hidden basic attitude, its secret tendency? Our reply is: a tendency toward devaluation. In every given case its efforts to evaluate the intellectual content of psychic acts are in truth efforts to devaluate. It is always trying to unmask. It evades all questions of validity—in the religious, artistic, or even scientific fields—by escaping from the realm of content to the realm of the act. Thus psychologism is ultimately shying away from the complexity of questions requiring knowledge and tasks demanding decisions; it is in flight from the realities and possibilities of existence.

Everywhere, psychologism sees nothing but masks, insists that only neurotic motives lie behind these masks. Art, it asserts, is "in the final analysis nothing but" flight from life or from love. Religion is merely primitive man's fear of cosmic forces. All spiritual creations turn out to be "mere" sublimations of the libido or, as the case may be, compensations for inferiority feelings or means for achieving security. The great creators in the realm of the spirit are then dismissed as neurotics. After we have been put through such a course of "debunking" by psychologism we can with complete complacency say that Goethe or St. Augustine, for instance, was "really only" a neurotic. This point of view sees nothing for what it is; that is to say, it really sees nothing. Because something at one time was a mask, or somewhere was a means to an end, does that make it forever a mask, or nothing but a means to an end? Can there never be anything immediate, genuine, original?

Individual psychology preaches courage, but it has apparently forgotten the humility that should accompany courage. Humility in the face of the spirit's powers, in the face of the spiritual realm as a sphere in itself whose nature and values cannot simply be projected psychologistically down into the psychological plane. Humility, if it is genuine, is certainly as much a sign of inner strength as courage.

"Debunking" psychotherapy—like all psychologism—avoids coming to terms with the problems of philosophical and scientific validity. For example, a psychoanalyst in the course of a private discussion attacked the non-psychoanalytic opinion of another psychotherapist and damned it by saying it was due to "complexes" on the part of his opponent. When it was pointed out to him that the non-psychoanalytic method had resulted in a cure, he argued that the "cure" was only another of the patient's symptoms. By such reasoning it is possible to escape all objective discussion and scientific debate.

Psychologism, then, is the favorite recourse of those with a tendency toward devaluation. But to our mind psychologism is a partial aspect of a more comprehensive phenomenon. It is this: the end of the nineteenth and the beginning of the twentieth century completely distorted the picture of man by stressing all the numerous restraints placed upon him, in the grip of which he is supposedly helpless. Man has been presented as constrained by biological, by psychological, by sociological factors. Inherent human freedom, which obtains in spite of all these constraints, the freedom of the spirit in spite of nature, has been overlooked. Yet it is this freedom that truly constitutes the essence of man. Thus, along with psychologism we have had biologism and sociologism,* all of which have helped set up a caricature of man. No wonder that in the course of intellectual history a reaction to this naturalistic view was forthcoming. This counter-view called attention to the fundamental facts of being human; it stressed man's freedom in the face of the obstacles imposed by nature. No wonder that the prime fact of being responsible has at last been restored to the center of our field of vision. The other prime fact, that of being conscious, was at least something that could not be slurred over by psychologism.

Existential philosophy deserves the credit for having pro-

---

* The genealogy of all these ideologies is as follows: the father of psychologism, biologism, and sociologism is naturalism. Out of the, as it were, incestuous connection between biologism and sociologism was begotten collective biologism. Another aspect of collective biologism is racism.

claimed the existence of man as a form of being *sui generis*. Thus Jaspers calls the being of man a "deciding" being, not something that simply "is" but something that first decides "what it is." That statement underscores a fact that has long been generally understood, though not always admitted. And only after it has been granted does an ethical judgment of human conduct become possible at all. For when man opposes the limitations of nature, when as a human being he "takes a stand" on them, when he ceases to be subjugated and blindly obedient to the constraints imposed by the biological factor (race), the sociological factor (class), or the psychological factor (characterological type)—only then can he be judged morally. The meaning of concepts like those of merit and guilt stands and falls on our belief in man's true capacity for not simply accepting as fated limitations all the above-mentioned constraints, on his capacity for seeing them instead as challenges bidding him shape his destiny and his life. Thus, a man who belongs to a given nation is obviously neither guilty nor meritorious by that fact alone. His guilt would begin only when, for example, he did not cultivate in himself the special talents of the nation, or took no part in national cultural values; while he would be acting meritoriously if he overcame in himself certain characterological weaknesses of the nation by a conscious process of self-education. Yet how many men fall into the error of using the character weaknesses of their nation as an excuse for their own weaknesses. They call to mind the anecdote about Dumas *fils*, to whom a lady of rank one day remarked: "It must vex you that your father lives in so loose a manner." Whereupon young Dumas replied: "Oh, no, Your Excellency; though he may not serve as an example to me, he serves as an excellent excuse for me." It would have been better had the son taken his father as a warning. Yet is it not equally common for persons to take pride in national virtues without their having personally any share in those virtues? Something for which a person cannot be made responsible cannot be accounted to his praise or blame. This perception lies at the heart of all Occidental thought since the classical philosophers, and certainly since the rise of Judaism and Christianity. In striking and conscious contrast to pagan thought, it is held that a man can be ethically judged only where he is free to decide and to act responsibly; he is not to be judged where he is no longer free.

We have endeavored first to deduce theoretically the necessity for logotherapy. It was shown that psychotherapy inevitably falls into the error of psychologism. In the following chapters we must demonstrate the practicability of logotherapy. Finally, in the last chapter we shall adduce proof for its theoretical possibility—that is, we shall answer the question already touched on: whether logotherapy can be practiced without the therapist's philosophy being imposed willy-nilly on the patient.

In the next chapter we shall be dealing with the problem of the technical practicability of logotherapy. We have already stressed the importance of the concept of responsibility as the foundation of human existence. We therefore propose that logotherapy lead the way in directing psychotherapy toward existential analysis, wherein human nature will be examined in terms of responsibility.

II

From
Psychoanalysis
to
Existential
Analysis

A   General Existential Analysis

Psychotherapy endeavors to bring instinctual facts to consciousness. Logotherapy, on the other hand, seeks to bring to awareness the spiritual realities. As existential analysis it is particularly concerned with making men conscious of their responsibility —since being responsible is one of the essential grounds of human existence. If to be human is, as we have said, to be conscious and responsible, then existential analysis is psychotherapy whose starting-point is consciousness of responsibility.

1   *On the Meaning of Life*

Responsibility implies a sense of obligation. A man's obligation can, however, only be understood in terms of a "meaning"—the specific meaning of a human life. The question of such a meaning is of supreme interest and comes up very frequently, whenever a doctor has to deal with a psychically ill patient who is racked by spiritual conflicts. The doctor himself does not bring up the subject; it is the patient who in his spiritual distress flings the question at the doctor.

Whether expressed or implicit, this is an intrinsically human question. Challenging the meaning of life can therefore never be taken as a manifestation of morbidity or abnormality; it is rather the truest expression of the state of being human, the mark of the most human nature in man. For we can easily imagine highly developed animals or insects—say bees or ants—which in many aspects of their social organization are actually superior to man. But we can never imagine any such creature raising the question of the meaning of its own existence, and thus challenging this existence. It is reserved for man alone to find his very existence questionable, to experience the whole dubiousness of being. More than such faculties as power of speech, conceptual thinking, or walking erect, this factor of doubting the significance of his own existence is what sets man apart from animal.

The problem of meaning in its extreme form can literally overwhelm a person. It takes on this overwhelming urgency particularly at puberty, when the essential uncertainty of human life is suddenly revealed to young people maturing and struggling spiritually. A science teacher in a junior high school was once explaining that the life of organisms, and so of man also, was "in the final analysis nothing but" a process of oxidation, of combustion. One of his students suddenly sprang to his feet and passionately threw at him the question: "If that's so, then what kind of meaning does life have?" This boy had correctly grasped the truth that man exists on a different plane of being from, say, a candle that stands on the table and burns down until it sputters out. The candle's being (Heidegger would say: *"Vorhanden-Sein"*) may be interpreted as a process of combustion. But man possesses a totally different form of being. Human existence takes the form of historical existence. It is—in contrast to the existence of animals—always placed in a historical space (a "structured" space, according to L. Binswanger) and cannot be extracted from the system of coordinates governing that space. And this frame of reference is always governed by a meaning, although that meaning may be unspoken, and perhaps altogether inexpressible. The activity of an anthill can be called purposeful, but not meaningful. And where meaning is absent, the historical factor cannot be present. An ant "nation" has no "history."

Erwin Straus (in his book *Geschehnis und Erlebnis*) has shown that the reality of man's life, what Straus calls the *"Werdewirklichkeit,"* is inconceivable apart from the historical time factor. This is especially true in neurosis where man "deforms" this *Werdewirklichkeit.* One type of this deformation is the attempt to desert the original human plane of being. Straus calls this attempt "presentist" existence. He is referring to the attitude which repudiates any sense of direction in life; to behavior, in other words, which is neither based upon the past nor guided toward the future, but related only to the unhistorical pure present. Thus many a neurotic expresses a preference for living "far from the struggle for existence" upon some solitary island where he would have nothing to do but lie in the sun. That may be fitting for animals, but not for men. Only in his self-forgetfulness can such a person imagine that in the long run (leaving aside, that is, all the "Dionysiac" moments of existence) such a life would be human, worthy of a man, and tolerable. The "normal" man (in the sense of both "average" and "conforming to an ethical norm") may and can take a presentist attitude only at certain times, and then only to a degree.

The time and occasion for this is a thing of conscious choice. One can, for example, at a festival, take a leave of absence from one's responsible life and consciously seek self-forgetfulness in intoxication. In such deliberately and artificially induced bouts of abandon, man from time to time consciously relieves the pressure of his real responsibility. But intrinsically and ultimately man, Occidental man at least, is permanently subject to the dictate of values which he must realize creatively. This is not to say that he cannot intoxicate himself in and with his own creativity, that he cannot use creativity to drown out his sense of obligation. Every type of human being is susceptible to this danger, which Scheler in his treatise on the *"bourgeois"* has characterized as getting so involved in the means of realizing values that the end (the values themselves) is forgotten. This class is swelled by those vast numbers of human beings who, hard at work all week long, on Sundays are overwhelmed by the emptiness and lack of content of their lives, which the day of idleness brings into consciousness. Victims of "Sunday neurosis," they get drunk in order to flee from their spiritual horror of emptiness.

While the urgent questioning of the meaning of life is most apt to occur during adolescence, it may also come later, precipitated

28

by some shaking experience. And as the adolescent's preoccupation with this question is not a morbid symptom, so the spiritual distress, the existential crises of a mature man struggling to find a content for his life have nothing pathological about them. Logotherapy and existential analysis undertake to deal with psychic sufferers who are not sick in the clinical sense. For our "psychotherapy in spiritual terms" is specifically designed to handle those suffering over the philosophical problems with which life confronts human beings. But even where there are actual clinical symptoms based on some disturbance, logotherapy can be helpful to the patient. For it can give him that firm spiritual support which the healthy, ordinary person does not so much need, but which a psychically insecure person urgently requires to bolster up his insecurity. In no case should the spiritual problems of a person be written off as a "symptom." In every case these are an "accomplishment" (to make use of Oswald Schwarz's antithesis)—representing a level of thoughtfulness the patient has already achieved, or one we are going to help him to attain. This applies especially to persons who are not psychically unstable for internal reasons (like neurotics) but have lost their psychic balance for purely external reasons. Among persons of this sort we would class, say, someone who had lost a loved one around whom his life revolved, and who then despairingly raises the question of whether his own life any longer has meaning. There is something particularly pitiable about the man whose faith in the meaningfulness of his own existence totters in such a crisis. He has been left without moral reserves. He lacks that spiritual fiber which can be supplied only by a world-view unqualifiedly affirmative toward life. Lacking this fiber (which need not be clearly conscious or formulated in definite terms in order to provide support), he is unable in difficult times to "take" the blows of fate and to set his own strength against them. He is left morally unarmed and unarmored, prey to the full terror inherent in the concept of fate.

How crucial is an affirmative attitude toward life, and how naturally it belongs to the biological side of man, is perhaps illustrated by the following example: A large-scale statistical survey of longevity showed that all the long-lived subjects had a "serene"— that is, an affirmative—view of life. The individual's philosophical attitude emerges in every case. For example, melancholiacs, though seeking to conceal their basic negation of life, can never wholly dissimulate. Given the right method of psychiatric exploration, the hidden ennui is immediately uncovered. If we suspect that a melancholiac is only pretending to be free of the urge to commit suicide, the following examination procedure is recommended.

First we ask the patient about thoughts of suicide, or whether he is still harboring suicidal yearnings he has expressed at some time in the past. He will always answer this question in the negative—with special vehemence if he is merely dissimulating. Whereupon we ask him a further question, from the answer to which we can gauge whether he is really shaking off his *tædium vitæ* or only pretending. We ask him—crude as the question may sound—why he does not have (or no longer has) ideas of committing suicide. A melancholiac who really is not harboring such intentions, or has overcome them, will answer without hesitation that he must consider his family, or think of his work, or something of the sort. The man who is trying to fool his analyst, however, will immediately fall into a typical state of embarrassment. He is actually at a loss for arguments supporting his "phony" affirmation of life. Characteristically, such dissimulating patients will try to change the subject, and will usually bring up their naked demand to be released from confinement. People are psychologically incapable of making up counterfeit arguments in favor of life, or arguments for their

30

continuing to live, when thoughts of suicide are surging up within them. If such arguments were really present, they would be ready at hand, and in that case the patient would *eo ipso* no longer be swayed by suicidal impulses.

The question of the meaning of life can be approached in various ways. At the start let us set aside the problem of the meaning and purpose of the world as a whole, or our perplexity at the destiny we experience, our protest against the events that befall us. For the positive answers to all these questions fall into the special precincts of religion. For the religious man who puts his faith in Providence, there may well be no such problems. For the rest of mankind, the first concern must be to put the question in some fitting form. We must first determine whether it is even permissible to ask about the meaning of the whole, whether such a question itself is meaningful.

Actually, our interrogation must be confined to the meaning of a part. We cannot begin to question the "purpose" of the universe. Purpose is transcendent to the extent that it is always external to whatever "possesses" it. We can therefore at best grasp the meaning of the universe in the form of a super-meaning, using the word to convey the idea that the meaning of the whole is no longer comprehensible and goes beyond the comprehensible. This concept of meaning would serve as a parallel to the Kantian postulate of reason; our minds require its existence at the same time that it is to our minds unfathomable.

Pascal long ago remarked that the branch can never grasp the meaning of the whole tree. Modern biology has shown that each living creature is locked within his specific environment and is unable to break out of it. For all that man may occupy an exceptional position, for all that he may be unusually receptive to the world, and that the world itself may be his environment—still, who can say that beyond this world a super-world does not exist? Just as the animal can scarcely reach out of his environment to understand the superior world of man, so perhaps man can scarcely ever grasp the super-world, though he can reach out toward it in religion —or perhaps encounter it in revelation. A domestic animal does not understand the purposes for which man employs it. How then could man know what "final" purpose his life has, what "super-meaning" the universe has? We differ with N. Hartmann's assertion that man's freedom and responsibility is counterposed against a purposiveness which is hidden from him, but to which he is subordinate. Hartmann himself admits that man's freedom is a "freedom despite dependence," insofar as the freedom of man's mind rises above the laws governing nature and operates in a higher "stratum of being" of its own which is "autonomous" in spite of its dependence upon the lower stratum of being. As we see it, an analogous relationship between the realm of human freedom and a realm superior to man is quite imaginable, so that man is endowed with free will in spite of the plans Providence may have for him—just as a domestic animal lives by its instincts even at the same time that it serves man. For man makes use of the very instincts of the animal for his own ends.

We will, then, visualize the relationship of the human world to a super-world as analogous to the relationship between the animal's "environment" (von Uexküll) and man's.* Schleich has most cogently and beautifully expressed this relationship where he says:

---

* The relationship between the (narrow) animal environment and the (wider) world of man, and between man's world and an (all-embracing) super-world, therefore corresponds, if you will, to the "golden section."

"God sat at the organ of possibilities and improvised the world. Poor creatures that we are, we men can only hear the vox humana. If that is so beautiful, how glorious the Whole must be."

It is self-evident that belief in a super-meaning—whether as a metaphysical concept or in the religious sense of Providence—is of the foremost psychotherapeutic and psychohygienic importance. As a genuine faith springing from inner strength, such a belief adds immeasurably to human vitality. To such a faith there is, ultimately, nothing that is meaningless. Nothing appears "in vain"; "no act remains unaccounted for" (Wildgans). The world appears to manifest something akin to a law of the conservation of spiritual energy. No great idea can vanish, even if it never reaches public circulation, even if it has been "taken to the grave." In the light of such a law, the drama and tragedy of a man's inner life never have unfolded in vain, even when played out in secret, unrecorded, uncelebrated by any novelist. The "novel" which each individual has lived remains an incomparably greater composition than any that has ever been written down. Every one of us knows somehow that the content of his life is somewhere preserved and saved. Thus time, the transitoriness of the years, cannot affect its meaning and value. Having been is also a kind of being—perhaps the surest kind. And all effective action in life may, in this view, appear as a salvaging of possibilities by actualizing them. Though past, these possibilities are now safely ensconced in the past for all eternity, and time can no longer change them.*

---

* Time that has passed is certainly irrecoverable; but what has happened within that time is unassailable and inviolable. Passing time is therefore not only a thief, but a trustee. Any philosophy which keeps in mind the transitoriness of existence need not be at all pessimistic. To express this point figuratively we might say: The pessimist resembles a man who observes with fear and sadness that his wall calendar, from which he daily tears a sheet, grows

In the foregoing we have dealt with the question of meaning as it applies to the meaning of the universe. Now we shall take up a consideration of the many cases where patients ask what is the meaning of their individual, their personal lives. There is a characteristic twist a good many patients give to this question, which inexorably leads them to ethical nihilism. The patient will flatly assert that, after all, the whole meaning of life is pleasure. In the course of his argument he will cite it as an indisputable finding that all human activity is governed by the striving for happiness, that all psychic processes are determined exclusively by the pleasure principle. This theory of the dominant role of the pleasure principle in the whole of the psychic life is, as is well known, one of the basic

---

thinner with each passing day. On the other hand, the person who takes life in the sense suggested above is like a man who removes each successive leaf from his calendar and files it neatly and carefully away with its predecessors—after first having jotted down a few diary notes on the back. He can reflect with pride and joy on all the richness set down in these notes, on all the life he has already lived to the full. What will it matter to him if he notices that he is growing old? Has he any reason to envy the young people whom he sees, or wax nostalgic for his own youth? What reasons has he to envy a young person? For the *possibilities* that young person has, the future that is in store for him? "No, thank you," he will think. "Instead of possibilities, I have realities in my past— not only the reality of work done and of love loved, but of suffering suffered. These are the things of which I am most proud —though these are things which cannot inspire envy."

All that is good and beautiful in the past is safely preserved in the past. On the other hand, so long as life remains, all guilt and all evil is still "redeemable" (Scheler, *Wiedergeburt und Reue*). This is not the case of a finished film (as, say, the relativity theory conceives the world process as the totality of four-dimensional world-lines), or an already existent film which is merely being unrolled. Rather, the film of this world is just being "shot." Which means nothing more nor less than that the past—happily—is fixed,

tenets of psychoanalysis; the reality principle is not actually opposed to the pleasure principle, but is a mere extension of the pleasure principle, and serves its purposes.

Now, to our mind the pleasure principle is an artificial creation of psychology. Pleasure is not the goal of our aspirations, but the consequence of attaining them. Kant long ago pointed this out. Commenting on the hedonist ethics, eudemonism, Scheler has remarked that pleasure does not loom up before us as the goal of an ethical act; rather, an ethical act carries pleasure on its back. The theory of the pleasure principle overlooks the intentional quality of all psychic activity. In general, men do not want pleasure; they

---

is safe, whereas the future—happily—still remains to be shaped; that is, is at the disposal of man's responsibility.

But what is responsibility? Responsibility is something we face and something we may try to escape. The wisdom inherent in common speech thus suggests that there are counterforces operating in human beings which attempt to relieve them of their natural responsibleness. And in truth there is something about responsibility that resembles an abyss. The longer and the more profoundly we consider it, the more we become aware of its awful depths—until a kind of giddiness overcomes us. For as soon as we lend our minds to the essence of human responsibility, we cannot forbear to shudder; there is something fearful about man's responsibility. But at the same time something glorious! It is fearful to know that at this moment we bear the responsibility for the next, that every decision from the smallest to the largest is a decision for all eternity, that at every moment we bring to reality—or miss—a possibility that exists only for the particular moment. Every moment holds thousands of possibilities, but we can choose only a single one of these; all the others we have condemned, damned to never-being—and that, too, for all eternity. But it is glorious to know that the future, our own and therewith the future of the things and people around us, is dependent—even if only to a tiny extent—upon our decision at any given moment. What we actualize by that decision, what we thereby bring into the world, is saved; we have conferred reality upon it and preserved it from passing.

---

*II From Psychoanalysis
      to Existential Analysis*

simply want what they want. Human volition has any number of ends, of the most varied sorts, whereas pleasure would always take the same form, whether secured by ethical or unethical behavior. Hence it is evident that adopting the pleasure principle would, on the moral plane, lead to a leveling of all potential human aims. It would become impossible to differentiate one action from another, since all would have the same purpose in view. A sum of money disbursed on good food or given in alms could be said to have served the same purpose: in either case the money went to remove unpleasurable feelings within the spender.

Define conduct in these terms and you devaluate every genuine moral impulse in man. In reality, an impulse of sympathy is already moral in itself, even before it is embodied in an act which allegedly has only the negative significance of eliminating unpleasure. For the same situation which in one person may arouse sympathy may stimulate a sadistic malicious joy in another, who gloats over someone's misfortune and in this manner experiences positive pleasure. If it were true that, for example, we read a good book only for the sake of the pleasurable sensation we feel during the reading, we might with equal justification spend our money on good cake. In reality, life is little concerned with pleasure or unpleasure. For the spectator in the theater it does not matter so much that he see a comedy or a tragedy; what allures him is the content, the intrinsic value of the play. Certainly no one will maintain that the unpleasure sensations which are aroused in the spectators who behold tragic events upon the stage are the real aim of their attendance at the theater. In that case, all theatergoers would have to be classed as disguised masochists.

But the argument that pleasure is the final goal of all (not merely the final effect of certain isolated) aspirations can be most effectively countered by reversing it. If, for example, it were true that Napoleon fought his battles only in order to experience the pleasure sensations of victory (the same pleasure sensations which the ordinary soldier might obtain by stuffing his belly, swilling, and whoring), then the reverse must also be true: that the "ultimate aim" of Napoleon's last disastrous battles, the "final purpose" of his defeats, could only have been the unpleasurable sensations which followed these defeats as surely as the pleasurable sensations followed the victories.

When we set up pleasure as the whole meaning of life, we insure that in the final analysis life shall inevitably seem meaningless. Pleasure cannot possibly lend meaning to life. For what is pleasure? A condition. The materialist—and hedonism is generally linked up with materialism—would even say pleasure is nothing but a state of the cells of the brain. And for the sake of inducing such a state, is it worth living, experiencing, suffering, and doing deeds? Suppose a man condemned to death is asked, a few hours before his execution, to choose the menu for his last meal. He might then reply: Is there any sense, in the face of death, in enjoying the pleasures of the palate? Since the organism will be a cadaver two hours later, does it matter whether it did or did not have one more opportunity to experience that state of the brain cells which is called pleasure? Yet all life is confronted with death, which should cancel out this element of pleasure. Anyone holding this hapless view of life as nothing but a pursuit of pleasure would have to doubt every moment of such a life, if he were to be consistent. He would be in the same frame of mind as a certain patient who was hospitalized after an attempted suicide. The patient in question described to me the following experience: In order to carry out his plan for suicide, he needed to get to an outlying part of the city. The street-cars were no longer running, and he therefore decided to take a cab. "Then I thought it over," he said, "wondering whether I ought to spend the few marks. Right away I could not help smiling at wanting to save a few marks when I would be dead so soon."

Life itself teaches most people that "we are not here to enjoy ourselves." Those who have not yet learned this lesson might be edified by the statistics of a Russian experimental psychologist who showed that the normal man in an average day experiences incomparably more unpleasure sensations than pleasure sensations. How unsatisfying the pleasure principle is in theory as well as practice is evident from a commonplace experience. If we ask a person why he does not do something that to us seems advisable, and the only "reason" he gives is: "I don't feel like it; it would give me no pleasure," we feel that this reply is distinctly unsatisfactory. It is apparent that the reply is insufficient because we can never admit pleasure or unpleasure as an argument for or against the advisability of any action.

The pleasure principle would remain untenable as a moral maxim even if it were actually what Freud claims it to be in his *Beyond the Pleasure Principle:* namely, a derivative from the general tendency of organic life to return to the peace of the inorganic. Freud thought he could prove the kinship of all pleasure-striving with what he named the death instinct. To our mind it is quite conceivable that all these psychological and biological primary tendencies might be reduced further, perhaps to a universal principle of tension reduction which operates to reduce all tensions in every realm of being. Physics recognizes a similar law in its theory of entropy as leading to a final phase of the cosmos. Nirvana might be considered the psychological correlate of entropy; reduction of all psychic tensions by liberation from unpleasure sensations might then be viewed as the microcosmic equivalent of macrocosmic entropy. Nirvana, that is, may be entropy "seen from within." The principle of tension reduction itself, however, would represent the opposite of a principle of individuation which would endeavor to preserve all being as individuated being, as otherness. The very existence of such a polarity suggests that such formulations of universal principles, such findings of cosmic laws lead us up a blind alley, as far as ethics is concerned. For these phenomena have little bearing on our subjective and moral lives. What commands us to identify ourselves with all these principles and tendencies? To what extent is our ethical system to assent to such principles, even if we discover them in our own psychic life? We might equally well take the stand that our moral task is to oppose the rule of such forces with all our strength.

The nature of our education, heavily weighted as it is on the side of materialism, has left most of us with an exaggerated respect for the findings of the so-called exact sciences. We accept without question the picture of the world presented by physics. But how real, for example, is the entropy with which physics threatens us— how real is this universal doom, or this cosmic catastrophe which physics predicts, and in the light of which all the efforts of ourselves and our posterity seem to dwindle to nought? Are we not rather taught by "inner experience," by ordinary living unbiased by theories, that our natural pleasure in a beautiful sunset is in a way "more real" than, say, astronomical calculations of the time when the earth will crash into the sun? Can anything be given to us more directly than our own personal experience, our own deep feeling of our humanity as responsibility? "The most certain science is conscience," someone once remarked, and no theory of the physiological nature of life, nor the assertion that joy is a strictly organized dance of molecules or atoms or electrons within the gray matter of the brain, has ever been so compelling and convincing. Similarly, a man who is enjoying supreme artistic pleasure or the happiness of love never doubts for a moment that his life is meaningful.

II From Psychoanalysis
to Existential Analysis

Joy, however, may make life meaningful only if it itself has meaning. Its meaning cannot lie within itself. In fact it lies outside of itself. For joy is always directed toward an object. Scheler has already shown that joy is an intentional emotion—in contrast to mere pleasure, which he reckons among non-intentional emotions in a category he calls "conditional" emotions. Pleasure, that is, is an emotional condition. Here we are again reminded of Erwin Straus's concept of the "presentist" mode of life. In that mode a person remains in the conditional state of pleasure (say, in intoxication) without reaching out to the realm of objects—which in this case would be the realm of values. Only when the emotions work in terms of values can the individual feel pure "joy." This is the explanation of why joy can never be an end in itself; it itself, as joy, cannot be purposed as a goal. How well Kierkegaard expressed this in his maxim that the door to happiness opens outward. Anyone who tries to push this door open thereby causes it to close still more. The man who is desperately anxious to be happy thereby cuts off his own path to happiness. Thus in the end all striving for happiness—for the supposed "ultimate" in human life—proves to be in itself impossible.

Value is transcendent to the act which intends it. It transcends the value-cognitive act which is directed toward it, analogous to the object of an act of cognition, which likewise is situated outside of this (in the narrower sense of the word cognitive) act. Phenomenology has shown that the transcendent quality of the object in the intentional act is always already present in its content. If I see a lit lamp, the fact that it is there is already given along with my perception of it, even if I close my eyes or turn my back to it. In the perception of an object as something real is already contained the implication that I recognize its reality independently of its perception by myself or anyone else. The same is true of the objects of value perception. As soon as I have comprehended a value, I have comprehended implicitly that this value exists in itself, independently therefore of whether or not I accept it.

Let us give a concrete example. Suppose a man observes that the apparently æsthetic attractions of his erotic partner are "given" to him only so long as he is in a particular condition, namely a state of sexual tension. He discovers that with the abatement of his sexual excitement all the apparent beauties, the æsthetic values, somehow vanish. He concludes from this that these beauties do not really exist, but merely result from the distortion of his senses by sensuality; that they therefore do not represent anything objective, but rather relative values which are dependent upon the particular state of his organism and are subjected to his own subjective instincts.

But this conclusion is wrong. Unquestionably a certain subjective state is the necessary condition for making certain values visible at all; and unquestionably a particular receptivity in the subject was the necessary medium or organon for the comprehension of the values. But that by no means disproves the objectivity of values; rather, it presupposes them. Æsthetic as well as ethical values are like objects of perception in that they require adequate acts in order to be comprehended; but these acts also, and simultaneously, reveal the transcendence of all these objects as against the acts which bring them to light, hence their objectivity. All this, however, does not alter the fact already touched upon: that our values as well as our philosophic attitude in any given case afford us a view of only a cross-section of the world. In other words, our vision is limited by our individual perspectives. Perhaps the law by which man's responsibilities are revealed only in concrete tasks is more general than we imagine. Objective values become concrete duties, are cast in the form of the demands of each day and in personal tasks. The values lying back of these tasks can apparently be reached for only through the tasks. It is quite possible that the whole, of which all concrete obligations are a part, never becomes visible to the individual person, who is limited by the perspective of his day-to-day responsibilities.

Every human person constitutes something unique; each situation in life occurs only once. The concrete task of any person is relative to this uniqueness and singularity. Thus every man at any given moment can have only one single task. But this very singularity constitutes the absoluteness of his task. The world of values is therefore seen from the perspective of the individual, but for any given situation there is only one single perspective, which is the appropriate one. Accordingly, absolute rightness exists not in spite of, but because of the relativity of individual perspectives.

We have therefore attempted to counter the basic skepticism so frequently expressed by our patients, and to develop the counter-arguments necessary to blunt the edge of ethical nihilism. But it often becomes necessary in addition to disclose the full richness of the world of values, and to make clear the extent of its domain. For in spite of our doctrine of the specific task, men must also be prepared to make shifts. It sometimes happens that one task will not yield to man's efforts, while another, with its complement of values, presents itself as an alternative. Man must cultivate the flexibility to swing over to another value-group if that group and that alone offers the possibility of actualizing values. Life requires of man spiritual elasticity, so that he may temper his efforts to the chances that are offered.

How often one of our patients bewails his life, which he says has no meaning since his activities are without any higher value.

This is the point at which we must reason with him, showing that it is a matter of indifference what a person's occupation is, or at what job he works. The crucial thing is how he works, whether he in fact fills the place in which he happens to have landed. The radius of his activity is not important; important alone is whether he fills the circle of his tasks. The ordinary person who really masters the concrete tasks with which his occupation and his family life present him is, in spite of his "little" life, "greater" than and superior to a "great" statesman who may decide the fate of millions with the stroke of a pen, but whose decisions are unscrupulous and evil in their consequences. And any unbiased judge will value such a "little" life higher than, for example, the existence of a surgeon in whose hands we placed the lives of many patients but who performs his highly specialized work without being sufficiently conscious of the tremendous responsibility he bears.

Values which are realized in creative action we should like to call "creative" values. In addition to these, there are values which are realized in experience: "experiential values." These latter are realized in receptivity toward the world—for example, in surrender to the beauty of nature or art. The fullness of meaning which such values bring to human life must not be underestimated. The higher meaning of a given moment in human existence can be fulfilled by the mere intensity with which it is experienced, and independent of any action. If any one doubts this, let him consider the following situation. Imagine a music-lover sitting in the concert hall while the most noble measures of his favorite symphony resound in his ears. He feels that shiver of emotion which we experience in the presence of the purest beauty. Suppose now that at such a moment we should ask this person whether his life has meaning. He would have to reply that it had been worth while living if only to experience this ecstatic moment. For even though only a single moment is in question—the greatness of a life can be measured by the greatness of a moment: the height of a mountain range is not given by the height of some valley, but by that of the tallest peak. In life, too, the peaks decide the meaningfulness of the life, and a single moment can retroactively flood an entire life with meaning. Let us ask a mountain-climber who has beheld the alpine sunset and is so moved by the splendor of nature that he feels cold shudders running down his spine—let us ask him whether after such an experience his life can ever again seem wholly meaningless.

We can also set up a third category of possible values. For life proves to be basically meaningful even when it is neither fruitful in creation nor rich in experience. The third group of values lies precisely in a man's attitude toward the limiting factors upon his life. His very response to the restraints upon his potentialities provides him with a new realm of values which surely belong among the highest values. Thus an apparently impoverished existence—one which is poor in creative and experiential values—still offers a last, and in fact the greatest, opportunity for the realization of values. These values we will call attitudinal values. What is significant is the person's attitude toward an unalterable fate. The opportunity to realize such attitudinal values is therefore always present whenever a person finds himself confronted by a destiny toward which he can act only by acceptance. The way in which he accepts, the way in which he bears his cross, what courage he manifests in suffering, what dignity he displays in doom and disaster, is the measure of his human fulfillment.

As soon as we add attitudinal values to the list of possible categories of values, it is evident that human existence can never be intrinsically meaningless. A man's life retains its meaning up to the last—until he draws his last breath. As long as he remains conscious, he is under obligations to realize values, even if these be only attitudinal values. As long as he has consciousness, he has responsibleness. This responsibility remains with him to the last moment of his existence. No matter how sparse the possibilities for realizing values may be—he has always the recourse to attitudinal values. Our starting-point, the proposition that being human means being conscious and being responsible, is reaffirmed in the moral sphere.

In life the opportunities to address oneself to this or that group of values vary from hour to hour. Sometimes life demands of us the realization of creative values; at other times we feel it necessary to turn to the category of experiential values. At one time we are called upon, as it were, to enrich the world by our actions, another time to enrich ourselves by our experiences. Sometimes the demands of the hour may be fulfilled by an act, at another time by our surrendering to the glory of an experience. Man can be "obligated" to experience joy. In this sense a person sitting in a streetcar who has the opportunity to watch a wonderful sunset, or to breathe in the rich scent of flowering acacias, and who instead goes on reading his newspaper, could at such a moment be accused of being negligent toward his obligations.

The possibility of realizing in a consistent series and in an almost dramatic manner all three categories of values was open to a patient the last phase of whose life took the following form. A young man lay in the hospital, suffering from an inoperable spinal tumor. He had long since had to abandon his profession; paralysis had handicapped his ability to work. There was for him therefore no longer any chance to realize creative values. But even in this state the realm of experiential values remained open to him. He passed the time in stimulating conversations with other patients—

entertaining them also, encouraging and consoling them. He devoted himself to reading good books, and especially to listening to good music on the radio. One day, however, he could no longer bear the pressure of the earphones, and his hands had become so paralyzed that he could no longer hold a book. Now his life took another turn; while before he had been compelled to withdraw from creative values to experiential values, he was forced now to make the further retreat to attitudinal values. How else shall we interpret his behavior—for he now set himself the role of adviser to his fellow sufferers, and in every way strove to be an exemplar to them. He bore his own suffering bravely. The day before his death—which he foresaw—he knew that the doctor on duty had been ordered to give him an injection of morphine at night. What did the sick man do? When the doctor came to see him on his afternoon round, the patient asked him to give him the injection in the evening—so that the doctor would not have to interrupt his night's rest just on his account.

Must we not ask ourselves now whether we are ever entitled to deprive an incurably ill patient of the chance to "die his death," the chance to fill his existence with meaning down to its last moment, even though the only realm of action open to him is the realizing of attitudinal values—the only variable the question of what attitude the patient, the "sufferer," takes toward his suffering when it reaches its climax and conclusion? The way he dies, insofar as it is really *his* death, is an integral part of his life; it rounds that life out to a meaningful totality. The problem we are touching on here is that of euthanasia, of "mercy killing." Euthanasia in the narrower and original sense of the word—providing an easy death —has never been a problem for doctors. That the doctor assuages the agonies of death by medication is taken for granted; determining the point at which such medication is indicated is merely a matter of tact and insight and needs no discussion of a basic and theoretical nature. But in addition to this, the attempt has repeatedly been made in various quarters to legalize the ending of lives supposedly no longer worth living.

In answer to such proposals we must first of all reply that it is not the doctor's province to sit in judgment on the value or lack of value of a human life. The task assigned to him by society is solely that of helping wherever he can, and alleviating pain where he must; of healing to the extent that he can, and nursing illness which is beyond cure. If patients and their near and dear were not convinced that the doctor takes this mandate seriously and literally, they would never trust him again. A patient would never know whether the doctor was still coming to him as a helper—or as an executioner.

This position rests on principle and admits of no exceptions whatsoever. It applies to incurable diseases of the mind just as well as to incurable diseases of the body. Moreover, who could undertake to say whether a psychosis now considered incurable will be permanent? We must bear in mind that though the psychiatrist may be absolutely positive in his diagnosis of an incurable mental illness, he can never be sure enough to pass judgment on the patient's right to be or not to be. We know of a case in which a man lay in bed for a full five years, kept alive by artificial feeding, until the muscles of his legs atrophied. A layman would characteristically have asked whether it would not be better to put an end to such an unfortunate. However, the case took an unexpected development. One day the patient asked to be allowed to eat in normal fashion, and wanted to get out of bed. He practiced walking until his atrophied muscles would support him again. A few weeks afterward he was discharged—and was soon delivering public lectures on travels he had undertaken before he fell ill. One day he spoke before a small group of psychiatrists, reporting his impressions in the course of his illness—much to the dismay of some attendants who had treated him not too well, never reckoning that in years to come this living corpse would be able to describe in sensible words everything that had happened to him.

Our opponents might take the following line: A psychotically ill person is in no condition to look after his own interests. Therefore, as delegates, so to speak, of his diseased will, we doctors ought to take the step of destroying him, since it must be assumed that the sick man would have wished to be spared the degradation of his state if mental illness had not beclouded his consciousness.

The logotherapist takes an entirely different stand. The doctor must act as agent of the sick man's will to live and as supporter of his right to live. It is not for the doctor to deny him that will or retract that right. An instructive case is that of a young doctor who developed a melanosarcoma, and correctly diagnosed the disease himself. His colleagues vainly tried to convince him that there was no sarcoma. They went so far as to deceive him, showing him negative urine reactions—after exchanging his urine for someone else's. The young doctor stole into the laboratory at night and himself conducted a urine test. As the disease progressed, his friends feared that he would attempt suicide. But instead the young doctor began increasingly to doubt his original correct diagnosis. When metastases of the liver had already set in, he began diagnosing the symptoms as those of a harmless liver affliction. Thus he unconsciously deceived himself—because in the last stages of the disease the will to live was rebelling against impending death. We must respect this will to live—not deny a man the right to life for the sake of some ideology.

Another argument is fairly common. It is pointed out that

patients suffering from incurable mental disease, especially those who have been born mentally deficient, constitute an economic burden upon society; that they are unproductive and parasitic. What can we say to this argument? In reality, idiots who at least push wheelbarrows in some institution are considerably more "productive" than, say, aged grandparents lingering out their last days in harmless senility—whose relatives would be horrified at the suggestion that these old folks should be done away with because their usefulness to society was over. (Yet those same good people who respect the aged may be proponents of the mercy killing of the unfit.) Everyone must admit that a person surrounded by loving relatives, a person who is the irreplaceable object of their love, is a person whose life has meaning, though that meaning may be only passive. Not everyone realizes, however, that just because of their helplessness, mentally retarded children are as a rule particularly loved and tenderly protected by their parents.

To our mind the duty of the doctor to save life wherever he can remains binding even when he confronts a patient who has tried to destroy himself and whose life now hangs by a thread. In this situation the doctor is faced with the question of whether he ought not leave the would-be suicide to the fate he has voluntarily chosen, whether he ought to frustrate the suicide's will, once it has been expressed in an act, or whether he ought to respect that will. It might be said that the doctor who intervenes in an attempt at suicide is taking on himself the role of arbiter of destiny, instead of letting destiny take its course. To which we reply: If "destiny"— or Providence—were intent on letting a person weary of life die, it would have found ways to make the doctor's intervention come too late. If destiny places the would-be suicide in the hands of a doctor before it is too late, this doctor must act as a physician, must never assume the role of judge and decide on personal philosophical grounds, or simply arbitrarily, whether his patient is to be or not to be.

———————

In the above discussion we have examined the problem of suicide from the point of view of the outsider—the doctor who may take any of a number of positions on the matter. We should now like to illuminate this problem from within, to attempt to convey it as the depressed person himself sees it, and to look into his motives and see whether there is any inner justification for them.

The phrase "balance suicide" is occasionally employed. The notion is that a person can rationally draw up a balance sheet of his whole life and decide on the basis of it to dispense with further existence. As we have indicated, insofar as pleasure is made identical with the credit side of life this balance will prove to be largely negative. The question is, however, whether the sum of such a balance sheet can ever turn out so negative that living on appears incontrovertibly without value.

In the first place we are inclined to doubt whether any man is able to draw up a balance of his life with sufficient objectivity. This is especially true when the conclusion he arrives at is that his problems are insoluble, or that suicide is the only solution for them. No matter how strong a conviction that conclusion may be, the conviction remains subjective. If, of the many persons who have attempted suicide out of the conviction that their situation is hopeless, only one should prove wrong, if in a sole case there should turn out to be an alternative solution after all—then every attempt at suicide would be *ipso facto* unjustified. For all who resolve on suicide have the same firm subjective conviction that this is the right course for them, and none of them can know in advance whether he is judging the situation objectively and correctly, or whether events of the very next hour may not show him to be mistaken—an hour he may not live to see.

It is certainly conceivable, theoretically, that suicide may sometimes be justified as a consciously offered sacrifice, that in such a case it may amount to a genuinely ethical act. We know empirically, however, that the motives of even such suicide arise in reality all too often from some resentment, or that at the end some other solution to the apparently hopeless situation would have turned up. We can therefore risk the generalization that suicide is never ethically justified. Not as atonement either. For suicide not only makes it impossible for a person to grow and to mature as a result of his own suffering (thus realizing attitudinal values), but it also makes it impossible for him ever to make up for the suffering he may have inflicted on someone else. Thus the suicide cannot expiate the past. Instead of wiping the slate clean of a past misfortune or injustice—he simply wipes out his own ego.

Let us turn now to cases in which the motives for suicide are based on a sick condition of the psyche. Rigorous psychiatric research might establish that no suicide ever takes place without some psychopathological basis, but we will not go into that question here. We are concerned here with demonstrating that it is our duty to convince the would-be suicide that taking one's own life is categorically contrary to reason, that life is meaningful to every human being under any circumstances. We believe this can be done by objective argument and analysis of the problem on its own terms—by the methods of logotherapy, that is.

It would have to be pointed out that the person's weariness with life is an emotional thing, and that emotions are never arguments. In ethical terms the question would remain whether the individual ought to surrender to such ennui. (In moral terms mere pleasure in life would constitute no argument at all for the meaningfulness of continuing to live.)

Where no psychopathological basis of motivation can be shown, and where, therefore, psychotherapy in the narrower sense of the word can find no point of departure, logotherapy is the indicated method. The difference in its approach from that of psychotherapy is clearly shown in the following case.

A "patient" was committed to a psychiatric institute because of suicidal intentions. He freely admitted such intentions after his hospitalization. The patient, however, had no apparent psychic symptoms. The arguments he presented to the director of the institute seemed logically impeccable. He maintained that every man possesses the freedom to decide whether or not he wishes to live. In dignified and moving words he protested against being deprived of his freedom when no trace of psychic illness could be imputed to him. The director ordered the negative diagnosis "no psychic illness" entered into the case history—and discharged the man as "well." The patient was already on his way out of the hospital and this life when one of the psychiatrists, convinced that he might be psychically sound but that he was spiritually astray, suggested that they have a talk. In a surprisingly short time this doctor succeeded in explaining to the man that human freedom is not a "freedom from" but a "freedom to"—a freedom to accept responsibility. In the course of the continuing conversation, all the pseudological reasons for suicide were dispelled.

Certainly this doctor was not proceeding in the traditional manner of the physician. Yet who can deny that he was justified in the course he took—that in fact he was constrained to take it. That philosophical disputation between the doctor and his patient was the only possible means by which the patient could be brought to an affirmation of life in the brief time that was left.

This conversation had both a logotherapeutic phase, dealing

with suicide on philosophical grounds, and a psychotherapeutic phase in the proper sense—in which the doctor attempted to clarify the psychological background of the man's decision. In the course of this psychotherapy it turned out that one of the man's motives for suicide was the desire to take revenge on a society which had dealt badly with him. It is significant that after treatment the man resolved to show others who he was, what he was worth, and how meaningful his life was. In the course of the talk he had stressed that his economic predicament was not the reason for his decision to end his life, that money would not help him. Rather, he "needed some content to his life" and was "escaping from this emptiness."

We have spoken of the freedom to accept responsibility. But this freedom itself predicates a sense of responsibility. Even in the most radical form of the flight from responsibility—flight from life itself in suicide—man cannot escape his sense of responsibility. For he commits the act of suicide in freedom (assuming, of course, that he is still sane). He cannot escape what he is fleeing from; his responsibility will not let him go. And what he is seeking he will not find: namely, the solution of a problem. For we must again and again stress to the would-be suicide that taking his own life can solve no problem. We must show him how much he resembles a chess-player confronted with a chess problem that seems too difficult, and who simply sweeps the pieces off the board. That is no solution to a chess problem. And it is no solution to a problem in life to throw one's life away. Just as the chess-player is violating the rules, a man who chooses suicide is violating the rules of the game of life. The rules of the game do not require us to win at all costs, but they do demand that we never give up the fight.*

---

* The often broached question of whether it takes courage or cowardice to commit suicide is not easy to answer. For we must in all fairness take cognizance of the inner conflict which usually precedes an attempt at suicide. Perhaps all we can say is: the suicidal person braves death—but funks life.

II From Psychoanalysis   53
to Existential Analysis

We want to teach our patients what Albert Schweitzer has called reverence for life. But our patients can only be persuaded that life has unconditional value if we can manage to give them some content for their lives, if we can help them find an aim and a purpose in their existence—in other words, if they can be shown the task before them. "Whoever has a reason for living endures almost any mode of life," says Nietzsche. The conviction that one has a task before him has enormous psychotherapeutic and psychohygienic value. We venture to say that nothing is more likely to help a person overcome or endure objective difficulties or subjective troubles than the consciousness of having a task in life. That is all the more so when the task seems to be personally cut to suit, as it were; when it constitutes what may be called a mission. Having such a task makes the person irreplaceable and gives his life the value of uniqueness. The sentence of Nietzsche's quoted above suggests that the "mode" of life—that is, its characteristic hardships and ennuis—retreats to the background the moment that, and to the extent that, the reasons for life come to the fore. But not only this. In view of the task quality of life, it logically follows that life becomes all the more meaningful the more difficult it gets. A natural analogy is the attitude of the true athlete. The athlete sets up his problem in such a way that he may prove himself by its conquest. Consider a hurdle race, or the practice of establishing handicaps in a race. Shall we not also test our mettle and grow in courage and strength through the difficulties in ordinary life?

Our aim must be to help our patient to achieve the highest possible activation of his life, to lead him, so to speak, from the state of a *"patiens"* to that of an *"agens."* With this in view we must not only lead him to experience his existence as a constant effort to actualize values. We must also show him that the task he is responsible for is always a specific task. It is specific in a twin sense: one, that the task varies from person to person—in accord with the uniqueness of each person. Two, that it changes from hour to hour, in accord with the singularity of every situation. We need only remind ourselves of what Scheler has called "situational values" in contrast to the "eternal" values which are valid at all times and for everyone. In a sense these situational values are always there, waiting until their hour strikes and a man seizes the single opportunity to actualize them. If that opportunity is missed, they are irrevocably lost; the situational value remains forever unrealized. The man has missed out on it.

We see, therefore, that the factors of uniqueness and singularity are essential constituents of the meaningfulness of human existence. To contemporary existentialist philosophy goes the honor of having shown that the existence of man is essentially concrete and subjective. It took the existentialist stress on these qualities to restore moral responsibility to the modern scene. Not for nothing has existentialist philosophy been termed the "summoning" philosophy. For the presentation of human life as singular and unique is an implicit summons to men to actualize in their own lives these unique and singular possibilities.

Existential analysis and logotherapy aim at bringing the patient to the point of highest possible concentration and dedication. It is our business, then, to show how the life of every man has a unique goal to which only one single course leads. Steering this course, man resembles the flier who is "piloted" into the airport through nocturnal mists to make a blind landing. The method for this is well known: the radio station at the airport sends out toward the approaching plane two different Morse signals, each covering a sector. At the boundary of the sectors—which marks the prearranged correct course—the pilot of the plane hears a steady signal tone. The marked course alone leads the pilot to his goal. Similarly, every man in all situations in life always has marked out before him a single and unique course by which he can attain to the realization of his most personal potentialities.

But if the patient should object that he does not know the meaning of his life, that the unique potentialities of his existence are not apparent to him, then we can only reply that his primary task is just this: to find his way to his own proper task, to advance toward the uniqueness and singularity of his own meaning in life. As for this matter of each man's inner potentialities—in other words, how a man is to go about learning what he ought to be from what he is—there is no better answer than that given by Goethe: "How can we learn to know ourselves? Never by reflection, but by action. Try to do your duty and you will soon find out what you are. But what is your duty? The demands of each day."

Now, there will be people who recognize the unique-task quality of life, and who wish to actualize its concrete, singular situational values, but who still consider their personal situation "hopeless." We must ask ourselves first of all: what does hopeless mean? After all, man cannot predict his future; he cannot do so if only because knowledge of the future would instantly influence his present conduct—the type of influence depending upon whether he was by temperament defiant or suggestible. Thus he would in any case always shape the future differently, so that the original prediction would no longer hold.

Because man cannot prophesy, he can never properly judge whether his future will contain possibilities for the realization of values. A Negro who had been condemned to a life sentence of forced labor was shipped out from Marseille to Devil's Island. On the high seas a fire broke out on the steamer. The convict, an unusually strong man, was released from his handcuffs—and saved the lives of ten persons. Later his sentence was commuted for this act of heroism. If this man had been asked at the quay in Marseille whether the rest of his life was likely to have any meaning, he would probably have shaken his head. No man can ever know what life still holds in store for him, or what magnificent hour may still await him.

No man is justified in insisting upon his own inadequacies—that is, in demeaning his own potentialities. No matter how discontented with himself a person may be, no matter how he torments himself with brooding on his own failings and how sternly he sits in judgment upon himself—the very fact that he is doing so proves that he is not so poor a creature as he thinks he is. Just as deploring the relativity and subjectivity of all knowledge and values assumes the objectivity of knowledge and values, so a man's moral self-condemnation assumes an ideal of personality, his private ought-to-be. Thus, the man who judges himself harshly has caught sight of a value and is taking part in the world of values. The moment he is able to apply the standard of an ideal to himself, he cannot be entirely valueless any longer. For by that fact he has reached a level of ethical values by which he is redeemed from worthlessness. "If our eye partook not of the sun, the sun it ne'er could see. . . ."

The same holds true for those generalizations of moral despair which cast fundamental doubt on the morality of mankind. This type of thinking holds that man is evil both in himself and at the root.* But this brand of ethical *Weltschmerz* also must not be allowed to paralyze anyone's ethical actions. Someone objects that "all men are ultimately nothing but egoists" and that occasional acts of altruism are in reality also egoism, since the seeming altruist is only trying to secure freedom from the unease born of sympathy. Our answer must be: in the first place, the elimination of sympa-

---

* We might even grant that the average man may well fall short of being good and that only individuals here and there are truly good. But if that is the situation, does it not impose upon each person the task of being better than the average, of becoming one of those rare individuals?

thetic pain is not a purpose, but a result; in the second place, the fact that sympathy is felt actually presupposes morality in the form of genuine altruism. Furthermore, what we have said of the life of the individual applies also to the life of mankind: that the peaks are decisive—in the history of a given era as in mountain ranges. A few model lives, a few intellectual or ethical geniuses, or even a single individual here and there whom we truly love, might provide justification enough for humanity as a whole.

If, finally, it is argued that the eternally great ideals of humanity are everywhere misused and employed as means for the ends of politics, business, personal erotic adventure, or private vanity—we may reply: that only testifies to the imperishable power of those ideals, and shows that they are binding upon everyone. For if a type of conduct must be cloaked with morality in order to be effective, that constitutes proof that morality really is effective, as nothing else is so prone to take effect upon human beings who themselves hold morality dear.

The task a man has to accomplish in life is therefore at bottom always present and in principle is always within the man's powers. Existential analysis accordingly is designed to help the individual comprehend his responsibility to accomplish each of his tasks. The more he grasps the task quality of life, the more meaningful will his life appear to him. While the man who is not conscious of his responsibility simply takes life as a given fact, existential analysis teaches people to see life as an assignment. But the following addendum must be made: There are people who go a step further, who, as it were, experience life in a further dimension. They also experience the authority from which the task comes. They experience the taskmaster who has assigned the task to them. In our opinion we have here an essential characteristic of the religious man: he is a man who interprets his existence not only in terms of being responsible *for* fulfilling his life tasks, but also as being responsible *to* the taskmaster.*

Finding their concrete, personal tasks in life is especially hard for neurotics because of their characteristic lack of instinctive sure-

---

* A concrete example will illustrate this deepening of the consciousness of responsibility in the religious person. We quote from an essay by L. G. Bachmann on the composer Anton Bruckner: "His sense of responsibility toward God was growing to infinite proportions. Thus he said to his friend Dr. Josef Kluger, canon of Klosterneuburg: 'They want me to write differently. I could, too, but I may not. Out of thousands God in His mercy chose me and endowed me with talent, me of all persons. Some day I will have to account to Him. And then how would I stand before our Lord if I followed the others and not Him?'"

It would be erroneous to maintain that the religious attitude necessarily makes for passivity. Quite the contrary, it may activate the individual to a tremendous extent. It certainly will have this effect upon that type of religious person whose existential attitude comprises a sense of his being, as it were, a soldier for God upon earth. He feels that everything is being "decided" here upon earth; •ipon this earth all conflicts are fought out, contested by and within each individual human being, and therefore by and within himself. In this connection there springs to mind as a parable that Chassidic tale of the sage who once said to his disciples: "Now tell us when and how a man knows whether Heaven has forgiven him for something." And he supplied the answer: "Man can recognize the forgiveness of Heaven for a sin only by his never committing this sin again."

The unique achievement of Mosaic monotheism may well consist in its conveying to the human race the permanent consciousness of a divine authority. Man is seen as a being standing before God, thereby intensifying man's consciousness of responsibility by presenting his life task to him as an assignment from the Divine. But we must not forget that the moral urge springing from this view was chiefly concerned with what we have called creative values. It must therefore appear all the more remarkable to us when we realize that Christianity has placed in the foreground of man's moral consciousness the kind of values we have called attitudinal

---

II From Psychoanalysis
to Existential Analysis

ness in sensing their tasks. For example, a woman suffering from obsessional neurosis did everything she could to block herself from studying psychology, for which she was distinctly talented, by exaggerating her maternal duties. Using her knowledge of individual psychology, she constructed the theory that psychology for her was only a "subsidiary theater of war," that her studies were a neurotic "arrangement." Only after she had cast aside this mistaken self-analysis and had subjected her life to an existential-analytical survey was she able to "know herself by acting" and meet "the demands of each day." When she had accomplished that, she found that she did not need to neglect either her child or her vocational field.

The neurotic inclines to play one life task off against the other. We find other types of mistaken behavior in the typical neurotic. For example, he may attempt to live "according to a program, point by point," as an obsessional neurotic woman once put it. We cannot really live with Baedekers in our hands; if we did so, we would overlook all chances in life that come only once; we would skirt our destiny and pass by situational values instead of actualizing them.

In the light of existential analysis there is no such thing as a

---

—the third of the three main categories of possible values. For the Christian existence, taken in the perspective of the cross, of the Crucified One, becomes ultimately and essentially a freely chosen imitation of Christ, a "passion." It remained for Protestantism to install the further element; by emphasizing the concept of grace, Protestantism deepened man's sense of responsibility in regard to the second category of values, experiential values. For in terms of the idea of grace, which is so cardinal a point in Protestant theology, all of man's encounters with valuational experiences constitute receiving a gift of God (grace). All this, it seems to us, suggests a coherent relationship between the three categories of values on the one hand and the three principal branches of Occidental religion on the other.

generally valid and universally binding life task. From this point of view the question of "the" task in life or "the" meaning of life is—meaningless. It reminds us of the question a reporter asked a grand master in chess. "And now tell me, maestro—what is the best move in chess?" Neither question can be answered in a general fashion, but only in regard to a particular situation and person. The chess master, if he took the question seriously, would have had to reply: "A chess-player must attempt, within the limits of his ability and within the limits imposed by his opponent, to make the best move at any given time." Two points must be stressed here. First, "within the limits of his ability"; that is to say, the inner state, what we call temperament, must be taken into consideration. And, secondly, the player can only "attempt" to make a move which is best in a concrete situation in the game—that is, in relation to a specific configuration of the pieces. If he set out from the start with the intention of making the best move in an absolute sense, he would be tormented by eternal doubts and endless self-criticism, and would at best overstep the time limit and forfeit the game.

A person who is confronted with the question of the meaning of life is in an analogous situation. For him, too, the question makes sense only if he asks it in reference to a concrete situation and to his own concrete personality. It would be ethically erroneous and psychologically morbid for him to take it into his head to perform an act of "supreme" value, instead of modestly "attempting" to do his best. That he must aim at the best is imperative; otherwise his efforts would come to nought. But at the same time he must be able to content himself with nothing more than approaching nearer and nearer, without ever quite attaining his goal.

Our remarks on the question of the meaning of life come down to a radical criticism of the question as such. To ask the meaning of life in general terms is to put the question falsely because it refers vaguely to "life" and not concretely to "each person's own" existence. Perhaps we ought to go far back and recollect the original structure of experience. In that case we must perform a kind of Copernican Revolution, and give the question of the meaning of life an entirely new twist. To wit:

It is life itself that asks questions of man. As was pointed out earlier, it is not up to man to question; rather, he should recognize that he is questioned, questioned by life; he has to respond by being responsible; and he can answer *to* life only by answering *for* his life.

It is perhaps to the point to mention here that developmental psychology also shows that "discovery of meaning" represents a higher stage of development than "conferring of meaning." Thus the argument we have endeavored to "develop" logically above corresponds to the course of psychological development: the paradoxical primacy of response as against question. It is based upon man's experience with himself as the questionee. The guide which guides man in his responses to the question life puts, in his taking the responsibility for his life, is conscience. Conscience has its "still small voice" and "speaks" to us—that is an undeniable phenomenological fact. What conscience says, however, is in every case a response. From the psychological point of view, the religious person is one who experiences not only what is spoken, but the speaker as well; that is, his hearing is sharper than the non-religious person's. In the dialogue with his conscience—in this most intimate of possible monologues—his God is his interlocutor.*

---

* We are speaking here, of course, only of the type of religious experience in which God is experienced as a personal Being, in fact as the very sum and prime image of personality, or—we might also say—as the first and last "Thou." For a person religious in this sense the experiencing of God means experiencing the ultimate "Thou."

(a)　On the Meaning of Death

In attempting to answer the question of the meaning of life
—that most human of all questions—man is thrown back upon
himself, must realize that he is questioned by life and has to answer
and be answerable with his life. That is, he is thrown back upon
the primal elements of human existence—being conscious and being
responsible. In existential analysis, which is analysis of the responsibility aspects of being human, responsibility has been shown to
arise out of the concreteness of person and situation and to grow
with this concreteness. Responsibility grows, as we have seen, with
the uniqueness of the person and the singularity of the situation.
Uniqueness and singularity, we have said, are fundamental components of the meaning of human life.

At the same time, the finiteness of man's existence is poign-
antly present in these two essential factors of his existence. Therefore, that finiteness must itself constitute something that gives
meaning to human existence—not something that robs it of meaning. This is a point that requires more discussion. First let us take
up the question of whether the finiteness of man in time, the
temporal finiteness of his life—the fact of death—can make life
meaningless.

How often we hear the argument that death does away with
the meaning of life altogether. That in the end all man's works are
meaningless, since death ultimately destroys them. Now, does death
really decrease the meaningfulness of life? On the contrary. For

what would our lives be like if they were not finite in time, but infinite? If we were immortal, we could legitimately postpone every action forever. It would be of no consequence whether or not we did a thing now; every act might just as well be done tomorrow or the day after or a year from now or ten years hence. But in the face of death as absolute finis to our future and boundary to our possibilities, we are under the imperative of utilizing our lifetimes to the utmost, not letting the singular opportunities—whose "finite" sum constitutes the whole of life—pass by unused.

Finality, temporality, is therefore not only an essential characteristic of human life, but also a real factor in its meaningfulness. The meaning of human existence is based upon its irreversible quality. An individual's responsibility in life must therefore be understood in terms of temporality and singularity. If, then, in existential analysis we wish to bring our patients to consciousness of their responsibility, we must try by parables to put before them the historical quality of life out of which responsibility flows. For example, the doctor might suggest to the patient that he pretend to be leafing through his own biography in the declining days of his life. Let the patient suppose that he has just opened to the chapter dealing with the present phase of his life and that by a miracle he has the power to decide what the contents of the next chapter shall be. He is to imagine, that is, that it still lies within his capacity to make corrections, as it were, in a crucial chapter of his unwritten inner life story.

In general, the leading maxim of existential analysis might be put thus: live as if you were living for the second time and had acted as wrongly the first time as you are about to act now. Once an individual really puts himself into this imagined situation, he will instantaneously become conscious of the full gravity of the responsibility that every man bears throughout every moment of his life: the responsibility for what he will make of the next hour, for how he will shape the next day.

Or else we instruct the patient to imagine his life as if it were a moving-picture which is just being "shot," but which he will not be permitted to "cut"; that is, anything once "taken" can never be retroactively changed. By such examples as these the physician can impress on the patient the irreversible quality of human life, the historical nature of his existence.

In the beginning life is still all substance, still unconsumed. As it unfolds, however, it loses more and more substance, is more and more converted into function, so that at the end it consists largely of what acts, experiences, and sufferings have been gone through by the person who has lived. Thus man's life is reminiscent of radium with its limited "span of life" during which its atoms disintegrate and its matter is steadily transformed into energy which never again returns and never again is reconverted into matter. For the process of atomic disintegration is irreversible, "directed"; with radium, too, the original substantiality increasingly decreases. Of life it may be said, similarly, that its original material quality more and more vanishes, until in the end it has become pure form. For man resembles a sculptor who chisels and hammers the un-shaped stone so that the material takes on more and more form. Man works the matter with which fate has supplied him: now creating, now experiencing or suffering, he attempts to "hammer out" values in his life—as many as he can of creative or experiential or attitudinal values.

We can also introduce the factor of time into this simile of the sculptor: We need only imagine that the sculptor has a limited span of time at his disposal for completing his work of art—but that he is not informed when his deadline is. Thus he never knows when he is going to be "called away," whether the summons may not come in the very next minute. He is therefore forced to use his time well in any case—lest his work remain abortive. That time runs out before the work is completed by no means makes it worthless, however. The "fragmentary quality" of life (Simmel) does not detract from its meaning. It is not from the length of its span that we can ever draw conclusions as to a life's meaningfulness. We cannot, after all, judge a biography by its length, by the number of pages in it; we must judge by the richness of the contents. The heroic life of one who has died young certainly has more content and meaning than the existence of some long-lived dullard. Sometimes the "unfinisheds" are among the most beautiful symphonies.

Man's position in life is like that of a student at a final examination; in both cases it is less important that the work be completed than that its quality be high. The student must be prepared for the bell to ring signaling that the time at his disposal is ended, and in life we must be ready all the time to be "called away."

In time and in finiteness man must *finish* something—that is, take finiteness upon himself and consciously accept an end as part of the bargain. This attitude is not necessarily the sole property of heroes; in fact we find such an attitude underlying the ordinary behavior of the average man. Going to the movies, for example, our average man will probably be more concerned that a picture have some kind of end than that it have a happy ending. The mere fact that the ordinary man needs motion pictures or the theater constitutes proof in itself of the meaningfulness of the historical element. If it were not important to explicate what matters—that is, to unfold it in time, represent it historically—people would be content to have "the moral of the story" conveyed in the briefest possible form, instead of bothering to sit for hours in the theater.

There is, then, no necessity to somehow exclude death from

life; rather, it belongs quite properly to life! Nor is there any way to "overcome it," as people sometimes think when they seek immortality through reproduction. For there is no truth in the statement that the meaning of life is to be found in future generations. First of all, our lives cannot be propagated *ad infinitum*. Families ultimately die out, and some day the whole of humanity may well have to die out—supposing that the human race lasts until some cosmic catastrophe wipes out the planet Earth. If life were rendered meaningless by the factor of its finiteness, it would not matter at all when the end came, or whether or not it were within the foreseeable future. To close one's eyes to the irrelevancy of the date of ultimate end is to be like the lady who cried out in horror when the astronomer told her that the world would probably come to an end in a billion years. And when she was reassured: "But not before a billion years," she sighed with relief and remarked: "Oh, I thought I heard you say just a million." Either life has a meaning and retains this meaning whether it is long or short, whether or not it reproduces itself; or life has no meaning, in which case it takes on none, no matter how long it lasts or can go on reproducing itself. If the life of a childless woman were really meaningless solely because she had no children, then humanity lives only for its children, and the sole meaning of existence is to be found in the next generation. But that is only a postponement of the problem. For every generation hands the problem on to the next generation unsolved. The only meaning in the life of one generation consists in raising the next. But to perpetuate something in itself meaningless is meaningless. If the thing is meaningless, it does not acquire meaning by being immortalized.

Even when a torch goes out, its light has had meaning; but there is no meaning in conducting an eternal torch race to infinity, passing on and on a torch that is not burning. "What is to give light must endure burning," Wildgans says. That is, it must suffer. We might also say that it must endure until it is burned, until it is burned "to the end."

We come, then, to the paradox that a life whose only meaning lay in its propagation would *eo ipso* be just as meaningless as the propagation. And on the other hand the propagation of life has meaning only when and if life in itself represents something meaningful. So that to elevate motherhood into the sole and ultimate meaning of woman's life is not only to denigrate the life of the childless woman, but to denigrate the life of the mother. The absence of posterity cannot render the existence of an important human being meaningless. What is more, the whole line of ancestors leading up to him might achieve its crowning meaning retroactively, simply through the importance of this one existence in which the line culminated. From all of which we see once again that life can never be an end in itself, and that its reproduction can never be its meaning; rather, it acquires meaning from other, non-biologic frames of reference: intellectual, ethical, æsthetic, and so on. These frames of reference therefore represent a transcendental factor. Life transcends itself not in "length"—in the sense of reproduction of itself—but in "height"—by fulfilling values—or in "breadth" in the community.

These arguments were presented to a patient for whom it was strictly inadvisable, for eugenic reasons, to have children. The patient, a teacher and writer, finally admitted of his own accord that his original views—namely, that his intellectually fruitful life lacked meaning because he could not have children—represented "actually a kind of materialism." Moreover, he was led to perceive that his original attitude was one of self-contempt: his own physical weakness had made him overestimate the importance of biological "immortality." It was necessary to ask him whether he could wish that his memory should live on in a son suffering from a hereditary disease or whether it would not be better if it should live on in whole generations of readers and pupils. After the patient had accepted all this, he was prepared to break off his projected marriage. Again, it was necessary for the physician to intervene and point out to him that reproduction has as little to do with the meaning of marriage as it has with the meaning of life. Instinctual gratification and biological reproduction are, after all, only two aspects of marriage—and not even the most important ones. The spiritual factor of love is more essential.

The correlate to the singularity of human existence is the uniqueness of every human being. But just as death as a temporal, outward limitation does not cancel the meaning of life but rather is the very factor that constitutes its meaning, so the inner limits only add to the meaning of man's life. If all men were perfect, then every individual would be replaceable by anyone else. From the very imperfection of men follows the indispensability and inexchangeability of each individual; for each is imperfect in his own fashion. No man is universally gifted; but the bias of the individual makes for his uniqueness.

A biological example will make this clear. As is well known, when one-celled life forms evolve into many-celled organisms they pay the price of losing their immortality. They also sacrifice their omnipotence. They exchange all-aroundness for specificity. The highly differentiated retinal cell, for example, performs a function that no other type of cell can perform. The principle of division of labor has deprived the cell of its functional versatility, but what it has lost in the way of independent functioning is offset by its relative indispensability within the organism.

In a mosaic, similarly, every particle, every individual piece of stone is incomplete, imperfect as it were, in form and color; its meaning follows only from its use in the whole. If each of the tesseræ contained the whole—like a miniature—each could be replaced by any of the others. A crystal may be perfect in its form, but for that very reason it is replaceable by any other specimen of the same crystal form; one octahedron is like any other.

The more highly differentiated a man is, the less he resembles the norm—norm both in the sense of average and in the sense of ideal. At the price of normality or, as the case may be, ideality, he has bought his individuality. The significance of such individuality, the meaning of human personality, is, however, always related to community. For just as the uniqueness of the tessera is a value only in relation to the whole of the mosaic, so the uniqueness of the human personality finds its meaning entirely in its role in an integral whole. Thus the meaning of the human person as a personality points beyond its own limits, toward community; in being directed toward community the meaning of the individual transcends itself.

There is an emotional gregariousness of human beings; but beyond this, community has its task quality. But an individual existence not only must have the community in order to become meaningful; vice versa, the community needs the individual existence in order for it itself to have meaning. Therein lies an essential distinction between community and the mere mass. Far from providing a frame of reference for the individual existence, the mass does not tolerate individuality. If the relationship of the individual to the community may be compared with that of a tessera to a whole mosaic, then the relationship of the individual to the mass may be equated with that of a standardized paving-stone to uniform gray pavement: every stone is cut to the same size and shape and may be replaced by any other; none has qualitative importance for the whole. And the pavement itself is not really an integral whole, merely a magnitude. The uniform pavement also does not have the æsthetic value of a mosaic; it possesses only utilitarian value—just as the mass submerges the dignity and value of men and extracts only their utility.

The meaning of individuality comes to fulfillment in the community. To this extent, then, the value of the individual is dependent upon the community. But if the community itself is to have meaning, it cannot dispense with the individuality of the individuals that make it up. In the mass, on the other hand, the single, unique existence is submerged, must be submerged because uniqueness would be a disrupting factor in any mass. The meaning of the community is constituted by individuality, and the meaning of individuality by community; the "meaning" of the mass is disrupted* by the individuality of the individuals composing it, and the meaning of individuality is submerged in the mass (while in the community it emerges).

We have said that the uniqueness of every human being and the singularity of all life are vital components of the meaning of existence. This singularity, however, must be distinguished from mere numerical singleness. All numerical singleness is in itself valueless. The fact that one man differs from all other men in the pattern of his fingerprints by no means establishes him as a personality. Whenever, therefore, we speak of uniqueness as a factor of meaning in human existence, we do not infer this kind of "fingerprint" uniqueness. We might then—analogous to Hegel's "good" and "bad" infinity—speak of a good and a bad uniqueness. "Good uniqueness" would be the kind that is directed toward a community for which a person has a unique significant value.

Personal existence constitutes a special mode of being. A

---

* Therefore the mass suppresses the individuality of the individuals composing it, and therefore it limits their *liberty* for the sake of *equality*. *Fraternity*, moreover, is replaced by the herd instinct.

house, for example, is made up of stories, and the stories of rooms. The house therefore can just as well be conceived as the sum of stories as a room can be conceived as the quotient of a story. We can therefore draw the limits of being more or less arbitrarily; we can deliberately delimit particular being and extract it from the totality of being. Only the being of a person, personal existence, is not subject to this arbitrary procedure; a person is something complete within himself, subsisting for himself—neither divisible nor addable.

The preferential position of man within being, the special quality of the human mode of being, can be described by referring to our original thesis, "to be equals to be different." We may formulate it thus: personal being (human existence) means absolute *being different*, absolute otherness. For the uniqueness of every individual human being means that he is different from all other human beings.

Man therefore cannot be integrated into any complex being of a high order without this being losing the particular quality of dignity which characterizes human existence. We see this most clearly in the phenomenon of the mass, the mob. The mass as such has no consciousness and no responsibility. Therefore it is without existence. To the extent that it is nevertheless operative, and in that sense "real," it never operates in and of itself. Sociological laws do not operate above the heads of individuals, but through them, by means of them. These laws may seem to be valid, but they are so only to the degree that probability calculations for the data of mass psychology are valid, and only to the extent that an average type is psychologically predictable. But this average type is a scientific fiction and not a real person; it fails to be a real person precisely because it is predictable.

By escape into the mass, man loses his most intrinsic quality: responsibility. On the other hand, when he shoulders the tasks set him by society, man gains something—in that he adds to his responsibility. To escape into the mass is to disburden oneself of individual responsibility. As soon as someone acts as if he were a mere part of the whole, and as if only this whole counts, he can enjoy the sensation of throwing off some of the burden of his responsibility. This tendency to flee from responsibility is the motif of all collectivism. True community is in essence the community of responsible persons; mere mass is the sum of depersonalized entities.

When it comes to evaluating people, collectivism leads us astray. For in place of responsible persons, the collectivist idea substitutes a mere type, and in place of personal responsibility, substitutes conformity to norms. In the process responsibility is whisked away not only for the object of judgment, but for the subject as well. Evaluation by type simplifies things for the person who judges, insofar as it relieves him of the responsibility for the judgment. If we evaluate a human being as a type, we need not take the individual case into account, and that is so convenient. It is as convenient as evaluating an automobile by its make or body type. If you drive a certain make of car, you know where you stand. If you know the brand of a typewriter, you know what to expect of it. You can even select your breed of dog in this way; a poodle will have certain inclinations and certain traits, a wolfhound will have others. Only in the case of man is this not so. Man alone is not determined by his origins; his behavior cannot be calculated from the type. The reckoning will not come out even; there is always a remainder. This remainder is the freedom of man to escape the conditioning factors of type. Man begins to be human only where he has the freedom to oppose bondage to a type. For only there, in freedom, is his being—being responsible; only there "is" man authentically, or only there is man "authentic." The more standardized a machine is, the better it is; but the more standardized a person is, the more submerged he is in his race, class, or characterological type, the more he conforms to a standard average —the more inferior is he from the ethical standpoint.

In the moral sphere the collective point of view leads to the idea of "collective guilt." Men are made responsible for something they are not actually responsible for. In judging or, as the case may be, condemning men in this manner, the person who judges evades the responsibility for his judgment. Of course it is ever so much more facile to evaluate or devaluate "races" wholesale, rather than rank every individual human being in one of the two morally relevant "races" to which all men belong: the "race" of the decent or the "race" of the rotten.

———————

Human responsibility, which existential analysis strives to make men aware of, is a responsibility springing from the singularity and uniqueness of each man's existence. Man's existence is a responsibility springing from man's finiteness. This finiteness of life, the limited time man has upon this earth, does not make living meaningless. On the contrary, as we have seen, death itself is what makes life meaningful. We have said that a part of the singularity of life is the singularity of every situation. Now, a part of the uniqueness of life is the uniqueness of every man's destiny. Like death, destiny is a part of life. No man can break away from the concrete, unique sphere of his personal destiny. If he quarrels with his destiny—that is to say, with what is beyond his power, for which he bears no responsibility or blame—he is overlooking the meaning of destiny. And there is a meaning to destiny—destiny is as essential to the meaning of life as is death. Within his own "exclusive" sphere of destiny every man is irreplaceable. This irreplaceability adds to the responsibility with which he has to shape his destiny. To have a destiny means in each case to have one's own destiny.

With his unique destiny each man stands, so to speak, alone in the entire cosmos. His destiny will not recur. No one else has the same potentialities as he, nor will he himself be given them again. The opportunities that come his way for the actualization of creative or experiential values, the tribulations which are destined to come his way—which he cannot alter and must therefore endure and in the enduring of them actualize attitudinal values—all these are unique and singular.

The paradoxical nature of any revolt against destiny becomes clear when a person asks what his life would have been like if someone other than his actual father had begotten him; he forgets, of course, that in that case he would not have been "himself," that the person undergoing this different destiny would have been someone else entirely so that it would no longer be possible to speak of "his" destiny. The question of the possibility of a different destiny is therefore untenable in itself, self-contradictory and meaningless.

An individual's destiny belongs to him in much the same way as the ground, which fetters him by its gravity, but without which walking would be impossible. We must accept our destiny as we accept the ground on which we stand—a ground which is the springboard for our freedom. Freedom without destiny is impossible; freedom can only be freedom in the face of a destiny, a free stand toward destiny. Certainly man is free, but he is not floating freely in airless space. He is always surrounded by a host of restrictions. These restrictions, however, are the jumping-off points for his freedom. Freedom presupposes restrictions, is contingent upon restrictions. Mind is contingent upon instinct, existence upon substance. But this contingency does not mean dependency. The ground on which a man walks is always being transcended in the process of walking, and serves as ground only to the extent that it is transcended, that it provides a springboard. If we wanted to define man, we would have to call him that entity which has freed itself from whatever has determined it (determined it as biological-psychological-sociological type); that entity, in other words, that transcends all these determinants either by conquering them and shaping them, or by deliberately submitting to them.

This paradox points up the dialectical quality of man, with his eternal incompleteness and his freedom of choice—his reality is a potentiality. What he is, he is not yet, but ought to be and should become.

Being human is being responsible because it is being free. It is a state of being that—as Jaspers says—first decides what it is; it is "deciding being." It is "existence." The table before me is and remains what it is, at least for its part—that is to say, unless a human being puts hand to it and changes it. But the human being who sits opposite me at this table decides in every case what he "is" during the next second, what he will say to me or conceal from me. There is a multitude of different possibilities in his being, of which he actualizes only a single one and in so doing determines his existence as such. (The human mode of being, called existence, might also be termed "the being that I am.") During no moment of his life does man escape the mandate to choose among possibilities. Yet he can pretend to act "as if" he had no choice and no freedom of decision. This "acting as if" constitutes a part of the human tragicomedy.

The Emperor Franz I of Austria, anecdote has it, had repeatedly rebuffed a petitioner who kept coming back with the same request. After still another rebuff the emperor turned to his adjutant and said: "You'll see, the fool will get his way in the end." What strikes us as funny in this anecdote? It is the fact that the emperor is pretending not to be free, to be powerless to decide whether or not "the fool" will really "get his way" next time.

The comic aspect of the person who is blind to his essential freedom of decision is one of the stock situations of humor. There is the story of the man who is complaining to his wife that people nowadays are without any moral fiber. To prove his point he says: "For instance, I found a wallet today. Do you think I would take it into my head to leave it at the Lost and Found?" What is the joke here? That anyone should speak of his own dishonesty as though he were not responsible for it. This man is pretending that he must simply accept his own lack of moral fiber as a given fact, just as he must accept that of others. He is acting as if he were not free and could not have decided whether to keep the wallet or surrender it at the Lost and Found.

We have mentioned the teacher who described the "essence" of life as a process of oxidation or combustion. A candle which is *"vorhanden"*—to use the terminology of existential philosophy— burns to the end without being in any way able to control this process of combustion. Man, on the other hand—having *"Dasein"* —is always free to decide on the nature of his being. The range of his power to decide extends even to the possibility of self-destruction; man can "extinguish himself." We will go so far as to say that this most radical challenging of oneself, to the extent not only of doubt-ing the meaning of life, but of taking action against that life—this fundamental possibility of choosing suicide, this liberty of man to decide whether he shall be at all, distinguishes his being from all other kinds of being and marks its contrast with the mode of being of animals.

The freedom of decision, so-called freedom of the will, is for the unbiased person a matter of course; he has an immediate experience of himself as free. The person who seriously doubts freedom of the will must either be hopelessly prejudiced by a deterministic philosophy or suffering from a paranoid schizophrenia, in which case he experiences his will as having been "made" unfree. In cases of neurotic fatalism, freedom of the will is concealed; the neurotic person himself blocks the realization of his own potentialities; he stands in the way of what he himself is "able to be." Thus he deforms his life. If, as we said at the start, to be human means to be different, we must now rephrase this formula: to be human means not only to be different, but also to be able to become different, that is, to change.

Freedom of the will is opposed to destiny. For what we call destiny is that which is essentially exempt from human freedom, that which lies neither within the scope of man's power nor his responsibility. However, we must never forget that all human freedom is contingent upon destiny to the extent that it can unfold only within destiny and by working upon it.

The whole of the past, precisely because it is unalterable, goes to make up man's destiny. What has passed is intrinsically fate. Nevertheless, man has some freedom even with regard to destiny as embodied in the past. Certainly the past does much to explain the present, but we are not to see the future as exclusively determined by that past. That is a characteristic error of the typical neurotic fatalist who reviews the mistakes committed in the past and considers that his unfortunate history absolves him from any faults he may commit in the future. As a matter of fact the mistakes of the past should serve as fruitful material for shaping a "better" future; the mistakes should have "taught a lesson." Man is free to take a purely fatalistic attitude toward his past, or to learn something from it. It is never too late to learn—but neither is it too soon; it is always "high time" we learned whatever is to be learned. To disregard this is to resemble the drunkard who was urged to quit drinking.

"It is already too late," he replied.

"But it is never too late."

"In that case I can quit some other time."

Human freedom is called into play by the unalterability of the past which has thus become destiny. Destiny must always be a stimulus to conscious, responsible action. As we have seen, man's position in life is such that at any moment he may select out of many possibilities a single one which by actualizing he rescues, as it were, transporting it safely into the realm of the past. In the realm of the past, what is past "remains"—paradoxical as that may sound—and it "remains" not in spite of being past, but precisely because it is past. As we have remarked earlier, the reality of the past is "saved" in the sense of "conserved." To have been is the "safest" form of being. By being past, possibilities are saved from passing away; only unrealized possibilities pass away. (Compare what has been said earlier in regard to singular situational values and the irrevocably passing opportunity to actualize them.) What has been conserved in the past is alone preserved from passing; reality is rescued from extinction by becoming past. The moment becomes eternity if the possibilities hidden in the present are converted into those realities which are held safely in the past "for all eternity." That is the meaning of all actualizing. In this sense man actualizes not only where he performs an act or creates a work "once and for all," but also where he simply experiences. As we see it, this objectivism enables us to say that what has been realized in experience can never be really annihilated, even if it should be forgotten, and indeed even if the memory of it is totally stamped out—by the death of the person experiencing it. As the counterpart to this, compare what we say

*II From Psychoanalysis
to Existential Analysis*

further (page 110) on the subjectivism or, as the case may be, psychologism of a person who, confronted with misfortune, stupe- fies himself by escaping into "unawareness" of the misfortune—by intoxication—or into absolute unawareness—death through suicide.

Destiny appears to man in three principal forms: (1) as his natural *disposition* or endowment, what Tandler has called man's "somatic fate"; (2) as his *situation*, the total of his external environ- ments; (3) disposition and situation together make up man's *position*. Toward this he "takes a position"—that is, he forms an attitude. This "position taken" or attitude is—in contrast to the basically destined "position given"—a matter of free choice. Proof of this is the fact that man can "change his position," take another attitude (as soon as we include the time dimension in our scheme, since a change of position means an alteration of attitude in the course of time). Included under change of position in this sense is, for example, everything we call education, learning, and self-im- provement, but also psychotherapy in the broadest sense of the word, and such inner revolutions as religious conversion.

Disposition represents the biological fate of man, situation his sociological destiny. In addition there is his psychological des- tiny. In the subsequent pages we will examine in turn how the biological, the psychological, and the sociological as factors of destiny obstruct human freedom.

Let us turn first to those cases or situations in which man is confronted with biological destiny. The question immediately arises of how far man's freedom extends in regard to his organism, or how deep down into the physiological realm the power of his free will reaches. We herewith approach the mind-body problem, though we will have to sidestep the interminable discussion of whether and to what extent the physical body of man is dependent on his psycho-spiritual being, and vice versa. We will confine ourselves to a comparison of a set of case histories, with the hope that these speak for themselves.

Lange, the psychiatrist, has reported the following case. He knew a pair of identical twin brothers who had been separated for many years. Almost at the same time that he was treating one of these brothers for paranoia, he received a letter from the other brother, who lived in a distant city. The letter betrayed a delusion identical in content with his twin's paranoia. Here was destiny indeed; the identical twins, who had developed from the same germ cell and had the same fundamental disposition, developed the same mental disease.

In the presence of such a case as this, is it not incumbent upon us to bow to the power of biological destiny? Given facts like these, which attest to the ability of organic forces to come to the fore in defiance of everything, how can we presume to doubt these forces? Is not man's destiny critically shaped by such biological factors, by the endowment he is born with? Where, then, is there room for the human spirit to take command? The results of research into the hereditary pathology of twins suggest fatalistic conclusions which are dangerous because they paralyze man's will to defy his inner destiny. The man who believes his fate is sealed is incapable of repealing it.

Now for the second case history. Working within the Vienna Neurological Clinic, Dr. Hoff and his associates hypnotized experimental subjects in order to evoke pure "crystallized" affects. Joyous experiences or sad experiences were suggested to the subjects at various times. When blood serum was taken at a time of joyful excitement, the agglutination titer against typhoid bacilli was found to be enormously higher than when blood was taken from the same subject in a saddened state. These researches throw light upon the lowered resistance to infection of an anxious hypochondriac. They also suggest why nurses at hospitals for contagious diseases, or even at leprosy stations, nurses who are filled with a sense of moral dedication, have escaped infection to such an extent that people hitherto have always spoken of their immunity as "miraculous."

In our opinion, there is little point in opposing the "power of the spirit" to the "power of nature." We have already indicated that both mind and matter are part of man, that both are contingent upon one another in his existence. For man is a citizen of more than one realm; he stands in life in a state of permanent tension, in a bipolar field of force. If we attempted to pit the two powers against one another, to test the power of one against the power of the other, the result would probably be a "dead heat." As is well known, a dead heat is the liveliest kind of race. The eternal combat between man's spiritual freedom and his inward and outward destiny is what intrinsically makes up his life. Without in the least undervaluing the element of destiny, especially biological destiny, we as psychotherapists consider destiny as the ultimate testing-ground for human freedom. For the sake of our work, at least, we must behave as if the sphere of destined compulsion did not infringe upon the field of free action; in that way we give ourselves the fullest possible benefit of our freedom.

Even where physiology is intimately linked with the psychic—in the pathology of the brain—a morbid physical change does not necessarily and unalterably fix a person's destiny; rather, the malady gives him a starting-point for a free shaping of destiny. In this sense the brain is said to be "plastic." We know, for instance, that in case of injury to extensive parts of the brain, other parts of this organ can leap into the breach, can serve vicariously, so that sooner or later the necessary functions can be restored. Dandy, the

American brain surgeon, has even been able to remove the entire right cerebral cortex (in right-handed persons) without producing permanent psychic disturbances of any significance. It is a separate question whether the permanent physical handicap resulting from such an operation—the entire left half of the body is paralyzed—will be accepted by the patient or his relatives. A problem such as this bears on the ultimate philosophical basis of medical practice.

At present we do not even know whether whole parts of the human cerebrum may not be lying fallow. It is still to be ascertained whether all ganglial cells are actually being utilized. (The fact that other parts can take over the functions of injured centers would seem to indicate that they are not.) Most important of all, recent research has shown that the phylogenetic development of the cerebrum takes place by leaps. That is, the number of ganglial cells does not gradually increase, but suddenly doubles at each stage of development. Who can say definitely that we men of today have tapped all the resources to be found in the human brain at its present stage of evolution? Is it not conceivable that functional development still lags behind the maximum potentialities of the organ?

Biological destiny is the material which must be shaped by the free human spirit. This, from the point of view of man, is what it exists for. We witness again and again how man meaningfully incorporates his biological destiny into the structure of his life. We constantly encounter persons who have succeeded in exemplary fashion in overcoming the original handicaps and barriers to freedom that biological factors have imposed, who have surmounted the initial obstacles to their spiritual development. The form of life they ultimately attain to resembles an artistic or an athletic achievement—the former in the sense that the resistant biological matter has been given form by free will; the latter in the sense in which we earlier represented the feats of the athlete as a prime example of what disciplined effort could do. The runner who has started behind his competitor with such-and-such a handicap may emerge from the race as the better runner, even though he does not cross the finish line first. No wonder that the English, that nation of sportsmen, have made the phrase "to do one's best" one of their commonest maxims. To do one's best implies that one also includes the relativity of an accomplishment in the judgment of its value. The accomplishment must be judged in reference to the starting-point, to the concrete situation with all its difficulties, all its outward obstacles and inner inhibitions.

A human life marked from the beginning by the individual's defiance of a biological handicap can be seen as one great record-breaking race. We know a man who as the result of a prenatal brain disease had all four extremities partially paralyzed. His legs were so crippled that all his life he was condemned to a wheel chair. Until late in his adolescence he was generally considered to be mentally retarded also, and he remained illiterate. Finally a scientist took an interest in him and arranged for him to be given tutoring. In an amazingly short time our patient not only learned reading, writing, etc., but acquired the equivalent of a university education in subjects of special interest to him. A number of prominent scientists and professors vied with each other for the honor of being his private tutor. At his home he held a literary salon, of which he himself was the much-admired star. Beautiful women competed for his sexual favors, losing their hearts to him to such a point that there were scandals and even suicides on his account. And this man was not even able to speak normally! A severe general athetosis had affected his articulation; perspiring from the effort, with contorted features, he had to struggle visibly over the pronunciation of every single word. What a *tour de force* this man's shaping of his life represented! And what an example he might be to our patients, who for the most part have had a far easier start than this man! For had his life gone according to his "destiny," he might equally well be vegetating away in an institution for mental deficients, some day to die there unnoticed.

We turn now to what we have termed man's psychological fate, meaning by this those psychic factors which stand in the way of spiritual freedom. Psychoanalysis in particular has stressed the deterministic aspects of psychic events, viewing these events as the products of more or less irresistible "mechanisms." But any unbiased observer must recognize the plain fact that the instincts only make proposals, so to speak, while the ego decides what to do about these proposals. The ego can decide—resolve, freely choose; the ego "wills." And it does so independently of where the id "drives" it.

Even Freud, of course, had to admit that the ego is essentially opposed to the instincts, to the id. On the other hand he attempted to derive the ego from the instincts. An analogy to his concept would be a court proceeding in which the defendant, after his testimony, is made to take the place of the prosecuting attorney and conduct the case against himself. Erwin Straus has already shown that the authority which exerts censorship upon the instincts cannot itself have arisen out of the instincts. And Scheler has characterized psychoanalysis as intellectual alchemy which holds that sexual instincts can be transmuted into moral will.

Certainly the ego, as the embodiment of deciding will, has need of the dynamics of instinct. But the ego is never simply "driven." Sailing does not consist in letting a boat be driven by the wind; rather, the art of the sailor is his ability to use the wind in order to be driven in a given direction so that he is able to sail even against the wind. The danger of the psychoanalytic conception of man's instinctuality is that it culminates in fatalism. Neurotics above all incline to a blind belief in fate anyway.

There is no such thing as an original weakness of will. For all that the neurotic is apt to attribute independent status to strength of the will, it in itself is nothing static, nothing which is given once and for all. Rather, it is a function of clear recognition of goals, honest resolution, and a certain degree of training in making decisions (which last the neurotic certainly often needs). So long as a person makes the mistake of reminding himself constantly, before making an effort, that the effort may fail, he is not likely to succeed—if only because he does not like to disprove his own expectations. It is therefore all the more important when formulating a resolution to bar from the start all the counter-arguments which spring up with such profusion. For example, if someone considers the possibility of cutting out drinking, he can expect all sorts of inner objections to crop up almost immediately—"But I have to" or "Still, I won't be able to resist it" and so on. If instead he simply tells himself repeatedly: "There will be no drinking—and that's all there is to it!" he will be on the right path.

How instructive—though unwittingly and unintentionally so—was the reply a schizophrenic patient gave to the question of whether she were weak-willed: "I am weak-willed when I want to be, and when I don't want to be I'm not weak-willed." This psychotic patient was skillfully pointing out that people are inclined to hide their own freedom of will from themselves by alleging weakness of will.

Neurotic fatalists, impressed by the ideas of individual psychology (which they misunderstand and misuse), are prone to blame childhood educational and environmental influences for "making" them what they are and having determined their destinies. These persons are attempting to excuse their weaknesses of character. They accept these weaknesses as given facts, instead of seeing that having had such unfortunate early influences only makes it more incumbent upon them to practice self-restraint and seek to school themselves differently. A patient who was placed in a psychiatric institute after an attempted suicide answered the remonstrances of his psychotherapist: "What can I do about it? I'm just a typical Adlerian 'only child.'" Properly understood, the ethics of individual psychology ought to require that each person free himself from the typical faults and characterological weaknesses that still infect him as the result of his rearing—free himself so completely that he will no longer bear the marks of having been an "only child" or whatever his particular situation was. Neurotic fatalism is only another disguised form of escape from responsibility; the neurotic fatalist is betraying his uniqueness and singularity when he seeks refuge in typicality and courts the unalterable destiny of belonging to a type. In this connection it does not matter whether the type under whose laws a person believes himself to fall is a characterological type, a racial type, or a class type—whether, in other words, the fate invoked was psychological or (collective) biological or sociological.

The "law" (of individual psychology) which our aforementioned patient was "obeying" (being an only child) is valid only theoretically, for the outsider; practically, existentially, it is valid only so long as its validity is granted, so long as it is taken not only as a fact, but as a fate—and that is a fatalistic fiction. A faulty upbringing exonerates nobody; it has to be surmounted by conscious effort.

That a person's spiritual attitude has free play not only with respect to his physical, but also with respect to his psychic nature, that in other words there is no need for him to blindly submit to psychological destiny, is perhaps most clearly and dramatically manifested in cases where people must choose an attitude toward morbid states of the psyche. In his *Zur Psychologie der Zwangs-neurose* (*The Psychology of Obsessional Neurosis*) Erwin Straus has examined the extent to which psychopathological events are "creatural," by which he means destined and impervious to free will. In the special case of obsessional neurosis he inclines toward the view that the illness may restrict existential freedom to such an extent that even the philosophical position of the obsessional neurotic is fatefully determined. We cannot agree with this and will have further comment to make on this subject in another chapter. Here, however, we shall present a few examples, which demonstrate the possibility of a person's freely taking a position in spite of a sick psyche.

A patient, a highly intelligent schoolteacher, was under clinical treatment for periodically recurring depressions due to organic causes. A drug was prescribed. That is, the approach used was somatic. However, in the course of a brief talk, it turned out that the depression of the moment was not really organic, but psychogenic; taken as a whole, the illness had a psychogenic component. For the patient was weeping over the fact that she was so tearful. An additional psychogenic component was now complicating the original organic disease. She was now depressed over her depression; her present depression, that is, was a reaction to the organic condition. In view of this reaction, additional therapy was now indicated—namely, psychotherapy to treat the psychogenic factors. In line with this, the patient was instructed to ignore as far as possible her depressive mood, and above all to avoid unhappy brooding about her depression, since such brooding understandably but unjustifiably would tend to give her a bleak view of her prospects. It was suggested that she let the depression pass by her as a cloud passes over the sun, hiding the sun from our eyes. She must remember that the sun continues to exist, even if we do not see it for the moment. Similarly, values continue even though a person blinded to values by depression is momentarily unable to observe them.

Once psychotherapy was introduced, much that this patient had locked within herself was released. She herself disclosed her whole spiritual distress—her low opinion of herself, the paucity of content and meaning in her life—the dreary existence of a person who felt herself hopelessly handicapped by these recurrent depressions to which fate had condemned her. What was now indicated was a procedure that went beyond psychotherapeutic treatment in the narrower sense of the word. Here was a case where logotherapeutic treatment was necessary. It was the doctor's business to show the patient that her very affliction—these fated (Straus would say "creatural") recurrent depressions—posed a challenge for her. Since men are free to take a spiritual position on psychic processes, she was free to take a positive attitude toward it—or, in other words, to actualize what we have called attitudinal values. In time the patient learned to see her life as full of personal tasks, in spite of her states of dejection. Moreover, she learned to consider these states as presenting one more task: the task of somehow getting along with them and being superior to them. After this existential analysis—for that was what it was—she was able, in spite of and even during further phases of endogenous depression, to lead a life that was more conscious of responsibility and more filled with meaning than before treatment—more so, probably, than if she had never fallen ill and never needed treatment. One day this patient was able to write to her doctor: "I was not a human being until you made me one." We are reminded again of that remark of Goethe's which we have already quoted, and which we called the finest maxim for any kind of psychotherapy: "If we take people as they are, we make them worse. If we treat them as if they were what they ought to be, we help them to become what they are capable of becoming."

In many cases of psychic illness the free attitude toward life can best be practiced in the form of a reconciliation with the fate of being sick. For the continual vain struggles against such "creatural" conditions are precisely what so often leads to an additional depression; whereas the person who simply accepts such disorders without agony can more easily ignore them and more quickly rise above them.

A patient had for decades suffered from the severest acoustic hallucinations. She was continually hearing horrible voices jeering at everything she did. One day she was asked how it was that she nevertheless kept in such good spirits. How did she feel about hearing voices? She replied: "I just think to myself: after all, to hear voices like this is a lot better than to be deaf." How much skill in the conduct of life and how much achievement (in the sense of attitudinal values) is contained in this simple woman's demeanor. How courageously she put up with tormenting schizophrenic symptoms which might have driven her to lose control of herself entirely. Does not this droll and profoundly clever remark bespeak an element of spiritual freedom in the face of psychic illness?

Every psychiatrist knows how different the conduct of persons suffering from the same psychosis can be, depending on their different spiritual attitudes. One paretic is irritable and hostile toward his fellow men, while another—though the basic disease is one and the same—is friendly, good-natured, and may even be quite charming. We know of the following case: In a barrack in a concentration camp lay several dozen men down with typhus. All were delirious except one who made an effort to avert the nocturnal deliria by deliberately fighting back sleep at night. He profited by the excitement and mental stimulus induced by the fever, however, to reconstruct the unpublished manuscript of a scientific work he had written, which had been taken away from him in the concentration camp. In the course of sixteen feverish nights he had recovered the whole book—jotting down, in the dark, stenographic cue words on tiny scraps of paper.

Always and everywhere the individual appears to us embedded in the social nexus. His personality is determined by the community in a twofold manner, insofar as he is conditioned by the total social organism and is simultaneously directed toward this organism. There thus exists both a social causality in the individual and a social finality of the individual. In regard to social causality, it must be stressed again that the so-called sociological laws never completely determine the individual—do not, that is, deprive him of his freedom of will. Rather, they cannot affect him without first passing through a zone of individual freedom where they leave their mark upon the individual's behavior. In respect to his social destiny there remains for man an area within which free decision is possible, as is the case with his biological or psychological destiny.

While we are on the subject of social destiny, we must point out an unfortunate error in the field of psychotherapy to which individual psychology is particularly prone. This is the view that all worth-while behavior of a man is ultimately nothing more than socially correct behavior. The argument that only those things are of worth which profit the community cannot be supported ethically. Such a premise would lead to an impoverishment of the values of human existence. It can easily be shown that in the realm of values there are whole areas which are the private preserve of the individual. These are values which can or must be actualized aside from and independent of all community. All that we have termed experiential values belong to this category. They lie completely outside the sphere of the community. The rich store of values which experiences with art or nature offer to the individual even in utter solitude is essentially and fundamentally personal; these values are valid whether or not the community profits from them. In saying this we are well aware that on the other hand there are a number of experiential values which by their nature are reserved to community experience. These may rest upon a broader basis (comradeship, solidarity, etc.) or upon erotic community, upon twoness.

So far we have been considering the social factor in human existence as a possible basis or goal of life. We must now turn to sociality as destiny proper—that is, as a more or less unalterable element which opposes the human will, challenging it to combat. Here, then, is the third area in which destiny confronts man; we must deal with sociology. Later we shall take up the question of shaping one's life vocationally, the problem of reaching an "active" settlement with the social environment. In the next subsection the social environment appears as a force which may well cause the individual suffering.

The recent past has supplied ample data on the psychology of such suffering from social circumstances. The First World War added to our knowledge of prison psychology: observations and experiences in prisoner-of-war camps led psychologists to draw up the clinical picture of what was called "barbed-wire disease." The Second World War familiarized us with the typical neuroses bred by the "war of nerves." The enforced collective life in concentration camps has thrown new light on the psychopathology of the masses.

(b)   On the Psychology of the Concentration Camp

In the concentration camps human existence underwent a deformation. So thoroughgoing was this deformation that it is questionable whether the observer, if he were himself an inmate in the camp, could possibly retain sufficient objectivity to draw any conclusions. Psychological and ethical warping must have taken place which would seriously impair his capacity to judge or evaluate himself or others. While the outsider was too far removed from the strange world of the concentration camp and could scarcely empathize, the person who was in the midst of it had grown hardened to its laws and had no distance at all. It can therefore be said that we have no adequate description of just what took place—since we have to allow for a considerable degree of distortion in the mentality of the viewer. To use an image from the theory of relativity, the standard of measurement applied to the deformed lives was itself deformed.

In spite of these reservations, specialists in psychopathology and psychotherapy have used the available material drawn from their own or others' observations, to formulate theories. And on the whole we must accept these theories, since a certain consistency can be found running through all of them.

The reactions of the camp inmate are found to fall into three phases: the phase of reception into camp, the phase of actual camp life, and the phase after discharge or liberation from the camp. The first phase is marked by so-called reception shock. This form of reaction to an unaccustomed and unusual environment is no novelty to the psychologist. The new inmate draws a line through his previous life. All his possessions have been taken away; he has nothing, except perhaps his glasses, which he was usually allowed to keep, to form an external link with his former life. The impressions that assail him agitate him deeply, or arouse his intense indignation. Faced with the constant threat of death, some make up their minds that they will "run into the wire" (the barbed-wire fence of the camp, charged with high-tension electricity) or attempt suicide in some other fashion.

After some days or weeks this stage is usually succeeded by the second phase, a profound apathy. This apathy is a kind of self-defense mechanism of the psyche. Everything that formerly excited or embittered the inmate, that aroused his indignation or drove him to despair, everything he is forced to watch or to take part in, now rebounds from a kind of armor he has put on. What has taken place is psychic adjustment to the strange environment; the events in that environment reach the consciousness only in blurred form. Affective life is tuned down to a lower level. Psychoanalytic observers interpreted the process as a regression to primitiveness. Interests are restricted to the most immediate, most urgent needs. All thinking seems to be concentrated upon a single point: to survive the particular day. Evenings after a day in the "work squads," when the freezing, hungry, and exhausted prisoners stagger under the eyes of their guards back over the snow-covered fields to camp, they can be heard saying with heaving sighs: "Well, that's another day we've got through."

Anything beyond the immediate questions of sheer self-preservation, beyond saving one's own and others' lives daily and hourly, must be considered a luxury. Everything is devalued. This far-reaching tendency toward devaluation is vented in the words that are about the most common in camp life: "It's all rot." All higher interests are put aside for the duration of the camp life—except, of course, for political and, remarkably, religious interests. Otherwise the inmate crawls off into a cultural hibernation.

The primitiveness of the inner life in a concentration camp is characteristically expressed in the inmates' typical dreams. Usually they dream of bread, cake, cigarettes, and a good warm bath in a tub. The talk is constantly about food. When the prisoners in "work squads" are standing close to one another, and the guard does not happen to be near, they exchange cooking recipes and vividly describe the favorite dishes they will serve one another some day, after their liberation, when they will invite each other to dinner. The best among them are longing for the day when this starvation will be over not for the sake of the good food they will enjoy but for the termination of this unworthy state in which they cannot think of anything but food.

If camp life leads to primitiveness, and undernourishment to the centering upon food of all thoughts and desires, undernourishment is probably also the principal cause for the widely noted indifference to sexual subjects in the concentration camps. Conversation steers clear of sex, there is no telling of "dirty jokes," and the sexual instinct does not even manifest itself in the prisoners' dreams.

That the psychic pattern of camp life represents a regression to a more primitive structure of instinctuality has not been the only interpretation. E. Utitz has interpreted the changes which he observed in camp inmates as a shift from the "cyclothymic" to the "schizothymic" character type. It struck him that most camp inmates manifested irritability as well as apathy, and these in a distinct ratio which corresponded completely to the pattern of the schizothymic temperament as defined by Kretschmer.

Aside from the psychological dubiety of any such character

change or shift of dominance, this apparent schizoidization can in our opinion be explained much more simply. The majority of the prisoners suffered on the one hand from lack of food, on the other hand from lack of sleep—a result of the plague of vermin caused by too many persons being thrown together in such close quarters. While undernourishment made the men apathetic, chronic sleeplessness made them irritable. In addition to these causal factors, there was another—the absence of those two toxins of civilization which in normal life mitigate both apathy and irritability: caffein and nicotine. For the camp command had forbidden the possession of coffee and tobacco.

These factors may well explain the physiological cause of the so-called "characterological changes." A psychic factor must be added. Most of the camp inmates suffered from certain complexes. The majority were tormented by inferiority feelings. These people had once been "somebodies" and were now being treated worse than "nobodies." A minority, however, who stuck together as a clique and consisted mainly of the *capos* (overseers of work squads), gradually developed a megalomania *en miniature*. This group, consisting of individuals selected for "negative" character traits, had been handed power altogether out of proportion to their sense of responsibility. Wherever the majority of the declassed and this minority of those newly come to power clashed—and camp life was only too full of such collisions—the already intensified irritability of the prisoners boiled over.

Does not all this support the view that a character type is marked out by the environment? Does it not prove that man cannot escape the destiny of his social surroundings? Our answer is: it does not. But if not, where does man's inner freedom remain? Consider his behavior—is he still spiritually responsible for what is happening to him psychically, for what the concentration camp has "made" of him? Our answer is: he is. For even in this socially limited environment, in spite of this societal restriction upon his personal freedom, the ultimate freedom still remains his: the freedom even in the camp to give some shape to his existence. There are plenty of examples—often heroic ones—to prove that even in these camps men could still "do differently"; that they did not have to submit to the apparently almighty concentration-camp laws of psychic deformation. In fact the weight of evidence tends to show that the men who typified the character traits of the camp inmates, who had succumbed to the character-forming forces of the social environment, were those who had beforehand given up the struggle spiritually. The freedom to take what attitude they would toward the concrete situation had not been wrested from them; they had themselves withdrawn their claim to use that freedom.* For whatever may have been taken from them in their first hour in camp— until his last breath no one can wrest from a man his freedom to take one or another attitude toward his destiny. And alternative attitudes really did exist. Probably in every concentration camp there were individuals able to overcome their apathy and suppress their irritability. These were the ones who were examples of renunciation and self-sacrifice. Asking nothing for themselves, they went about on the grounds and in the barracks of the camp, offering a kind word here, a last crust of bread there.

This puts the whole symptomatology of the concentration camp in a new light. A while back we were regarding the symptoms as the apparently fated result of an enforced development, as springing from physical and psychic causes. Now it appears that the symptoms can be shaped by the spirit. On the psychopathology of the concentration camp we can make the same comment that

---

* Freedom is not something we "have" and therefore can lose; freedom is what we "are."

we shall apply in a later chapter to the neurotic symptom in general: that the symptom is never merely a consequence of some somatic factor and the expression of some psychic factor, but is also a mode of existence—and this last element is the crucial one. The character changes in the concentration-camp inmate are both the consequences of physiological changes of state (hunger, lack of sleep, etc.) and expression of psychological data (inferiority feelings, etc.). But ultimately and essentially they are a spiritual attitude. For in every case man retains the freedom and the possibility of deciding for or against the influence of his surroundings. Although he may seldom exert this freedom or utilize this opportunity to choose—it is open to him to do so. Those upon whom the concentration-camp environment had inflicted psychic scars still had it within their power, within reach of their responsibility, to surmount those influences. But what were the reasons that made these people let themselves go spiritually, so that they surrendered without a struggle to the physico-psychic influences of their surroundings? We may put the answer this way: they let themselves go because and only if they had lost their spiritual support. This is a subject that needs some elaborating.

Utitz has already characterized the life of camp inmates as a "provisional existence." In our opinion the term must be further qualified—camp existence was not only provisional, but provisional without a time limit. Before the future prisoners were consigned to the camp, their frame of mind was often that of men facing the Beyond from which no one has yet returned. As far as people knew, these camps were places from which nobody returned. No information had yet trickled out of what was actually going on in these camps. Once the prisoner was in camp, his chief fear was somewhat calmed. There was an end to uncertainty (about what awaited him). But he now had to face uncertainty about the end. For none of the prisoners knew how long he would have to stay in the camp. The innumerable rumors that raced daily and hourly among these masses of herded human beings, many of them concerning an "end" soon to come, ultimately produced thorough skepticism. The indefiniteness of every man's discharge date aroused in the prisoner the sense of practically life imprisonment. As a result, in time he began to feel alienated toward the world outside the barbed wire. Through the barbed wire he looked upon people and things outside as if they were not part of his world, or, rather, as if he were not part of their world, as if he had utterly lost touch with that world. The world of non-prisoners looked to his eyes as the here and now might look to a dweller in the hereafter: unreal, inaccessible, unattainable—ghostly.

The monotonous quality of life in the concentration camp led to the sensation of "futurelessness." A prisoner marching in a long column to a new camp remarked that he felt as if he were walking in a funeral procession behind his own dead body—so strong was his sense that his life was now without a future, that it consisted entirely of past, was just as past as the life of a dead man. The lives of such "living corpses" become mainly existences in retrospect. Their thoughts fasten again and again upon the same details of past experiences; the most commonplace trivialities of the past are transfigured and mythified.

But man cannot really exist without a fixed point in the future. Under normal conditions his entire present is shaped around that future point, directed toward it like iron filings toward the pole of a magnet. Lacking that, inward time, lived time forfeits its entire structure. When he loses "his future" a person must drift through a presentist, vegetative existence—something like that described by Thomas Mann in *The Magic Mountain:* the life led by incurable consumptives who also do not know when they will be

*II From Psychoanalysis
to Existential Analysis*

discharged. Or the prisoner may be overcome by that sense of emptiness and meaninglessness of his existence which so often affects the unemployed. For the jobless man, too, suffers a disintegration in the structure of his experience with time, as psychological studies of unemployed miners have conclusively shown.

The Latin word *finis* means both end and goal. The moment a person cannot foresee the end of a provisional stage in his life, he is unable to set himself any further goals, is unable to assign himself a task. Life consequently loses all content and meaning in his eyes. And, vice versa, envisioning the "end" and a goal in the future constitutes that very spiritual support which the camp prisoner so badly needs because such spiritual support alone can keep him from succumbing to the character-marring and type-forming forces of the social environment—can save him, that is, from utterly giving in. One camp inmate, for example, instinctively chose a good method for getting through the worst situations in camp life by imagining each time that he was standing on the podium before a large audience and lecturing on the things he was at the moment experiencing. By means of this trick he succeeded in experiencing things *quadam sub specie æternitatis*—"as if under the aspect of eternity"—and so enduring them.

Psychic degeneration because of spiritual emptiness, the onset of total apathy, was a phenomenon both familiar to and feared by all concentration-camp prisoners. It sometimes took such a galloping course that it reached its disastrous climax within a few days. The day would come when the apathetic inmates would simply lie on their bunks in the barracks, would refuse to rise for roll call or for assignment to a work squad, would not bother about mess call, and ceased going to the washroom. Once they had reached this state, neither reproaches nor threats could rouse them out of their apathy. Nothing frightened them any longer; punishments they accepted dully and indifferently, without seeming to feel them. This lying passively on their cots—sometimes in their own excreta—was endangering their lives, not only because of the forms disciplinary action might take, but in an even more direct sense. This was sufficiently proved by numerous cases in which the experience of "interminability" ran its inevitable course. Here is one example:

One day a prisoner told his fellows he had had a strange dream. He dreamed that a voice spoke to him and asked whether he wanted to know anything at all—it could foretell the future. He answered: "I should like to know when this Second World War will end for me." Whereupon the dream voice replied: "On March 30, 1945." It was the beginning of March when the prisoner narrated this dream. At the time he was very hopeful and in good spirits. But as the thirtieth of March came closer and closer, it began to seem less and less probable that the "voice" would be right. In the last days before the prophesied deadline the man gave way more and more to discouragement. On March 29 he was taken to the infirmary with a high fever and in a state of delirium. On the crucial thirtieth of March—the day when the Second World War was to end "for him"—he lost consciousness. Next day he was dead of typhus. We have already remarked how extremely dependent the organism's immunity is upon affective states. Courage for living or weariness with life, disillusionment or blighted hopes gravely influence immunity. We can therefore assume in all seriousness that the prisoner's disappointment over his dream voice's "false" prophecy brought about a rapid decline of his organism's defenses, thus permitting the organism to succumb to a dormant infection.

Our view of this case is supported by an observation on a larger scale reported by a camp doctor. The prisoners in his camp, he said, had generally subscribed to the hope that they would be back home by Christmas of 1944. Christmas came, and newspaper reports were anything but encouraging to the camp inmates. The consequence? During the week between Christmas and New Year's Day there was unprecedented mass mortality in this concentration camp. No outward occurrence, such as change of weather or harsher working-conditions or a sudden onset of infectious diseases, could have been sufficient explanation for it.

It should be clear, then, that even under concentration-camp conditions psychotherapy or mental hygiene could not possibly be effective unless directed toward the crucial factor of helping the mind find some goal in the future to hold on to. For healthy living is living with an eye to the future. In "practice" it was often not too difficult to encourage some prisoners by turning their attention toward the future. For example, a conversation with two camp inmates disclosed that both of them were haunted by the feeling that they "no longer had anything to expect from life." Here was a chance to bring about that "Copernican revolution" of which we have already spoken, that change of attitude which eliminates once and for all the futile questioning about the meaning of life, and substitutes for it a concern with the concrete problems life poses, the need to be responsive and responsible to life. And in fact it soon turned out that—beyond what the two prisoners had to anticipate in life—each of them had a life with quite concrete tasks awaiting him in the outside world. One of them had published a series of books on geography, but the series was still incomplete. The other had a daughter abroad who loved him devotedly. That is, a task was waiting for the one, a human being for the other. Accordingly, both were reassured as to that singularity and irreplaceability which impart meaning to life in spite of suffering. The one was indispensable for his work; no one could take the other's place in his daughter's affections.

Occasionally it was possible to practice "mass psychotherapy" even in concentration camp, though within modest limits. For example, we know of a psychotherapeutically trained neurologist who was himself a prisoner. In the evenings, when his fellow inmates lay in the dark in their crowded huts, exhausted from work, he would give little talks about their common problems which restored to a good many of his fellow prisoners the courage and will they needed to go on.

The liberated prisoner is still in need of psychic care. For the liberation itself, the *sudden* release, the throwing off of the burden of psychic pressure constitutes a psychological hazard of prime magnitude. The characterological effects of liberation can be as drastic as the effects of caisson disease, the "bends." Here we have come to the third phase to be considered in this brief examination of the psychology of the concentration-camp prisoner.

The prisoner's reaction to release can be summed up as follows: at first everything seems to him like a lovely dream; he hardly dares to believe it. After all, he has been deceived by beautiful dreams in the past. How often he dreamed of his liberation—dreamed of coming home, embracing his wife, greeting his friends, sitting down at table and beginning to tell the story of his experiences, to describe how he had longed for this moment of reunion, to say how many times he had dreamed of this moment, until at last it had become reality. And then the three blasts of the whistle shrilled in his ears, the whistle for the morning rising, and wrenched him out of the dream. How terrible it was to be brought back to harsh reality. But finally the day dawns when what has been longed for and dreamed of actually comes true. The liberated prisoner is still dominated by a sense of depersonalization. He cannot really enjoy life yet—he has to learn all over again how to be happy, for he has forgotten. But if on the first day of freedom the present seems like a lovely dream, in time he reaches the point where the past seems to be nothing more than a nightmare. When that time comes, he himself can no longer understand how he was able to survive the imprisonment. Henceforth he enjoys the precious feeling that after all he has experienced and suffered, there is nothing left in the world that he need fear—except, perhaps, his God. For a good many men learned in concentration camp, and as the result of concentration camp, to believe in God again.

2   On the Meaning of Suffering

We have said that man's being consists of being conscious and being responsible. His responsibility is always responsibility for the actualization of values: not only "eternal" values, but also "situational values" (Scheler). Opportunities for the actualization of values change from person to person just as much as they change from hour to hour. The requirement that values be actualized—a requirement that radiates from the world of values into the lives of men—thus becomes a concrete demand for every single hour and a personal summons to every single person. The possibilities that every person has exclusively for himself are just as specific as the possibilities presented by every historical situation in its peculiar singularity. Thus the various values merge to form a concrete task for the individual. That merging gives them the uniqueness whereby every man feels himself personally and validly addressed. Until he learns what constitutes the singularity and uniqueness of his own existence, he cannot experience the fulfillment of his life task as something binding upon him.

In discussing the question of the meaning of life we have set up three categories of values. While the values of the first category are actualized by doing, experiential values are realized by the passive receiving of the world (nature, art) into the ego. Attitudinal values, however, are actualized wherever the individual is faced with something unalterable, something imposed by destiny. From the manner in which a person takes these things upon himself, assimilates these difficulties into his own psyche, there flows an incalculable multitude of value-potentialities. This means that *human life can be fulfilled not only in creating and enjoying, but also in suffering!*

Those who worship the superficial cult of success obviously will not understand such conclusions. But when we pause and consider our everyday judgments upon human existence, we see that we ascribe value and dignity to many things independently of the success or failure which may attend them. Great artists, in particular, have understood and described this phenomenon of inner fulfillment in spite of outward failure. An example that comes readily to mind is Tolstoy's story *The Death of Ivan Ilyich.* The story concerns a respectable government official the abysmal meaninglessness of whose life only dawns upon him when he is faced with unexpected death. But with insight into this meaninglessness the man grows far beyond himself in the last hours of his life; he attains an inner greatness which retroactively hallows all of his previous life—in spite of its apparent futility—and makes it meaningful. Life, that is, can receive its ultimate meaning not only as the result of death (the man who is a hero), but in the very process of death. Not only the sacrifice of one's life can give life meaning; life can reach nobility even as it founders on the rocks.

The untenability of the cult of success becomes obvious as soon as we consider the moral problem of sacrifice. Insofar as a sacrifice is "calculated," performed after careful reckoning of the prospects of its bringing about a desired end, it loses all ethical significance. Real sacrifice occurs only when we run the risk of having sacrificed in vain. Would anyone maintain that a person who plunges into the water to save someone has acted less ethically, or unethically, because both are drowned? Do we not rather presuppose this risk when we assign a high ethical standing to the rescuer's action? Consider what a high ethical rating we place upon the life of a man who has fought vainly but heroically—and has died heroically but not vainly.

Lack of success does not signify lack of meaning. This also becomes obvious when we look back upon our own past and consider, say, the times we have been in love. Let anyone honestly ask himself whether he would be prepared to strike his unhappy love affairs, with all their self-doubt and suffering, out of the record of his life. Almost certainly he would not. The fullness of suffering did not seem to him lack of fulfillment. On the contrary, the suffering matured him; he grew as a result of it; his ill-fated love gave him more than many an erotic success might have given him.

In general, people are inclined to overestimate the positive or negative aspects, or the pleasant or unpleasant tone of their experiences. In giving an exaggerated importance to these aspects, they are apt to cultivate an unjustified self-pity in respect to fate. We have already discussed the numerous senses in which man is "not in this world for enjoyment." We have pointed out that pleasure is incapable of giving meaning to man's life. If this is so, lack of pleasure in life does not detract from its meaning. Once again art comes to our aid with examples: we have only to recall how irrelevant with regard to artistic merit is the question of whether a melody is in the major or minor modes. Not only are the unfinished symphonies among the finest, as we have mentioned in another connection; so also are the *"pathétiques."*

We have said that in creating, man actualizes creative values; in experiencing, experiential values; and in suffering, attitudinal values. Beyond that, however, suffering has a meaning in itself. In suffering from something we move inwardly away from it, we establish a distance between our personality and this something. As long as we are still suffering from a condition that ought not to be, we remain in a state of tension between what actually is on the one hand and what ought to be on the other hand. And only while in this state of tension can we continue to envision the ideal. As we have already seen, this even applies to the person who has despaired of himself; by the very fact of his despair he has cast off some of the blame attaching to himself, since he is evaluating his own reality in terms of an ideality and the fact that he can at all envision values (even though unrealized ones) implies a certain value in himself. He could not sit in judgment upon himself if he did not already possess the worth and dignity of a judge—of a man who has perceived what ought to be as against what at the moment is. Suffering therefore establishes a fruitful, one might say a revolutionary, tension in that it makes for emotional awareness of what ought not to be. To the degree that a person identifies himself with things as they are, he eliminates his distance from them and forfeits the fruitful tension between what is and what ought to be.

Thus there is revealed in man's emotions a deep wisdom superior to all reason, which in fact runs counter to the gospel of rationalistic utility. Consider, for instance, the affects of grief and repentance. From the utilitarian point of view both necessarily appear to be meaningless. To mourn for anything irrevocably lost must seem useless and foolish from the point of view of "sound common sense," and this holds also for repenting an irredeemable wrong. But for the inner biography of man, grief and repentance do have meaning. Grieving for a person whom we have loved and lost in a sense continues his life, and repentance permits the culprit to rise again, as it were, freed of guilt. The loved person whom we grieve for has been lost objectively, in empirical time, but he is preserved subjectively, in inner time. Grief brings him into the mind's present. And repentance, as Scheler has shown, has the power to wipe out a wrong; though the wrong cannot be undone, the culprit himself undergoes a moral rebirth. This opportunity to make past events fruitful for one's inner history does not stand in opposition to man's responsibility, but in a dialectical relationship. For guilt presupposes responsibility. Man is responsible in view of the fact that he cannot retrace a single step; the smallest as well as the biggest decision remains a final one. None of his acts of commission or omission can be wiped off the slate as if they had never been. Nevertheless, in repenting man may inwardly break with an act, and in living out this repentance—which is an inner event—he can undo the outer event on a spiritual, moral plane. Only to the most superficial view is there any contradiction between these two statements.

Schopenhauer, as is well known, complained that human life dangles between trouble and boredom. In reality both have their profound meaning. Boredom is a continual reminder. What leads to boredom? Inactivity. But activity does not exist for the purpose of our escaping boredom; rather, boredom exists so that we will escape inactivity and do justice to the meaning of our life. The struggle of life keeps us in "suspense" because the meaning of life depends upon whether or not we fulfill the demands placed upon us by our tasks. This suspense is therefore different in nature from the type engendered by a neurotic passion for sensation or a hysterical hunger for stimulus.

The meaning of "trouble" is also that it is a reminder. On the biological plane, as we know, pain is a meaningful watcher and warder. In the psycho-spiritual realm it has a similar function. Suffering is intended to guard man from apathy, from psychic *rigor mortis*. As long as we suffer we remain psychically alive. In fact, we mature in suffering, grow because of it—it makes us richer and stronger. Repentance, as we have just seen, has the power to undo, and the significance of undoing, an outer event in the moral sense, within the biography of the individual; grief has the power to perpetuate, and the significance of perpetuating, the past in the present. Both thus serve to correct the past, so to speak. In so doing they solve a problem—as diversion and narcotization cannot do. The person who tries to "take his mind off" a misfortune or narcotize his feelings solves no problem, comes to no terms with misfortune; all he does is get rid of a mere aftereffect of the misfortune: the sensation of unpleasure. By diversion or narcotization he makes himself "ignore" what has happened—he no longer knows it. He tries to escape reality. He takes refuge, say, in intoxication. But this is to commit a subjectivistic, in fact a psychologistic, error: the error of acting as if "silencing" the feeling by narcotization also makes an end of the object of the emotion; as if what has been banished to non-consciousness were thereby banished to unreality. But the act of looking at something does not create that thing; neither does the act of looking away annihilate it. And so the suppression of an impulse of grief does not annul the thing that is grieved over. Mourners, in fact, ordinarily rebel against, say, taking a sedative instead of weeping all through the night. To the trite suggestion that he take a sleeping-powder the grief-stricken person commonly retorts that his sleeping better will not awaken the lost one whom he mourns. Death—that paradigm of the irreversible event—is not wiped off the slate by being pushed out of consciousness, any more than when the mourner himself takes refuge in absolute non-consciousness—the non-consciousness and the non-responsibility of his own death.

As contrasted with narcotization, intoxication has positive aspects. The essence of intoxication is a turning away from the objective world and a turning toward a subjective world. Narcotization, on the other hand, leads only to non-consciousness of unhappiness, to "happiness" in Schopenhauer's negative sense, to a nirvana mood. Narcotization is spiritual anesthesia. But just as surgical anesthesia can induce death, so spiritual anesthesia can lead to a kind of spiritual death. Consistent suppression of intrinsically meaningful emotional impulses because of their possible unpleasurable tone ends in the killing of a person's inner life. A sense of the meaning of emotional experiences is deeply rooted in human beings, as the following example indicates. There is a type of melancholia in which sadness is conspicuous by its absence. Instead, the patients complain that they cannot feel sad enough, that they cannot cry out their melancholy, that they are emotionally cold and inwardly dead. Such patients are suffering from what we call *melancholia anæsthetica.* Anyone acquainted with such cases knows that greater despair can scarcely exist than the despair of such persons because they are unable to be sad. This paradox again makes it plain that the pleasure principle is a mere construct but not a phenomenological fact. Out of his emotional *"logique du cœur"* man is actually always striving, whether his emotions be joyful or sad, to remain psychically "alive" and not to sink into apathy. The paradox that the sufferer from *melancholia anæsthetica* should suffer from his incapacity to suffer is therefore only a paradox for psychopathology. For existential analysis it is no paradox at all, since existential analysis recognizes the meaning of suffering, installs suffering in a place of honor in life. Suffering and trouble belong to life as much as fate and death. None of these can be subtracted from life without destroying its meaning. To subtract trouble, death, fate, and suffering from life would mean stripping life of its form and shape. Only under the hammer blows of fate, in the white heat of suffering, does life gain shape and form.

The destiny a person suffers therefore has a twofold meaning: to be shaped where possible, and to be endured where necessary. Let us also remember that "inactive," passive enduring still retains the immanent meaning of all suffering. On the other hand, man must be on his guard against the temptation to lay down his arms prematurely, too soon accepting a state of things as destined and bowing his head before a merely imaginary fate. Only when he no longer has any possibility of actualizing creative values, when there is really no means at hand for shaping fate—then is the time for attitudinal values to be actualized; then alone does it have meaning for him to "take his cross." The very essence of an attitudinal value inheres in the manner in which a person resigns himself to the inevitable; in order therefore for attitudinal values to be truly actualized, it is important that the fate he resigns himself to must be actually inevitable. It must be what Brod has called "noble misfortune" as against the "ignoble misfortune," the latter being something which is either avoidable, or for which the person himself is to blame.*

One way or another, then, every situation holds out the opportunity for the actualization of values—either creative or attitudinal values. "There is no predicament that we cannot ennoble either by doing or enduring," says Goethe. We might say that even in enduring there is a kind of doing implicit, provided that the enduring is of the right kind, that what must be endured is a fated situation that cannot be either altered by doing or avoided by not

---

* The difference between evitable or blameworthy destiny ("ignoble misfortune") on the one hand and inevitable, immutable destiny ("noble misfortune") on the other hand (to suffer the latter alone provides opportunities for the realization of attitudinal values) has its parallel in the distinction mountaineers make between subjective and objective dangers. For the mountaineer it is not discreditable to succumb to objective perils (such as a falling rock), while it is considered shameful to be halted by a subjective failure (such as faulty equipment, lack of skill, or inadequate climbing-experience).

doing. This "right" enduring is the kind which constitutes a moral achievement; only such unavoidable suffering is meaningful suffering. This moral achievement implicit in suffering is something that the ordinary person in his simple, straightforward way knows quite well. He can well understand, for example, the following incident:

Some years ago when prizes were to be awarded to British Boy Scouts for highest accomplishments, the coveted awards went to three boys hospitalized for incurable diseases who nevertheless remained brave and cheerful and steadfastly endured their suffering. Their record of suffering was recognized as greater in accomplishment than the records in athletics, etc., of so many other Boy Scouts.

"Life is not anything; it is only the opportunity for something." This maxim of Hebbel's seems to cover the subject. For the alternatives are either to shape fate (that is, one's unalterable situation) and so realize creative values, or, if this should really prove to be impossible, to take such an attitude toward fate that, in the sense of attitudinal values, there is achievement in suffering. It sounds like a tautology to say that illnesses give people the "opportunity" for "suffering." But if we understand "opportunity" and "suffering" in the above sense, the matter ceases to be obvious. It is above all not obvious because a fundamental distinction must be made between sickness—including psychic illness—and suffering. On the one hand, people can be sick without "suffering" in the proper sense. On the other hand, there is a suffering beyond all sickness, a fundamental human suffering, the suffering which belongs to human life by the very nature and meaning of life. Consequently, cases may arise where existential analysis is called upon to make a person capable of suffering—whereas psychoanalysis, for instance, aims only at making him capable of pleasure or capable of doing. For there are situations in which man can fulfill himself only in genuine suffering, and in no other way. And just as men can miss the "opportunity for something" which life means, so can they miss their opportunity for genuine suffering, with its opening for the actualizing of attitudinal values. In the light of this we can agree with Dostoevsky when he said that he feared only one thing: that he might not be worthy of his torment. And we can now appreciate what an accomplishment there is in the suffering of patients who appear to be struggling—to be worthy of their torment.

An extraordinarily brilliant young man was abruptly forced to give up his active professional life. An abscess of the spinal cord caused by tubercular affection had produced symptoms of paralysis in the legs. An operation (laminectomy) was considered. Friends of the patient consulted one of the foremost neurosurgeons of Europe. He was pessimistic about the prognosis and refused to undertake the operation. This decision was reported in a letter to another of the sick man's friends, who was caring for him at her country house. The unsuspecting servant girl handed the letter to her mistress while the latter was breakfasting with her sick guest. What followed is described by the patient in a letter of his from which we take the following passages: ". . . In the situation Eva could not help letting me read the letter. And so I was informed of my death sentence, which was obvious from the surgeon's remarks.—I recall the movie about the *Titanic*, which I saw many years ago. What I particularly recall is the scene in which the paralyzed cripple, played by Fritz Kortner, reciting the Lord's Prayer, ushers a small group of fellow victims toward death, while the ship sinks and the water rises higher and higher around their bodies. I came out of the movie deeply shaken. What a gift of fate it must be, I thought at the time, consciously to go toward one's death. And now here was fate granting me that! I get this last chance to test my fighting spirit, only this is a fight where the question of victory is ruled out at the start. Rather, it's a last exertion of simple strength, a last gymnastic drill, as it were. . . . I want to bear the pain without narcotics as long as it is at all possible. . . . 'A fight for a lost cause?' In terms of our philosophy, that phrase has to be stricken off the books. The fighting alone is what counts. . . . There cannot be any lost causes. . . . In the evening we played Bruckner's *Fourth*, the *Romantic Symphony*. I was filled with emotion of love for all mankind, a sense of cosmic vastness.— For the rest, I work away at mathematics and don't give way to sentimentality."

At another time illness and the approach of death may draw forth the ultimate capacities from a man who has hitherto wasted his life in "metaphysical frivolity" (Scheler) and let his own potentialities lie fallow. A young woman who had led an utterly pampered existence was one day unexpectedly thrown into a concentration camp. There she fell ill and was visibly wasting away. A few days before she died she said these very words: "Actually I am grateful to my fate for having treated me so harshly. In my former middle-class existence I certainly had things a great deal too easy. I never was very serious about my literary ambitions." She saw death coming and looked it squarely in the eye. From her bed in the infirmary she could catch a glimpse of a chestnut tree in blossom outside the window. She spoke of this tree often, though from where the sick woman's head lay just one twig with two blossoms was visible. "This tree is my only friend in solitude," the woman said. "I converse with it." Was this a hallucination? Was she delirious? Did she think the tree was "answering" her? What strange dialogue was this; what had the flowering tree "said" to the dying woman? "It says: 'I am here, I am here—I am life, eternal life.' "

Viktor von Weizsäcker once remarked that the patient, as the sufferer, is superior to the doctor. Certainly I had that feeling when I left this patient. A doctor who is sensitive to the imponderables of a situation will always feel a kind of shame when attending a patient with an incurable disease, or a dying person. For the doctor himself is helpless, incapable of wresting this victim from death. But the patient has become a hero who is meeting his fate and holding his own by accepting it in tranquil suffering. That is, upon a metaphysical plane, a true achievement—while the doctor in the physical world, in his physician's realm, has his hands tied, is a failure.

3   On the Meaning of Work

The meaning of life, we have said, is not to be questioned but to be responded to, for we are responsible to life. It follows from this that the response should be given not in words, but in acting, by doing. Moreover, the correct response depends upon the situation and the person in all his concreteness. The response, so to speak, must have incorporated that concreteness into itself. The right response will therefore be an active response within the actual conditions of everyday living, within the area of human responsibility.

Within that area every man is indispensable and irreplaceable. We have already discussed the importance of the individual's being conscious of his uniqueness and singularity. We have seen the reasons why existential analysis works toward bringing responsibility to consciousness, and how consciousness of responsibility arises above all out of awareness of a concrete personal task, a "mission." Without perception of the unique meaning of his singular existence, a person would be numbed in difficult situations. He would be like the mountain-climber who enters a dense fog and, lacking the goal before his eyes, is in danger of succumbing to a total weariness. If the fog lifts and he catches sight of the shelter hut in the distance, he at once feels a surge of renewed strength. Every climber has experienced fatigue, the flagging energy that attacks him when he is "in the wall" and cannot tell whether he may not be taking a wrong route, whether he has not perhaps entered a blind crevice—until suddenly he sees the escape chimney. Then, realizing that he is only a few rope-lengths below the peak, he feels fresh strength coursing into his arms as he reaches out cheerfully for new holds.

As long as creative values are in the forefront of the life task, their actualization generally coincides with a person's work. Work usually represents the area in which the individual's uniqueness stands in relation to society and thus acquires meaning and value. This meaning and value, however, is attached to the person's work as a contribution to society, not to the actual occupation as such. Therefore it cannot be said that this or that particular occupation offers a person the opportunity for fulfillment. In this sense no one occupation is the sole road to salvation. It is true that many persons, mostly those with a neurotic tinge, insist that they could have fulfilled themselves if only they had gone into a different occupation. But that assertion is either a misunderstanding of what occupation means, or is self-deception. If there are cases where the actual occupation does not allow a sense of fulfillment to arise, the fault is in the person, not in the work. The work in itself does not make the person indispensable and irreplaceable; it only gives him the chance to be so.

A patient once declared that she thought her life meaningless and therefore did not want to get well; but that everything would be different and fine if only she had a job that fulfilled her— if, for example, she were a doctor or a nurse or a chemist or were engaged in some kind of scientific research. It was necessary to show this patient that the job at which one works is not what counts, but rather the manner in which one does the work. It does not lie with the occupation, but always with us, whether those elements of the personal and the specific which constitute the uniqueness of our existence are expressed in the work and thus make life meaningful.

What, really, is the doctor's condition? What gives meaning to his activities? Practicing all the arts of medicine? Giving an injection in this case or prescribing a medicine in that? To practice all the arts of medicine is not to practice the art of medicine. The medical profession merely provides a framework wherein the doctor finds continual opportunities to fulfill himself through the personal exercise of professional skill. The meaning of the doctor's work lies in what he does beyond his purely medical duties; it is what he brings to his work as a personality, as a human being, which gives the doctor his peculiar role. For it would come to the same thing whether he or a colleague gave injections, etc., if he were merely practicing the arts of medicine, merely using the tricks of the trade. Only when he goes beyond the limits of purely professional service, beyond the tricks of the trade, does he begin that truly personal work which alone is fulfilling.

And what about the work of nurses, which our patient so envied? They sterilize syringes, carry bedpans, change bedding—all highly necessary acts, but scarcely enough in themselves to satisfy the human spirit. But when a nurse does some little thing beyond her more or less regimented duties, when, say, she finds a personal word to say to a critically ill person—then and only then is she giving meaning to her life through her work. Every occupation allows for this, so long as the work is seen in the proper light. The indispensability and irreplaceability, the singularity and uniqueness issue from the person, depend on who is doing the work and on the manner in which he is doing it, not on the job itself.

In addition, it was necessary to point out to our patient who maintained she could not find fulfillment in her occupation that she also had the chance to bring to bear uniqueness and singularity, as factors giving meaning to existence, outside of her occupation, in her private life: as a lover and loved one, as a wife and mother, who in these relationships is indispensable and irreplaceable to her husband and child.

People's natural relationship to their employment as the area for possible actualization of creative values and self-fulfillment often is distorted by prevailing conditions of work. There are, for example, those who complain that they work eight or more hours a day for an employer, and in his interest alone, doing nothing but add interminable columns of figures or stand at an assembly line and perform the same movement, pull the same lever on a machine —and the more that the job is reduced to impersonal and standardized movements, the more pleasing it is to the employer. In such circumstances, it is true, work can be conceived only as a mere means to an end, the end of earning money—that is, earning the necessary means for real life. In this case real life begins only with the person's leisure time, and the meaning of that life consists in giving form to that leisure. To be sure, we must never forget that there are people whose work is of such exhausting quality that afterward they are good for nothing but falling into bed. The only form they can give to their leisure is to use it as a period for recovering their strength; they can do nothing more sensible with it than sleep.

But the employer also is denied the full use of his leisure time; he also is involved in the distortion of man's natural relationship to work. We all know the type of factory manager or financial magnate who is entirely devoted to earning money, who is so busy earning the means for living that he forgets life itself. The pursuit of wealth has become an end in itself. That kind of person has a great deal of money, and his money still has a use, but his life no longer has a direction. In such a person livelihood overshadows life.

The existential importance of work is most clearly seen

where work is entirely eliminated from a person's life, as in unemployment. Psychological studies of the unemployed have arrived at the concept of *unemployment neurosis*. Remarkably enough, the most prominent symptom of this neurosis is not depression, but apathy. The unemployed become increasingly indifferent and their initiative more and more trickles away. This apathy is not without grave dangers. It makes such people incapable of grasping the helping hand which may be extended to them. We recall, for example, the following case:

A man was sent to a psychiatric institute after an attempted suicide. There a doctor who knew him came upon him. Several years before, the doctor, working with the man at a psychological counseling clinic, had been able to help him out economically also. The doctor asked in astonishment why the man had not turned to him again. To which the patient replied: "I just didn't give a damn about anything."

The jobless man experiences the emptiness of his time as inner emptiness, as an emptiness of his consciousness. He feels useless because he is unoccupied. Having no work, he thinks life has no meaning. Just as idle organs in the body may become the hosts for rampant growths, so idleness in the psychological realm leads to morbid inner developments. Unemployment becomes a culture medium for the proliferation of neuroses. When the human spirit idles at full throttle, so to speak, a permanent Sunday neurosis may result.

Apathy as the chief symptom of unemployment neurosis is, however, not only the expression of psychic emptiness or unfillment. It is, as is in our opinion every neurotic symptom, in addition a consequence of a physical condition—in this concrete case the consequence of undernourishment, which is the usual concomitant of unemployment. Occasionally it can also be—like neurotic symptoms in general—a means to an end. That is especially the case in persons who already have a neurosis which is exacerbated by the concurrent unemployment, or into which they relapse. For them the fact of unemployment provides material for the neurosis, is incorporated into the neurosis as part of the neurotic content and "neurotically processed." In such cases the unemployment is a welcome alibi for all the neurotic's failures in life (not only in his working life). It serves as a scapegoat on whose head is heaped all the blame for a "bungled" life. The person's own faults are interpreted as the fated results of unemployment. "Oh, if only I weren't unemployed everything would be different, everything would be fine and dandy," such neurotics declare. Then they would do this or do that. A jobless existence permits them to live life as a temporary expedient; it lures them into succumbing to a provisional modality of existence. They think nothing ought to be demanded of them. And they demand nothing of themselves. The misfortune of being unemployed seems to them to wipe out all responsibility to others and to themselves as well, to cancel their responsibility to life. This misfortune is blamed for failures on all planes of existence. Apparently it somehow does a person good to imagine that the shoe pinches only in one spot. To explain everything as the result of a single factor which, moreover, is fixed by fate, has a great advantage. For then no task seems to be assigned to one; one has nothing to do but wait for the imaginary moment when the curing of this one factor will cure everything else.

Like every neurotic symptom, then, unemployment neurosis is at one and the same time a consequence, an expression of something else, and a means to an end. We may therefore expect that from the ultimate and decisive point of view it will prove to be, like every other neurosis, also a mode of existence, a "position taken" by man, an existential decision. For unemployment neurosis is by no means the unconditional fate the neurotic wishes to believe it is. The jobless man need not necessarily succumb to unemployment neurosis. Here again we see that men can "do other," that they can decide whether or not to surrender psychically to the forces of social destiny. There are plenty of examples to prove that the state of mind accompanying unemployment is not unequivocally shaped and determined by fate. For in addition to the neurotic type noted above, there is another sort of unemployed person who, forced to live under the same adverse economic conditions as the neurotics, nevertheless remains free of unemployment neurosis. He seems to be neither apathetic nor depressed, seems in fact to retain a certain cheerful serenity. Why should this be? If we examine the matter, we discover that such persons have put themselves to work elsewhere when they do not have their regular jobs. For example, they are busy as voluntary assistants in various organizations and adult education courses, serving as unpaid helpers in public libraries. They have formed the habit of attending lectures and hearing good music. They are reading a good deal and discussing what they have read with their friends. If they are young people, they are active in youth clubs, take part in community athletics, do gymnastics, go on hikes, play games, and so on. Such persons give meaningful form to their surplus of leisure time and stock their consciousness, their time, their life with content. Often they have to tighten their belts just as much as that other group of unemployed who become neurotic, but nevertheless they take an affirmative attitude toward life and are far from hopeless. They know how to lend interest to life and wrest meaning from it. They have grasped the fact that the meaning of human life is not completely contained within paid work, that unemployment need not compel one to live meaninglessly. They have stopped making an equation between living and having a job. What actually reduces

*II   From Psychoanalysis
      to Existential Analysis*

the neurotic unemployed to apathy, what ultimately underlies unemployment neurosis, is the erroneous view that working is the only meaning of life. There is a false identification of one's calling with the life task to which one is called. This incorrect equating of the two necessarily makes the unemployed person suffer from the sense of being useless and superfluous.

A young man once told us that throughout a long spell of unemployment, which drove him to despair and almost to suicide, he experienced only one good hour. One day he was sitting alone in a park and noticed on the next bench a weeping girl. He went over to her and asked her what was the matter. She told him her troubles and declared that she was firmly resolved to commit suicide. The young man summoned up all his powers of persuasion to talk the girl out of her intention, and finally succeeded. That moment—the only moment of joy in a long time and the one bright spot for a long time to come—at last gave back to him the feeling of having a task to face and of being able to accomplish something. And that feeling pulled him out of his apathy, although he was to experience many a backsliding still.

It follows from all we have said that the psychic reaction to unemployment is hardly fated at all. There still remains much room in which man's free spirit can operate. In the light of our existential analysis of unemployment neurosis it becomes clear that the same situation of unemployment is given different form by different people, or rather that one person permits his psychic reactions and character to be marked and shaped by social destiny while the non-neurotic type undertakes to shape his social destiny. Every individual unemployed person can therefore always decide which type he will be, whether he will keep his chin up or become completely apathetic.

Unemployment neurosis is not, then, a direct consequence of

unemployment. In fact we sometimes find that it is quite the other way around, that unemployment is a consequence of the neurosis. For it is quite evident that a neurosis will influence the social destiny and the economic situation of the neurotic. Other things being equal, an unemployed person who maintains his morale will have better chances in the competitive struggle than a person who has become apathetic. He will, for example, be more likely to get a job which both apply for.

The effects of unemployment neurosis are not only social, but definitely physical. For just as a proper grasp of one's task in life gives structure and organization to the activity of the mind, so does it also affect the body. And on the other hand, the sudden loss of inner structure which accompanies the conviction that life is meaningless and without content leads to organic signs of deterioration. Psychiatrists, for example, are familiar with the typical psychophysical deterioration which takes place in retired people—the marks of old age emerge very rapidly. A similar phenomenon has been observed in animals. Trained circus animals which are assigned "tasks" generally live longer than members of the same species which are kept in zoos and have no "occupation."

Since, then, unemployment neurosis is not fatally linked with the lack of a job, something can be done about the neurosis. Considerable assistance can be given to these people. As with the treatment of would-be suicides, which has already been discussed, we can distinguish here also among the somatic, psychic, social, and spiritual approaches. "Somatic" aid would consist simply in providing the patient with enough to eat; social assistance would involve getting him a job. But so long as unemployment and its consequences (including unemployment neurosis) remain with us, for reasons that are outside the province of the psychotherapist, and so long as isolated individuals are powerless to extend somatic assistance of the kind indicated in any effectual fashion, the only alternative remains a psychotherapeutic procedure.

There will be those who cast scorn on the idea that there can be a psychotherapeutic approach to the problem of unemployment. But let them remember the frequently heard cry of the jobless, particularly of young people: "What we want is not money but some content to our lives." In the light of this, it is also apparent that psychotherapy in the narrower, the non-logotherapeutic sense —a "depth-psychological" approach, say—would be not only hopeless in such cases, but ludicrous. For if a man's problem is on the one hand plain hunger and on the other hand the meaning of his existence, the content or lack of content in his life, he cannot help but be outraged when somebody comes to him with psychological detective stories and starts hunting hidden complexes. How far more appropriate is existential analysis, which shows the jobless person the way to inner freedom in spite of his unfortunate situation and teaches him that consciousness of responsibility through which he can still give some content to his hard life and wrest meaning from it.

As we have seen, both unemployment and employment can be misused as means to a neurotic end. We must carefully differentiate between a neurotic attitude, which misuses work as a means to a neurotic end, and the normal attitude, which uses work as a means to the end of meaningful living. For the dignity of man forbids his being himself a means, his becoming a mere instrument of the labor process, being degraded to a means of production. The capacity to work is not everything; it is neither a sufficient nor essential basis for a meaningful life. A man can be capable of working and nevertheless not lead a meaningful life; and another can be incapable of working and nevertheless give his life meaning. In general the same may be said for the capacity for enjoyment.

Certain persons seek the meaning of life mainly in one area and to that extent restrict their experience; in such cases we must ask whether such a self-imposed restriction is objectively founded or, as in the case of neurosis, whether it was really needless. The neurotic needlessly renounces his capacity for pleasure in favor of the capacity for work, or vice versa. To such neurotic persons we might quote a penetrating remark made by the German novelist Alice Lyttkens: "Where love is lacking, work becomes a substitute; where work is lacking, love becomes an opiate."

The satisfactions of work are not identical with the creative satisfactions of life as a whole. Nevertheless, the neurotic sometimes tries to escape from life in general, from the frightening vastness of life, by taking refuge in his work or profession. The real emptiness and ultimate poverty of meaning of his existence come to the fore, however, as soon as his vocational activity is halted for a certain period: on Sundays. Everyone is familiar with the woe, which can scarcely be hidden, expressed on the faces of people who on their one free day a week may have missed an appointment or are too late to get a seat in the movies. It is clear that they feel utterly at a loss. The opium of "love" does not happen to be at hand. The week-end amusements are not available at the moment—the special kinds of week-end activity which are supposed to fill the inner void. The person who is wholly wrapped up in his work, who has nothing else, needs that week-end bustle. In any city, Sunday is the saddest day of the week. It is on Sunday, when the tempo of the working week is suspended, that the poverty of meaning in everyday urban life is exposed. The emphasis on a fast tempo in the personal life is reminiscent of the clinical picture of "unproductive mania"; the yield of all the to-do is zero. We get the impression that these people who know no goal in life are running the course of life at the highest possible speed so that they will not notice the aimlessness of it. They are at the same time trying to run away from themselves—but in vain. On Sunday, when the frantic race pauses for twenty-four hours, all the aimlessness, meaninglessness, and emptiness of their existence rises up before them once more.

What lengths they go to then to escape this experience. They flee to a dance hall. There the music is loud and boisterous, which saves the trouble of talking. They do not even have to make the effort that used to be involved in the polite ballroom conversation of former days. And there is no necessity to think either, since all attention can be directed toward the dancing.

Sports provide another "refuge" for the Sunday neurotics. They can pretend, for example, that the most important thing in the world is which football team wins a game. Twenty-two men play—and thousands of times that number look on. In a boxing-match only two persons are active—though the battle is all the more intense for that reason and an element of sadism enters into the voyeurism of the inactive spectator.

Let this not be interpreted as a condemnation of healthy athletics. But it is important that we determine what inner value must be ascribed to sports. Let us take, for example, the attitude of a mountain-climber. Mountain-climbing means active participation; passive onlooking is out of the question. There is genuine accomplishment; as far as physical prowess goes, the climber is forced in certain situations (of extreme peril) to draw on the utmost that is in him. There are psychic "accomplishments" as well, for the climber learns to overcome psychic weaknesses such as timidity or fear of heights. It must be remembered, however, that the climber does not seek danger for its own sake; rather he "tempts" it—as Erwin Straus has pointed out. Moreover, the rivalry which in other sports leads to the mania to set records is transmuted in mountain-climbing into the superior form of "outdoing oneself." Finally, the comradeship of men clinging to the same rope provides a further positive element—the social factor.

But even in the unsound mania for records a truly human trait can be detected, insofar as this mania represents a form of the common human striving for uniqueness and singularity. A like urge, incidentally, underlies other manifestations of mass psychology, as, for example, fashion. There, too, people are seeking originality at any cost—only the uniqueness and singularity they seek is limited to superficial externals.

Art can be neurotically misused just as sports can be. While true art or genuine artistic experience enriches a person and guides him to his own deepest potentialities, neurotically misused art only diverts the person from himself. Art then serves as simply one more opportunity for self-intoxication and narcotization. If, for example, a person wishes to flee from himself, to escape the experience of existential hollowness, he is apt to pick up the most thrilling detective story he can find. If his eagerness to know "how it turns out," his breathless state of suspense, is a type of pleasure, it is the negative pleasure of getting away from displeasure—a type which Schopenhauer erroneously considered to be the only possible pleasure. We have already said that displeasure, tension, struggle are not here in order to provide the experience of negative pleasure when they are dispelled. We do not fight the struggle for existence in order to undergo a series of new sensations. Rather, the struggle for existence is a struggle "for" something; it is purposeful, and only in so being is it meaningful and able to bring meaning into life.

To the person hungry for excitement the greatest possible sensation is death—in art as well as in reality. The dullard newspaper-reader sitting at his breakfast table is avid for stories of misfortune and death. But mass misfortunes and deaths en masse cannot satisfy him; apparently the anonymous mass seems too abstract. And so your newspaper-reader may feel the need to go to a movie and see a gangster film. His pattern is like that of every addict: his hunger for sensation requires a nervous jolt to satisfy it; the jolt to the nerves engenders a more intense hunger, and so the dose must be constantly stepped up. What such a person really gets out of these vicarious deaths is the contrast effect: it seems as though other people are always the ones who must die. For this type of person is fleeing what most horrifies him: the certainty of his own death—which his existential emptiness makes unbearable to him. The certainty of death terrifies only the person who has a guilty conscience toward his life. Death marking the end of a lifetime can frighten only the person who has not lived his lifetime to the full. Such a person cannot face death at all. Instead of filling the finite time of his life with some meaning and so fulfilling himself, he takes refuge in a kind of delusion that he will be let off—like the man sentenced to death who in his last hour begins to believe he still has a chance to be pardoned. This type of person takes refuge in the delusion that nothing can happen to him personally; death and disaster are trials that only affect others.

Neurotic escape into the world of novels and identification with fictional "heroes" give the neurotic still another chance. The athlete obsessed with record mania is at least desirous of resting on his own laurels, but the addict of cheap fiction is content to have someone else, even if only a fictional character, perform feats for him. Yet the greatest mistake we can make in life is to rest upon laurels. We must never be content with what has already been achieved. Life never ceases to put new questions to us, never permits us to come to rest. Only self-narcotization keeps us insensible to the eternal pricks with which life with its endless succession of demands stings our consciences. The man who stands still is passed by; the man who is smugly contented loses himself. Neither in creating nor experiencing may we rest content with achievement; every day, every hour makes new deeds necessary and new experiences possible.

II From Psychoanalysis
to Existential Analysis

4   *On the Meaning of Love*

We have seen how the meaningfulness of human existence is based upon the uniqueness and singularity of the human person. We have seen further that creative values are actualized in the form of accomplishments that bear on community. Community in its turn confers existential meaning upon personal uniqueness and singularity. But community can also be a rich field of human experience. This is especially so with "twoness," the intimate community of one self with another. Let us put aside all the more or less vague ideas about love and consider it in the light of existential meaning. Seen so, it proves to be the area in which experiential values are especially realizable. Love is living the experience of another person in all his uniqueness and singularity.

It thus appears that there are two ways to validate the uniqueness and singularity of the self. One way is active, by the realization of creative values. The other is, as it were, passive, in which everything that a person otherwise has to win by action falls into his lap. This way is the way of love—or rather, the way of being loved. Without any contribution of his own, without effort or labor—by grace, so to speak—a person obtains that fulfillment which is found in the realization of his uniqueness and singularity. In love the beloved person is comprehended in his very essence, as the unique and singular being that he is; he is comprehended as a Thou, and as such is taken into the self. As a human person he becomes for the one who loves him indispensable and irreplaceable without having done anything to bring this about. The person who is loved "can't help" having the uniqueness and singularity of his self—that is, the value of his personality—realized. Love is not deserved, is unmerited—it is simply grace.

But love is not only grace; it is also enchantment. For the lover, it casts a spell upon the world, envelops the world in added worth. Love enormously increases receptivity to the fullness of values. The gates to the whole universe of values are, as it were, thrown open. Thus, in his surrender to the Thou the lover experiences an inner enrichment which goes beyond that Thou; for him the whole cosmos broadens and deepens in worth, glows in the radiance of those values which only the lover sees. For it is well known that love does not make one blind but seeing—able to see values.

In addition to the grace of being loved and the enchantment of loving, a third factor enters into love: the miracle of love. For through love the incomprehensible is accomplished—there enters (via a detour through the realm of biology) into life a new person, itself complete with the mystery of the uniqueness and singularity of its existence: a child!

We have already spoken of the phased and layered structure of the human being. And we have also emphasized that we see man as a physical-psychic-spiritual totality. We have called upon psychotherapy to recognize this totality as such, so that not only the psyche, but the spiritual aspects of man will be taken into account.

Now, however, we wish to show how man as lover, as experiencer of love, and as experiencer, in love, of another person's self, can react differently to the many-layered structure of the human person. For just as there are the three layers of the human person, so are there three possible attitudes toward it. The most primitive attitude concerns itself with the outermost layer: this is the sexual attitude. The bodily appearance of the other person happens to be sexually arousing, and this arousal sets off the sex drive in the sexually disposed person, directly affecting that person's physical being. Standing one step higher in the ranking of attitudes toward the partner is the erotic—for the sake of our analysis here we are making a sharp distinction between eroticism and sexuality. The erotically disposed person, in this special sense of the word "erotic," is not just sexually excited, not just sexually desirous. His attitude does not stem only from a sex drive and is not provoked by the other as a mere sexual partner. If we think of the partner's physical being as his or her outermost layer, it can be said that the erotically disposed person penetrates deeper than the one who is only sexually disposed. Eroticism penetrates into the next deeper layer, enters into the psychic structure of the other person. This attitude toward the partner, considered as one phase of the relationship, is identical with what is commonly called "infatuation." The physical traits of the partner stir us sexually, but we are also "infatuated" with the other's psychic characteristics. The infatuated person, then, is no longer in a state of mere physical excitation; rather, his psychic emotionality is stirred—stirred by the peculiar (but not unique) psyche of the partner; let us say, by particular character traits of the partner. The merely sexual attitude, then, is directed toward the partner's physical being and does not wish to go beyond this layer. The erotic attitude, the attitude of infatuation, is directed toward the psychic being; but it too does not penetrate to the core of the other person. This is done only by the third possible attitude: love itself. Loving (in the narrowest sense of the word) represents the end stage of eroticism (in the broadest sense of the word), since it alone penetrates as deeply as possible into

134

the personal structure of the partner. Loving represents a coming to relationship with another as a spiritual being. The close connection with spiritual aspects of the partner is the ultimate attainable form of partnership. The lover is no longer aroused in his own physical being, nor stirred in his own emotionality, but moved to the depths of his spiritual core, moved by the partner's spiritual core. Love, then, is an entering into direct relationship with the personality of the beloved, with the beloved's uniqueness and singularity. The spiritual core is the carrier of those psychic and bodily characteristics toward which the erotic or sexually disposed person is attracted; the spiritual core is what lies back of those physical or psychic appearances; it is what "appears" in those appearances. The bodily and psychic lineaments of the personality are, so to speak, the outer "dress" which the spiritual core "wears." While the sexually disposed person or the infatuated person feels attracted by the physical characteristics or psychic traits "of" the partner— that is, something this other person "has"—the lover loves the beloved's self—not something the beloved "has," but what he "is." The lover's gaze looks through the physical and the psychic "dress" of the spiritual core, looks to the core of the other's being. He is no longer interested in an alluring physical "type" or attractive temperament; he is concerned with the person, with the partner as unique, irreplaceable, and incomparable.

The tendencies we encounter in "infatuation"—which, as we have indicated, are not strictly of a sexual nature—have been termed by psychoanalysis "aim-inhibited" tendencies. The term is quite apt —though in an opposite sense from that intended by psychoanalysis. The psychoanalysts consider these tendencies aim-inhibited because according to their theory the instinctual aim is genito-sexual. To our mind these tendencies are aim-inhibited in a different sense— inhibited from passing on to the next higher attitudinal form, genuine love; inhibited from penetrating to the next deeper layer of the partner's personality, the spiritual core.

That the true lover really seeks the uniqueness and singularity of his partner's spiritual core can be made plain even to the person whose ideas are based on simple empiricism. Let us ask the skeptic to imagine that the one he loves is lost to him forever, either through death or departure and permanent separation. He is then offered a double of the beloved person—someone who in body and temperament perfectly resembles her. We then ask whether the lover can transfer his love to this other person—and he will have to admit that he would be unable to do so. Such a "transfer" of true love is inconceivable. For the true lover does not "care about" particular psychic or physical characteristics "of" the beloved person, he does not care about some trait that she "has," but about what she "is" in her uniqueness. As a unique person, she can never be replaced by any double, no matter how perfect a duplicate. But someone who is merely infatuated could probably find a double satisfactory for his purposes. His affections could be transferred without difficulty to the double. For his feelings are concerned only with the temperament the partner "has," not with the spiritual person that the partner "is."

The spiritual core as the object of the true attitude of love is, then, irreplaceable and inexchangeable for the true lover, because it is unique and singular. It follows from this that true love is its own warrant of permanence. For a physical state passes, and a psychological state is also impermanent. Sexual excitement is only temporary; the sex drive vanishes promptly after gratification. And infatuation, too, is seldom of long duration. But the spiritual act by which the person comprehends the spiritual core of another outlasts itself; to the degree that the content of that act is valid, it is valid once and for all. Thus true love as a spiritual relationship to the other person's being, as the beholding of another peculiar essence, is exempt from the transitoriness which marks the merely temporary states of physical sexuality or psychological eroticism. Love is more than an emotional condition; love is an intentional act. What it intends is the essence of the other person. This essence is ultimately independent of existence; *essentia* is not contingent upon *existentia*, and insofar as it has this freedom, it is superior to *existentia*. That is why love can outlast the death of the beloved; in that sense we can understand why love is "stronger" than death. The existence of the beloved may be annihilated by death, but his essence cannot be touched by death. His unique being is, like all true essences, something timeless and thus imperishable. The "idea" of a person—which is what the lover sees—belongs to a realm beyond time. These considerations, it is true, go back to scholastic or Platonic philosophy. But let us not imagine that they are therefore too far removed from the simple empiricism which, we must also recognize, has its intellectual validity and dignity. For example, we have the following narrative by a former concentration-camp inmate:

"All of us in camp, my comrades and myself as well, were certain that no happiness on earth could ever in the future make up for what we were compelled to endure during our imprisonment. If we had drawn up a balance sheet of happiness, the only choice left to us would have been to 'run into the wire'—that is, to kill ourselves. Those who did not do so were acting out of a deep sense of some obligation. As far as I was concerned, I felt duty-bound toward my mother to stay alive. We two loved one another beyond all else. Therefore my life had a meaning—in spite of everything. But I had to count upon death any minute of every day. And therefore my death also should somehow have meaning—as well as all the suffering that I would have yet to go through before it came. And so I made a pact with Heaven: if I should have to die, then let my death preserve my mother's life; and whatever I should have to suffer up until the time of my death was to purchase for her a sweet and easy death when her time came. Only by imagining it in terms of such a sacrifice was my tormented existence endurable. I could live my life only if it had a meaning; but I also wanted to suffer my suffering and die my death only if suffering and death also had a meaning."

The prisoner then goes on to recount that whenever time and conditions in the camp permitted, he dwelt upon the inner personality of his mother. We might put it this way: while in his actual situation it was impossible for him to realize creative values, he was learning the inner enrichment and fulfillment of devoted love; in loving contemplation and loving memory he was realizing experiential values. The continuation of his account strikes us as wholly remarkable: "But I did not know whether my mother herself was still alive. All the time I was in camp we were without news of one another. Then it struck me that when, as I so frequently did, I was holding imaginary dialogues with my mother, the fact that I did not even know whether she was alive hardly disturbed me!"

That is, at no time did this man know whether the person he loved still had physical existence, and nevertheless this so little affected his feeling for her that he stumbled upon the question of her "existence" only incidentally—without its being a stumbling-block. Love is so little directed toward the body of the beloved that it can easily outlast the other's death, can exist in the lover's heart until his own death. The true lover can never really grasp the death of the loved one, any more than he can "grasp" his own death. For it is well known that no one can ever fully realize the fact of his own death, which is fundamentally as inconceivable as the fact of not having been before one's own birth. Anyone who really believes or claims that he can grasp the death of a person is deceiving himself. For what he would have us believe is ultimately incomprehensible: that a personal entity is removed from the world simply because the organism which is its vehicle has become a cadaver, and that thereafter no form of being pertains to it. Scheler in a posthumously published essay on the survival of personality after the death of the body has pointed out that even in a person's lifetime we apprehend far more of the person—as soon as we really "intend" him—than "the few scraps of sensuous data" his physical appearance gives us. The latter is all we miss after death! When that is gone, it is far from the same as saying that the person himself no longer exists. The most we can say is that he can no longer manifest himself, for manifestation requires physical forms of expression (speech, etc.). Once more, then, we see why and in what sense the true intending of love, the intending of another personality as such, is independent of the person's physical presence—independent, in fact, of the person's bodily existence altogether.

All this, of course, is not to say that love has no desire to "embody" itself. But it is independent of the body to the extent that it does not need the body. Even in love between the sexes the body, the sexual element, is not primary; it is not an end in itself, but a means of expression. Love as such can exist without it. Where sexuality is possible, love will desire and seek it; but where renunciation is called for, love will not necessarily cool or die. The spiritual self takes form in giving shape to its psychic and physical modes of appearance and expression. That is, in the totality which is centered around the personal core the outer layers serve as means by which the inner layers are expressed. A person's body expresses his character and his character expresses the person as spiritual being. The spirit attains to expression—and demands expression—in the body and the psyche. Thus the bodily appearance of the beloved person becomes for a lover a symbol, a mere token for something behind it which manifests itself in the external appearance but is not fully contained in that. True love in and for itself needs the body neither for arousal nor for fulfillment, though it makes use of the body for both. Arousal in a man of healthy instincts is stimulated by the partner's body—although his love is not directed toward the partner's body. But in given circumstances the partner's body as expression of the spirit will guide the lover's choice in that, with the sureness of instinct, he prefers one person to another. Certain physical characteristics or traits of character would then lead the lover to a particular partner—to the one particularly meant for him. While the "shallow" person sees only the partner's surface and cannot grasp the depths, the "deeper" person sees the surface itself as an expression of the depths, not as an essential and decisive expression, but as a significant one. In this sense love uses the body for arousal. We have said that it also uses the body for fulfillment. For in fact physically mature lovers will in general be impelled toward a physical relationship. But for the real lover the physical, sexual relationship remains a mode of expression for the spiritual relationship which his love really is, and as a mode of expression it is love, the spiritual act, which gives it human dignity. We can therefore say: as the body is for the lover the expression of the partner's spiritual being, the sexual act is for the lover the expression of a spiritual intention.

A person's physical appearance, then, has comparatively little to do with his being loved. His actual physical traits and temperamental features acquire their erotic significance from love itself; it is love which makes these characteristics "lovable." For this reason we must take a reserved and critical view of the use of cosmetics. For even blemishes are an essential part of the personality. Insofar as externals affect the lover, they do not affect him in themselves, but as part of the beloved person. A patient, for example, was considering plastic surgery to beautify ugly breasts, hoping thereby to assure her husband's love. She asked her doctor for advice. The doctor warned against the projected operation; he remarked that since her husband really loved her, he loved her body just as it was. An evening dress, he pointed out, does not affect a man "in itself"; he thinks it beautiful only when the woman he loves is wearing it. Finally the patient asked her husband his opinion. And he did indicate that the result of the operation would only be troubling to him; he would be forced to think: "Somehow this is no longer my wife."

Psychologically, of course, it is understandable that an unattractive person will painfully and artificially seek what seems to come so easily to the attractive. The ugly person will overestimate the love life—and the less joy he has in his own love life, the more he will exaggerate its importance. In fact love is only one of the possible ways to fill life with meaning, and is not even the best way. Our existences would have come to a sad pass and our lives would be poor indeed if their meaning depended upon whether or not we experienced happiness in love. Life is infinitely rich in chances to realize values. We need only remember the primacy of creative realization of values. But the individual who neither loves nor is loved can still shape his life in a highly meaningful manner. The only question is whether the failure to achieve love is really imposed by destiny and is not a neurotic failure, one for which the person has himself to blame. We have already discussed those cases where the actualization of creative values must be put aside, and attitudinal values cultivated in their stead. We have emphasized that the renunciation must not be arbitrary or premature. The same point may be made in regard to renouncing the experiential values of love. The danger of premature resignation is on the whole considerable. For people tend to forget how relatively unimportant outward attractiveness is, how much more important personality is to the love life. We all know shining (and consoling) examples of unattractive or unprepossessing persons who by virtue of their charm and temperament had successful love lives. We may recall our case of the cripple who under the most unfavorable circumstances was remarkably successful not only intellectually, but erotically also. To be unattractive is not a sufficient reason for being resigned. And resignation has a bad side-effect: resentment. For a neurotic person who fails to gain fulfillment in a particular realm of values ends either by overvaluing or devaluing that particular aspect of life. Neurotic straining after "happiness" in love leads, precisely because of the strain involved, to "unhappiness." The person who has a fixation on overvalued eroticism tries to force open that "door to happiness" of which we have remarked, with Kierkegaard, that it "opens outward" and does not yield to violent assault. On the other hand, the person who is negatively fixated on the love life, who devalues it in an effort to make himself feel better about what he has not attained and considers unattainable— such a person also blocks his own way to erotic happiness. Inner resentment coupled with renunciation brings about the same result as revolt and protest against fate: both reaction patterns rob the individuals of their own chance. On the other hand, the easy, unresenting attitude of someone who is sincerely but not irrevocably resigned permits the color of his personality to shine through and so offers a last chance for love to come his way. There is much truth to the old maxim: "By abstaining we obtain."

Stress on appearance leads to general overestimation of the value of "beauty" in erotic life. At the same time the person as such is devalued. There is something insulting in identifying a woman as "beautiful." Does not the use of this adjective ultimately mean that we are deliberately refraining from using any others, from judging the qualities of her mind, say? A high rating in a category of relatively low valuation arouses the suspicion of tacit unwillingness to give any rating in a category of higher valuation. Stressing externals, moreover, implies not only a devaluation of the person being judged, but also of the one who delivers the judgment. For if I talk about a woman's beauty, that suggests not only that I have nothing favorable to say about her personality, but that I am not interested in her personality—because I do not value qualities of the personality.

All flirtation, all the common, ordinary gallantries of the past and present, disregard the partner's inner personality with unconscious intent. The uniqueness and singularity of the other person is deliberately left out of such encounters. People who go in for such superficial eroticism flee from the obligations of real love, from any sense of having true ties with the partner—because such ties involve responsibility. They take refuge in a collective concept, preferring a "type"; their partner at any given time is a more or less chance representative of that type. They choose the type rather than any particular person. Their love is directed toward typical but impersonal "looks." A feminine type very commonly preferred is that of the chorus girl. This can easily be understood when we consider how thoroughly depersonalized a type she is. The chorus girl is, so to speak, a symbol of girls "wholesale." She is a component part of a precision mechanism: the chorus line. She is a member of a dance troupe, therefore part of a collective group. As such she cannot step out of her framework, cannot drop out of her role among the others who are tripping in step across the stage. In life as well she must keep in step. Today's average man takes this type of woman for his erotic ideal because she cannot, in her impersonality, burden him with responsibility. The type is ubiquitous.

Just as one chorus girl in the revue can be replaced by any other, so in life this type of woman is easily replaceable. The chorus-girl type is impersonal woman with whom a man need have no personal relationship, no obligations; a woman he can "have" and therefore need not love. She is property, without personal traits, without personal value. Only the human person can be loved; the impersonality of the chorus-girl type cannot be loved. With her, no question of faithfulness is involved; infidelity follows from impersonality. Not only is infidelity in such erotic relationships feasible; it is necessary. For where the quality of happiness in love is lacking, the lack must be compensated by quantity of sexual pleasure.

This kind of eroticism represents a crippled form of love. The use of such a phrase as "I have 'had' this woman" fully exposes the nature of such eroticism. What you "have" you can swap; what you possess you can change. If a man has "possessed" a woman, he can easily exchange her, can even "buy" himself another. This relationship of "having" has its counterpart in the woman's attitude. For such superficial eroticism which regards only the partner's surface, the outward appearance, is equally a surface matter for the woman. What a person "is" as such does not count, only how much sex appeal the person has as a possible sexual partner. What you have can be altered, and a woman's "surface" can likewise be changed—by make-up. Thus the woman's attitude corresponds to the man's. The woman will do her best to conceal all personal qualities, in order not to bother the man with them, and in order to give the man what he is looking for: his preferred type. The woman—or, rather, the contemporary urban "doll" is completely engrossed in her appearance. She wants to be "taken"—but she does not want to be taken seriously, to be taken for what she really is: a human person in all her uniqueness and singularity. She wants to be taken as a member of a sex, and therefore she puts her body, with all its unspecific quality, in the forefront. She wants to be impersonal and to represent whatever type happens to be the fashion, happens to be going well in the market place of erotic vanities. As slavishly as possible, she will attempt to imitate that popular type, and in so doing she must necessarily be unfaithful to herself, to her self.

She may, for example, choose her type from the world of the film stars. She compares herself again and again with the type—which represents her own or her male partner's present ideal woman—in order to make herself as like it as possible. She has no urge at all to assert the personality which is unique and incomparable in all human beings. She does not even long to create a new type of woman herself, has no ambition to set the fashion. Instead of creating a type, she is content to represent one. Gladly, of her own free will, she presents herself to the man as the type he prefers. She never gives herself, never lovingly surrenders her self. Proceeding from such assumptions, proceeding along such a course, she wanders further and further from true, fulfilling erotic experience. For the man who chooses her does not want her at all; he is in reality choosing only her type. Submissive to the man's desires, she readily gives him what he needs and wants to "have." And both part empty-handed. Instead of seeking one another and so finding each other's selves, finding the uniqueness and singularity which alone make each other worth loving and their own lives worth living, they have settled for a fiction. For in his creative work each man displays his uniqueness and singularity, but in loving he takes the uniqueness and singularity of his partner into himself. In the mutual surrender of love, in the giving and taking between two people, each one's own personality comes into its own. The love impulse breaks through to that layer of being in which every individual human being no longer represents a "type," but himself alone, not comparable, not replaceable, and possessing all the dignity of his uniqueness. This dignity is the dignity of those angels of whom some scholastics maintained that they do not represent a kind; rather, there is only one of each kind.

If the attitude of true love represents the directing of the core of one person toward another, that is also the sole guarantee of fidelity. In other words, out of love itself comes the assurance of its duration. But something more comes out of it: its "eternality." Love can only be experienced *sub specie æternitatis*. The real lover, in the moment of loving, in his surrender to that moment and to the object of his love, cannot conceive that his feeling will ever change. This is understandable when we consider that his feelings are directed toward the essence of the beloved person and that person's worth, just like any other spiritual act—like, say, cognition or the recognition of values. Once I have comprehended that $2 \times 2 = 4$, I have comprehended it once and for all. "That's all there is to it." And once I have truly comprehended the inner nature of another person by seeing that person in the illumination of love, that is all there is to it: I must abide by the truth of it, must abide by this love, and this love must abide with me. The moment we experience true love, we experience it as valid forever, like a truth which we recognize as an "eternal truth." In exactly the same way, as long as love lasts in ordinary time it is necessarily experienced as "eternal love."

Yet in all of his searchings for truth, man can make mistakes. And in the matter of loving, individuals may deceive themselves. A person may think that love has made him see, when in fact he may be blinded by mere infatuation. But no one can start out assuming that a subjective truth is a possible error because it is "only subjective"; it can turn out to be an error only later on.

Similarly, it is impossible for anyone to love "for a while," temporarily; it is impossible to intend a temporary state as such and to set a definitive term to love. A person can at most love at the risk of having the object of his love turn out to be unworthy afterward, so that his love "dies" as soon as the worth of the beloved is no longer there in the lover's vision.

A mere possession can be changed. But since true love is not directed toward the aspect of the other person which can be "possessed," toward what the other "has"; since true love is rather directed toward what the other "is"—such real love, and it alone, leads to a monogamous attitude. For the monogamous attitude presupposes comprehension of the partner in all his uniqueness and singularity, comprehending the core and the worth of his personality, going beyond all bodily and temperamental peculiarities, since these are not unique and singular and can be found in other persons of more or less the same cast.

The obvious conclusion from this is that mere infatuation, being by its nature a more or less fleeting "emotional state," must be considered virtually a contra-indication to marriage. This is by no means the equivalent of saying that real love in itself is a positive indication for marriage. Marriage is more than a matter of personal experience. It is a complex structure, an institution of social life legalized by the state or, as the case may be, sanctioned by the church. That is, it reaches deep into the societal realm, and certain societal conditions ought to be met before a marriage is sealed. In addition there are biological conditions and circumstances which in given cases may make marriage inadvisable. Eugenic considerations may enter into the decision. These factors may not disqualify the love as such, but the parties to such a marriage should be content to view their marriage as a spiritual partnership and to stop short of the usual concomitant of marriage—i.e., reproduction.

On the other hand, if motives in themselves extraneous to real love determine a marriage, the marriage can at most partake of the nature of "eroticism"—eroticism as we have defined it: as being directed toward "having," toward possession. In particular, where economic motives play a major part in the decision, the materialistic desire to "have" is preponderant. It is to such motives that institutions like marriage-brokerage owe their existence. For matchmaking of this sort the social factor of marriage is considered in isolation, is in fact considered the paramount and single issue. The degradation of human relationships that this entails is visited, as it were, upon the next generation. We know a young man who left home to escape the continual quarrels between his parents, who always dragged him into their disputes. With the naïveté and earnestness of youth he planned to devote his life to setting up some kind of institution whose sole purpose would be to prevent marriages between incompatible people like his parents.

Real love in itself constitutes the decisive factor of a monogamous relationship. But there is another factor, that of exclusiveness (Oswald Schwarz). Love means a sense of inward union; the monogamous relationship, in the form of marriage, is the outward tie. Being faithful means maintaining this tie in all its definitiveness. The exclusiveness of the tie, however, makes it the more imperative that a person form the "right" tie; not only must he be prepared to bind himself, but also he must know whom he is binding himself to. It becomes supremely important that he decide in favor of the right partner. Erotic maturity in the sense of being inwardly mature enough for a monogamous relationship thus involves a dual requirement: the ability to select a partner; and the ability to remain definitively faithful to that partner.

Youth is a time of preparation for one's erotic life as well as for life in general. Youth must explore, seek for the right partner, and find one. Youth must also "learn" in good time to be faithful. These two demands sometimes run counter to each other. For on the one hand, in order to develop the ability to choose a partner, the young person must acquire a degree of erotic insight and erotic practice. On the other hand, in developing the ability to be faithful, the young person must endeavor to grow beyond mere shifts of mood, stick to one person, and maintain the relationship. In some cases he (the pronoun is arbitrary here and stands for both sexes) will not know whether to abandon a particular relationship in order to have the experience of as many different relationships as possible so that he can finally choose the right one; or whether to preserve the given relationship as long as possible in order to learn fidelity as soon as may be. In practice the best advice to give a young person confronting this dilemma is to suggest that he formulate the question negatively. Let him ask himself whether he wishes to "drop" an existing and valuable relationship because he is afraid of being tied down and is trying to escape responsibility; or in the other case let him ask himself whether he is frantically clinging to an already moribund relationship because he is afraid of having to be alone for a few weeks or months. If he looks into his subjective motives in this way, he will find an objective decision easy to make.

Scheler defines love as a spiritual movement toward the highest possible value of the loved person, a spiritual act in which this highest value—which he calls the "salvation" of a person—is apprehended. Spranger makes a similar comment: that love perceives the value potentialities in the beloved person. Von Hattingberg expresses it differently: love sees a person the way God "meant" him. Love, we may say, reveals to us the valuational image of a human being. In so doing, it performs a metaphysical act. For the valuational image revealed to us in the course of the spiritual act of love is essentially the "image" of something invisible, unreal—unrealized. In the spiritual act of love we apprehend a person not only as what he "is" in his uniqueness and singularity, his *hæcceitas* in Scholastic terminology, but also as what he can and will be: his *entelechy*. Let us call to mind the definition of human reality as a possibility—the possibility of realizing values, of self-realization. What love sees is therefore no more and no less than this "possibility" of a human being. We may remark parenthetically that psychotherapy also must aim to see the human beings with whom it deals in their own most personal possibilities, to anticipate the potential values in them. It is part of the metaphysical mystery of the spiritual act we call love that out of the beloved's essential image it succeeds in reading the potential image. For to discover potential values on the basis of essential facts is not a matter of calculation. Facts can be calculated; potentialities are by their nature incalculable.

Awareness of values can only enrich a person. In fact, this inner enrichment partly constitutes the meaning of his life, as we have seen in our discussion of experiential values. Therefore, love must necessarily enrich the lover. This being so, there can be no such thing as "unrequited, unhappy love"; the term is self-contradictory. Either you really love—in which case you must feel enriched, whether or not the love is returned; or you do not really love, do not actually intend the inner being of another person, but rather miss it completely and look only for something physical "about" him or some (psychological) character trait which he "has." In such a situation your feelings may well be unrequited, but you are then not a lover. We must remember this: that infatuation makes us blind; real love enables us to see. Love permits us to see the spiritual core of the other person, the reality of the other's essential nature and his value potentialities. Love allows us to experience another's personality as a world in itself, and so extends our own world. While it thus enriches and "requites" us, it also does the other person good in leading him to those potential values which can be seen and anticipated only in love. Love helps the beloved to become as the lover sees him. For the loved one wants to be worthier of the lover, a worthier recipient of such love, by growing to be more like the lover's image, and so he becomes more and more the image of "what God conceived and wanted him to be." While, therefore, even "unrequited" love enriches us and brings happiness, "requited" love is distinctly creative. In mutual love, in which each wishes to be worthy of the other, to become like the other's vision of him, a kind of dialectical process takes place in which each outbids the other and so elevates the other.

We have shown that unrequited or unhappy love is a contradiction in terms. From the psychological point of view, the expression is fraught with self-pity. The pleasurable or unpleasurable significance of an experience is simply being overestimated. In erotic matters, above all, the hedonistic point of view has no justification. Like spectators in the theater, life's actors generally find that tragedies are more profound experiences than comedies. Even when our experiences in love turn out unhappily, we are not only enriched, but also given a deeper sense of life; such experiences are the chief things which foster inner growth and maturity.

Of course the inner enrichment which a person experiences in love may be accompanied by tension. Neurotics fear these tensions and shy away from anything which may tend to produce them. The experience of unhappy, unrequited love has a definite use—the end being to protect the burned child from the fire of Eros. For those who have once had this unpleasant experience, there is a tendency not to repeat it. The phrase "unrequited love" is therefore not only an expression of self-pity, but of perverted enjoyment of misery. In an almost masochistic fashion the thoughts of the infatuated wretch circle round and round his unhappiness. He barricades himself behind his first—or last—failure so that he will never have to burn his fingers again. He hides behind his lack of success; he escapes into the unhappiness of the past to avoid the possibility of happiness in the future. Instead of continuing to look until he finds, he gives up the search. Instead of remaining open-eyed to the wealth of opportunities that love can offer, he puts on blinkers. Spellbound, he fixes his eyes on his unhappy experience in order not to have to see life. He wants to be secure, not receptive. He cannot recover from his one unhappy experience because he does not want to chance another.

Such a person must be re-educated; he must learn to be always ready and receptive to the multitude of opportunities that may come his way. For the probability is that in the life of the average person there will be nine unhappy love affairs to a single happy one. He must simply wait for that one, not put obstacles in its path by perversely using unhappiness as a pretext for shutting out happiness. Psychotherapeutic treatment of so-called unrequited love must therefore consist in bringing this flight tendency into the open and in demonstrating the task quality not only of life in general, but of the love life in particular.

Even love which is reciprocated is not always free of unhappiness. Among other things, there are the torments of jealousy. Jealousy is an aspect of the erotic materialism we have spoken of.

At its root is the attitude toward the object of love as property. The jealous man treats the person he allegedly loves as if this person were his possession; he degrades her to a piece of property. He wants to have her "only for himself"—thereby proving that he thinks of her in terms of "having." There is no room for jealousy within a real love relationship. It is ruled out by very definition, since real love presupposes a mutual feeling of the uniqueness and singularity of the partners. The rivalry so feared by the jealous lover assumes the possibility that he can be replaced by a competitor, assumes that love can be transferred to another. But that is impossible in real love, for the beloved one cannot be compared with any other person.

There is another well-known type of jealousy which is jealousy of the partner's past, of predecessors. Persons plagued by this kind of jealousy always want to have been the "first." There is more modesty in those who are content to be the "last." But in another sense this is not greater modesty; rather, it is a more demanding attitude. For such a lover, while not worried about priority with respect to all his predecessors, nevertheless regards his love as a proof of his sovereign position. All who are prey to any of these forms of jealousy overlook the fundamental fact that each human being is not comparable with any other in his innermost being. To compare yourself with anyone else is to do an injustice either to yourself or to the other person. That, incidentally, is true outside of the love life also. For everyone has a different kind of start. But the person whose start was more difficult, whose fate was less kind, can be credited with the greater personal achievement, other things being equal. Since, however, all aspects of the situation imposed by fate can never be assessed, there is simply no basis and no standard for a comparison of achievements.

Where a relationship does not reach the level of real love,

where therefore a person is not loved so that his incomparability is part of the relationship, there is absolutely no place for jealousy at all. For in that case the love relationship really is not present. Jealousy is consequently foolish in every case, since it comes either too soon or too late. Either it is unjustified because the partner is committed to faithfulness, or it is well founded because the partner is actually unfaithful. In the latter case jealousy is certainly pointless, since the exclusive partnership exists no longer.

It may be added that from a tactical point of view jealousy is a dangerous emotion. The jealous person engenders the very thing he fears: the withdrawal of love. Doubting himself because of previous failures brings to the doubter more and more failures (just as confidence not only comes from inner strength but leads to still greater strength). The jealous person, doubting his ability to hold his partner, may actually lose out, may actually drive his partner into the arms of another, forcing infidelity because he has cast question on the beloved's fidelity. Thus he brings about what he believes to be true. Certainly fidelity is one of love's tasks; but it is always a task only for the lover and can never be a demand directed at the partner. Posed as a demand, it will eventually be taken as a challenge. It will drive the partner into an attitude of protest from which sooner or later infidelity may well result. Trust in another makes for self-confidence just as much as trust in oneself, so that in general this trust will prove to be justified. On the other hand, distrust makes for a lack of mutual confidence, so that in the end distrust will also prove justified.

Trust must have its counterpart, on the partner's side, in honesty. But just as trust follows a dialectical law in making true what it believes to be true, so honesty is also paradoxical: one can lie with truth and, on the other hand, tell the truth with a lie— even make something true by a lie. An example familiar to every doctor can serve to illustrate this. Suppose we take a patient's blood pressure and find it slightly high. The patient asks us to tell him the reading. But if we do, he will be so alarmed that his blood pressure will rise, will actually go higher than it already is. If, however, we do not tell the truth but give him a lower figure than the true reading, we will reassure him and his blood pressure will actually drop—so that in the end our sham lie (not white lie) will be an exact statement. Throughout life in general, and especially in the love life, fanatical adherence to truth at all costs is affected by this paradox. Consider the following example: A patient asked her doctor for advice on whether or not to confess to her husband a wholly harmless and abortive instance of infidelity. The doctor was of the opinion that she should not mention it. In the first place he knew that she wanted to confess her "infidelity" only for neurotic reasons—that in fact she had had her little adventure only to provoke her husband, to "test" him. In the second place, objectively (that is, on the merits of the matter and disregarding motivation and psychogenesis) the doctor thought that by telling the "truth" the patient would only be deceiving her husband. For her confession would be misleading, in that the husband would be forced to believe that there was more behind the matter than she was willing to admit, since otherwise she would not have felt impelled to confess anything. The woman did not follow her doctor's advice, and the result was a divorce which was legally and humanly needless.

Let us turn now from the problem of suspected infidelity to that of actual unfaithfulness. We at once encounter the double standard of morality: marital infidelity by the man and by the woman are commonly judged in different terms. A woman is generally blamed much more harshly for adultery than a man. Perhaps the injustice of this double standard is only apparent. For psychologically the attitude of the sexes toward sexual life differs considerably. Allers, for example, has pointed out this difference in the formula: the man lends himself to love; the woman gives herself in love.

Finally, we must not overlook the sociological reason for the double standard. For a woman who has "had affairs" with several men can never know for certain who the father may be if she has a child; whereas a husband who has been unfaithful to his wife, but to whom his wife has remained faithful, can be perfectly sure of the paternity of his child.

The conclusions which may be drawn from the partner's infidelity are numerous. The variety of possible attitudes toward infidelity makes it an occasion for actualizing attitudinal values. One person will avenge the hurt which has been inflicted on him by breaking up the relationship; another will forgive and make up; a third will try to conquer the partner anew, to win him back.

———

A materialist eroticism not only makes the partner a possession, but the sex act itself a commodity. This emerges most plainly in prostitution. As a psychological problem, prostitution is as much the affair of the prostitutes as of the "clients." What we have said earlier in another connection is relevant here also: that economic necessity forces a particular type of conduct upon no one. That is, necessity would not force a psychologically and morally normal woman to prostitution. On the contrary, it is amazing how frequently women resist the temptation to prostitution in spite of economic necessity. That solution for economic distress simply is out of the question for them, and their resistance seems as natural to them as soliciting seems to the typical prostitute.

As for the prostitute's client: he is seeking precisely the sort of impersonal and non-binding form of love life which the relationship to a commodity will give him. From the standpoint of psychological hygiene, prostitution is as dangerous as it is from the standpoint of bodily hygiene. The psychological dangers, however, are less easily guarded against. The chief peril is that it nurtures precisely the attitude toward sex which wise sex education tries to prevent. This is the attitude that takes sex to be a mere means to the end of pleasure—a thoroughly decadent sensualism. Sexuality, which should be the means of expression for love, is made subservient to the pleasure principle, and gratification of the instincts, sexual pleasure, becomes an end in itself.

Faulty upbringing is often to blame when a young person yearning for love develops into a sex-starved adult. We know of a case in which a mother sent her son to prostitutes in order to wean him from his love for a girl whom the mother considered economically and socially "beneath" him. Turning the impulses of love into the bypath of prostitution, degrading sex to mere instinctual gratification and reducing the partner to a mere instinctual object, is likely to block the way to the right kind of love life, in which sex is no more than the expression—and no less than the crowning glory—of love. When through habituation to prostitutes a young man becomes fixated upon sexual pleasure as an end in itself, his whole future marital life may be damaged. For then when he really loves, he can no longer go back—or, rather, he can no longer go forward, can no longer attain the proper attitude of the real lover toward sex. For the lover the sexual act is the physical expression of a psycho-spiritual union. But when a man has been accustomed to sex not as a means of expression but as an end in itself, he divides women sharply into two classes—the class of the madonna and that of the whore—with consequent psychological difficulties. Such cases are well known in the annals of psychotherapy.

For the woman, too, there are patterns which hinder her normal development toward experiencing sex as an expression of love. And here, too, the damage done is hard to correct. In one such case a girl at first had a platonic relationship with her young man; she refused to enter into sexual relations with him because she did not feel any impulse to do so. Her partner insisted more and more, and let fall the remark: "I guess you must be frigid." Whereupon she began to worry that he might be right. Troubled by this fear, she decided to give herself to him—in order to prove to him and to herself that he was wrong. The result of this experiment was, inevitably, a total inability to experience pleasure. For the impulse had not yet germinated; it had not awakened and could not be aroused. Instead of waiting for it to develop gradually and spontaneously, the girl entered into this first sexual act with the desperate intent to prove her capacity for pleasure, but at the same time with the secret fear that she might turn out to be incapable of it. The very artificiality of the situation would in itself have inhibited any instinctual impulses that might have been aroused. Under such circumstances it is hardly surprising that the girl, anxiously keeping watch on herself, could not possibly be yielding and responsive. The possible effect of such a disappointment on a woman's future love life or marriage may well be psychogenic frigidity of the anticipatory-anxiety-neurosis type.

The "mechanism" of what is termed anticipatory anxiety is all too familiar to the psychotherapist. Something goes wrong when the consciousness attempts to regulate acts which normally take place, so to speak, without thought. The stutterer is acutely conscious of the way he speaks—he concentrates on saying, not on what he wants to say; he observes the how instead of the what. And so he inhibits himself—as though his speech were a motor into which he attempts to poke his fingers when he should simply start it up and let it run of its own accord. It is often sufficient to teach the stutterer that he need only switch over, so to speak, to thinking aloud. If only he will think aloud, the mouth will talk of its own accord—the more fluently when the least observed. If he can be taught this, he is well along on the way to a cure. As will be demonstrated in the more systematic setting of a later, clinical chapter, the psychotherapy of insomnia works along analogous lines. If a person mistakenly fixes his mind upon the process of falling asleep, if he desperately wills sleep, he creates an inner tension which makes sleep impossible. Fear of sleeplessness is an anticipatory anxiety which in such cases hinders falling asleep, thus confirming the fact of insomnia, which in turn reinforces the anticipatory anxiety—a vicious circle.

A similar process takes place in all persons who have become insecure sexually. Their self-observation is sharpened and they start out with the fear of not succeeding. This anxiety itself leads to sexual failure. The sexual neurotic no longer fixes his mind upon his partner (as does the lover), but upon the sexual act as such. Consequently the act fails, must fail, because it does not take place "simply," is not performed naturally, but is willed. In such cases the task of psychotherapy is to break the hapless vicious circle of sexual anticipatory anxiety by eliminating this fixation upon the act itself. The patient should be instructed never to let himself feel obligated to perform a sexual act. Everything which the patient might feel as a "compulsion to sexuality" must be avoided. Such a compulsion might arise from his partner (if she is an "impulsive," sexually demanding woman) or from his own ego (making a

"resolution" to have sexual intercourse on a certain particular day)
or from a situation (accompanying others to a brothel, etc.).

When all these types of compulsion which affect the sexual
neurotic adversely have been eliminated, the patient must learn
spontaneity until he has achieved naturalness in his sexual practices.
But even before such psychotherapy is undertaken, the effort should
be made to show the patient that his original "sick" response was
quite understandable in human terms. Thus the patient can be
freed of the feeling that he is suffering from a fated pathological
condition. In other words, he must learn to recognize the unwhole-
some influence of anticipatory anxiety and the vicious circle in
which he has been caught, and he must learn that his reaction is a
common human failing.

A young man came to a doctor because he was worried
about his virility. It seemed that after a conflict lasting for years
he had finally persuaded his partner "to be his." She promised to
give herself to him during the Whitsun holidays. This promise
was made two weeks before Whitsuntide. During all those two
weeks the young man could hardly sleep for tension and anticipation. Then the two set out on a week-end excursion; they were
going to spend the night in an Alpine shelter hut. At night, when
the patient climbed the stairs to their common room, he was so
agitated—by anticipatory anxiety, not by sexual excitement—that
as he later described it his heart was pounding so hard and he was
trembling so violently that he could scarcely walk. How in the
world could he possibly have been potent!

The doctor had to explain how impossible sexual success
was in such an outer and inner situation, and how understandable
the patient's reaction had been. His reaction had been normal, not
pathological, behavior. The patient finally saw that his was not a
case of real impotence, as he had feared (the fear creating an

anticipatory-anxiety neurosis and thus becoming the starting-point for a fateful vicious circle). Understanding this was enough to restore his self-confidence. He realized that it was not the sign of a very grave sickness for a man to be unable to do two things at once: to be lovingly devoted to his partner (the prerequisite for the capacity to respond and perform sexually) and at the same time to be watching himself with anxious anticipation.

The function of such a psychotherapeutic procedure is to put to flight anticipatory anxiety when it is just getting started. The dangerous autosuggestion which comes from such anxiety is not permitted to develop, is arrested right at the start.

Again, then, in this realm of sex life, in the psychology and pathology of men's sexual behavior, we see how misguided all striving for happiness is, how the desperate attempt to achieve happiness, to achieve pleasure as such, is condemned to miscarry. We have already said in another connection that the striving for happiness is not one of man's basic drives; that, in general, life is not directed toward pleasure at all. Kant has remarked that man wants to be happy, but that what he ought to want is to be worthy of happiness. We hold, however, that man does not want to be happy. Rather, he wants to have a reason for being happy. Which is to say that all deflection of his desire from the object to the desire itself, from the aim (the reason for being happy) to the pleasure (the consequence of attaining the aim), represents a derivative mode of human striving. This derivative mode lacks immediacy. It is such lack of immediacy that characterizes all neurotic experience. We have already seen how it can lead to neurotic and especially to sexual disturbances. The immediacy and therefore the genuineness of sexual intention is the indispensable prerequisite for potency in the man. In connection with sexual pathology Oswald Schwarz has coined the word "exemplariness" to express the genuineness of an intention. Typical of the exemplary person is that he does not easily become embarrassed; with characteristic sureness of instinct he avoids all situations which he could not cope with, keeps out of all environments into which he might not fit. Strikingly non-exemplary, on the other hand, would be the behavior of a sensitive man who visits a prostitute and then finds himself impotent. There is nothing pathological about this behavior in itself; it is not yet characteristically neurotic. Sexual failure in such a situation is rather to be expected of a cultured man. But that such a man gets himself into this kind of situation where his impotence is the only way to get out of it again—that is evidence that he is not "exemplary."

We have dealt so far with questions of the nature of love. We turn now to its origins. Psychosexual maturity first begins in puberty. With physiologic maturation, sex (in the narrower sense of the word) enters the human consciousness so suddenly that—in analogy to Schilder's formulation in regard to psychosis—we can speak of an "invasion of the psyche by the organic realm." The adolescent child is unprepared for this sudden invasion of sexuality into his psyche, and the natural reaction is often some sort of shock. The psychological troubles of adolescence which follow are therefore not pathological.

At the time sexuality makes this invasion into the adolescent personality it is not as yet anything intrinsically psychological. It ought rather to be termed a psychic reaction to a somatic event, merely a psychic consequence of an endocrine upheaval, or the psychic expression of glandular tensions. This physiologically determined sexuality is originally amorphous, has not yet been shaped by the personality. In other words, it is not yet *integrated*. Only with increasing psychosexual maturity is sexuality organized by the personality, and assimilated into the life of the individual. At the beginning sex is not yet a personal tendency; rather, it is a mere urge without aim or direction. In the course of further development and maturity this urge becomes more and more directed; there is an increase in intentionality. Sexuality is brought closer and closer to the personal center, more and more within the field of force generated by personal strivings. The first step is when the sexual urge acquires a goal: detumescence, discharge of the state of tension by "contrectation" (A. Moll) with a partner of the other sex—any one will do. Thus the aimless sexual urge becomes the real sex instinct directed toward an instinctual aim. Later an additional directional factor enters in: the sex instinct is directed toward a definite person, a particular representative of the opposite sex: there is now a specific object. The aimless drive has first become aim-directed; then the aim-directed impulse has become person-directed. To the unspecific instinctual aim (genito-sexual in nature) has been added the specific object: the partner as a—beloved—person. Sexual urge, sexual instinct, sexual striving thus mark the phases of psychosexual maturing, each phase being characterized by increasing intentionality. Thus, in the course of the individual's maturation, sexuality grows increasingly expressive of the personality.

What is the origin of this directional factor? What furnishes the instinct with its direction toward a particular person? That cannot possibly come out of itself. The instinct, sexuality in general, acquires its intentionality from a tendency different in nature and origin (that is, not merely the result of sublimation), from an immanent erotic striving. It must be called "immanent" because its presence can always be shown, no matter how deeply buried it is. Even in cases where it is no longer conscious, the germs of it can be discovered in the past. This striving must at the same time be termed "erotic" because it presents a contrast to all sexual strivings. In young people, for example, it appears in the form of a longing for comradeship, tenderness, intimacy, and mutual understanding. Young people yearn for companionship in a psycho-spiritual sense —an entirely different thing from real sexual strivings. Thus the erotic striving is "erotic" in the narrower sense of the word. It is primary, and is not derivative from sexuality.

Even a man who is apparently interested in sexual pleasure alone has at some time or other experienced those finer strivings which Freud has called aim-inhibited tendencies, but which we consider to be properly erotic tendencies and more likely to attain the goal of true satisfaction than the unqualified sex drive. At some time or other even the devotee of mere sexual gratification made higher demands upon his partner, demanded qualities of the mind as well as the body. And all such impulses and requirements come to the fore even when buried deep in the rubble of vulgar sexual debauchery. Interesting in this connection is what a night-club dancer once reported: that when she brought a drunken man home with her he would typically propose that the two of them should pretend they were happily married and the husband was just coming home from work and the wife was being sweet to him— all this absolutely in conscious contrast to sexuality, and not even intended as a prelude. Here an element that has been all but repressed breaks through. For love had been repressed, the erotic tendency thrust into the background by the sexual instinct. And even in this debased, crippled form of erotic life—the relationship between a night-club dancer and her partner—the inborn yearning for a higher type of eroticism breaks through.

The immanent erotic tendency, then, is what impels sexuality to move from the merely physical urge via the psychological impulse to the spiritual striving which emanates from the self and is directed toward the self of another. In the normal or ideal course of psychosexual maturation there is a gradual conversion of sexual desire into the erotic tendency, until at last sex merges with eroticism and there is a congruency of the contents of the erotic tendency with the sexual desires. A successful synthesis of sexuality and eroticism is achieved. The instinct which has acquired its goal from the erotic tendency—namely, its direction toward a particular person—then fastens itself to this person.

This process of maturing therefore leads by logical steps to a monogamous attitude. The sexual desire has been turned toward one single partner, as the erotic tendency dictates. The really mature person, therefore, will feel sexual desire only when he loves; he will consider a sexual relationship only where sex is the expression of love. In this sense, then, the inner capacity for a monogamous relationship is the real criterion of sexual-erotic maturity. The monogamous attitude is at once the culmination of sexual development, the goal of sex education, and the ideal of sexual ethics. As an ideal it is achieved only seldom; usually it is only approached closely. Like all ideals, this one too is only a governing principle; "It is set up like the bull's-eye of the target, which must always be aimed at even if it is not always hit" (Goethe). Just as it is the rare person who is capable of real love, so it is the rare person who attains to the highest developmental state of the mature love life. But, after all, every human task is an "eternal" one and human progress is endless, an advance into infinity, toward a goal located in infinity. And even then it is a matter only of each individual's progress in his own personal history. For it is questionable whether and in what sense there is true progress within humanity's history. The only kind we know for certain is technological progress, and perhaps this impresses us as an advancement only because we happen to live in a technological age.

It is easier for women than for men to realize this ideal goal of the normal process of maturation. That, of course, is true only as a generalization and under present conditions. For a woman to feel sexual desire only where the physical longing is conjoined with a desire for psycho-spiritual union is the height of normality. Every "unspoiled" woman knows that this is how she feels. A man, on the other hand, does not attain this stage without some struggle. The woman is aided by a further factor: if she remains virginal until she has physical union with the man she finally and really loves, a monogamous relationship is henceforth easier for her, since—from the inception of sexual relations with her husband—both her eroticism and her sexuality are almost automatically centered on her partner's personality, and her sexual reactions are released almost like a conditioned reflex exclusively by him.

Normal psychosexual maturing is subject to various types of disturbances. Three different kinds of disturbed development can be distinguished, the presence of each one marking a different type of sexual neurotic.

The first type is represented by young people who are already well on the way to accomplishing the transformation of the formless sexual urge into a person-directed erotic tendency. They have achieved successively higher forms of eroticism and increasingly "deep" attitudes toward their partners until they are almost at the culminating point where sexual drive and erotic tendency merge and are directed toward a single goal: the inner personality of the beloved. At this last stage of development a setback occurs, produced perhaps by some disappointment. An unhappy love affair may so discourage a young person that he is blocked from continuing his normal development to the highest form of love life. He can no longer believe he will ever, or ever again, find someone whom he can at the same time respect as a person and desire sexually. And so he plunges into pure sexual pleasure; in sexual intoxication he tries to forget his erotic unhappiness. Quantity of sexual pleasure and instinctual gratification must take the place of quality: deeper fulfillment in the love life. Accent is shifted from eroticism to sexuality. The sex instinct suddenly demands gratification, as much of it as possible. In procuring such satisfaction for himself, the young man departs more and more from the goal of psychosexual maturation, becomes less and less capable of mastering the synthesis of eroticism and sexuality. The disappointing experience drives him down to the lower plane of mere sexuality; he reverts to an earlier stage of development. Since this type of disturbance of psychosexual maturation derives from an experience with disappointment, we call it the "resentment type."

The diary of a delinquent which we happen to have read reveals much about the inner workings of the "resentment type." While still a young boy, he was led into taking part in sex parties. At these sexual orgies he was also subjected to homosexual abuse. (Considering the essential aimlessness of the sexual urge, it is quite understandable that in this stage of psychosexual development perverse instinctual goals and instinctual objects are also accepted.) The young boy associated with the worst kind of companions, including criminals—and not sexual deviants alone—until one day he happened to meet up with a club of young people who were enthusiastic mountaineers and political idealists. Here he met a girl with whom he fell in love. Instantly his whole life changed, and especially his sex life. From the first he had no sexual aims toward this girl he loved. An abrupt shift of accent from sexuality to eroticism had taken place. In spite of his premature experiences with sex, he now took the step forward to the stage of non-sexual eroticism. One day, however, when this girl rejected him, he plunged back into his former life of crude pleasure-seeking, sexual and otherwise. His social as well as his sexual behavior retrogressed. The words he wrote in his journal ring out like a cry of despair, words imaginarily addressed to his girl: "Do you want me to be again what I once was, to go back to my former life, sitting around in dives, drinking and whoring?"

The second type of aberrant psychosexual maturing is represented by persons who have never achieved a truly erotic attitude or relationship. People of this type restrict themselves from the start to mere sexuality. They do not even attempt to unite sexual demands with erotic (in our sense) demands; they do not try to respect or love the sexual partner. They consider it impossible to have a real love relationship; they do not expect to experience love —or to be able to inspire it. Instead of undertaking the task of synthesizing sexuality and eroticism, they resign themselves. In contrast to the resentment type we will call this type the "resignation type." Because people of this type do not believe in the possibility of love for themselves, they do not believe in love at all. They maintain that it is an illusion. In reality, they say, all is sex; love occurs only in novels and is an unrealizable ideal.

The so-called Don Juan type belongs to this class. Simple souls are impressed by him, think of him as an erotic hero. But in reality he is a weakling who has never dared to attempt a truly fulfilling love life. For all the amount of sexual pleasure and the numbers of sexual partners he can total up, he remains inwardly empty. His world is emptier than that of the real lover and his life more unfulfilled than other lives.

The third and last type we will call the "inactive type." Persons of the resentment type and the resignation type never achieve more than sex; the inactive type does not even achieve that in the sense of sexual contact with a partner. While the resentment type experiences, at least initially, erotic partnership, and the resignation type at least experiences sexual partnership, the inactive type experiences no partnership at all, shunning it entirely. He is neither erotically nor sexually active. He remains in isolation, as it were, with his sex instinct, and the expression of this isolation is masturbation. That is the form that sex life takes in lonely people. Sexuality is experienced in an undirected way; the act of masturbation entirely lacks any object outside of the self, any directedness toward a partner.

Masturbation is, to be sure, neither a disease nor a cause of disease; rather, it is the sign of a disturbed development or misguided attitude toward the love life. Hypochondriacal ideas about its morbid consequences are unjustified. But the hangover which generally follows the act of masturbation has a reason, quite aside from these hypochondriacal theories. The underlying reason is that guilt feeling which comes upon one whenever one flees from active, directional experience to passive, non-directional experience. We have already named this kind of escape as the underlying motif of intoxication. It therefore seems all the more significant that masturbation—like drunkenness—is followed by a mood of hangover.

Aside from the practitioners of masturbation, the inactive class also includes all those young people who suffer from so-called sexual frustration. Sexual frustration should be understood as the expression of a more general psychological distress. It is the problem of a person who is "alone" with his drive and therefore experiences intense frustration—but only so long as he is alone with it. Whenever the erotic element is dominant, as it is in normal development, sexuality does not build up to any dangerous extent, and the conflict between the erotic element and sexuality does not occur. Only when a displacement arises in the course of deviant development—when, for example, the above-mentioned shift in accent from eroticism back to sexuality occurs—do there arise those conflicts and psychic tensions which make up sexual frustration. The phrase is deceptive in that it sounds as if the unsatisfied sex instinct were the source of the frustration, as if frustration therefore were necessarily bound up with sexual abstinence. In reality, abstinence as such is far from equivalent to frustration. We shall have more to say on this subject later on. That is true only of maturing young people, not of adults. But insofar as a young person suffers from sexual frustration, this is an indication that his sex instinct is not yet (or is no longer) subordinated to an erotic tendency and so integrated into the total system of his personal strivings.

The shibboleth of sexual frustration is occasionally called forth for purposes of sexual propaganda. In this sense it is a misconception and vulgar misinterpretation of psychoanalysis. The implication is that the ungratified sex instinct itself—rather than the repression of that instinct—must necessarily lead to neurosis. The harmfulness of sexual abstinence has been preached to youth. Such doctrines have done a good deal of injury by nourishing neurotic sexual anxiety. The slogan has been sexual intercourse at any cost, even among young people, when, on the contrary, sexuality should be permitted to mature tranquilly and to advance toward a healthy and meaningful eroticism consonant with human dignity, eroticism in which the sexual element is the expression and crown of a love relationship. This kind of eroticism must necessarily precede the commencement of sexual relations. But if the realm of mere sexuality is entered prematurely, a young person is incapable of proceeding to the synthesis of sexuality and eroticism.

Let us consider what can be done in the way of therapy for the so-called sexual frustration of youth. This question is relevant if only because a successful method of treating such sexual frustration throws light upon its psychogenesis. The therapy is of the simplest. It suffices to introduce the young person in question into a mixed company of people his age. There the young man will sooner or later fall in love—that is, he will find a partner—in the erotic and not in the sexual sense. Once this happens, his sexual frustration promptly vanishes. Such young men often admit that, for example, they have literally "forgotten" to masturbate. Their longing to be together with the girl of their choice is quite free of sexual promptings; not in their boldest daydreams, or even in their actual dreaming about her, do they have a direct desire for sexual gratification. The moment they fall in love, crude sexuality automatically drops into the background. Eroticism moves into the foreground. There is an abrupt shift in accent from sexuality to eroticism, a sudden alternation in dominance between the sexual and erotic tendencies which are to some extent antagonistic in young people. In treating young people suffering from sexual frustration we must take note of the reciprocal relationship between sexuality and eroticism. This reciprocal relationship and the resultant diminishing and cessation of suffering from the ungratified sex instinct in spite of sexual abstinence seems to be, as far as young people are concerned, a phenomenon governed by definite laws. The broad experience of psychological counselors who have worked with young people has confirmed the regularity of this phenomenon, as have discussions with large numbers of young people in connection with talks on sex education to youth groups. Among many thousands of young persons who have been questioned, not a single one failed to admit the effect of this shift in accent from sexuality to eroticism.

As we have suggested, the problem takes a different form with mature people. In adults sexual desires go hand in hand with the erotic tendencies, since as a result of that synthesis of sexuality with eroticism which comes with maturity, the two have become fused. Nevertheless, sexual abstinence need by no means lead to neurotic symptoms in the adult. If we do actually find neurotic symptoms in the sexually abstinent adult, we need not take these as the direct consequence of continence, but rather as co-ordinate with it. For in such cases it usually turns out that the abstinence is itself a symptom, one among others, of an underlying neurosis.

Among those young people who have been liberated from sexual frustration as a result of the accentual shift from sexuality to eroticism, the sex instinct will sooner or later come to the fore again, with the growth of maturity, and will make its claims felt. The question of sexual gratification has only been thrust into the background temporarily. But something vital has been achieved by this postponement, for the young person has been given time to mature. Now, under the dominance of the erotic tendency, he can build up an erotic relationship within the framework of which sexual relations can then be considered. A love relationship now exists for which eventual sexual intercourse may signify a means of expression—which is precisely the goal we were aiming at. But something has been accomplished even beyond that. The young man's sense of responsibility has meanwhile matured to the point where he can decide on his own and his partner's behalf whether and when he ought to enter into a serious sexual relationship with her. We can then turn this decision over to him with an easy conscience. For if such a relationship is reached, its sexuality will assume its appropriate form—that of physical expression of a spiritual content, the expression of love.

Let us then sum up the doctor's position on the problem of sexual intercourse between young people. What should he recommend in regard to continence or intercourse for the young? We find the following general guiding principles.

In the first place, from the somatic, medical point of view, neither continence nor intercourse is contraindicated—given a degree of physical maturity. In this respect the doctor ought to be entirely neutral, since he knows that neither sexual relations nor sexual abstinence can do any physical harm. But in terms of mental hygiene he ought not to be neutral; from this point of view he must take a stand. He must oppose sexual relations, must veto them if he can, whenever young people want sexual intercourse without real love. Where this is the case (and only where this is the case) he must take a negative stand. Sexual intercourse between young people who are sexually but not psychosexually mature is contraindicated.

Another point of view from which this question of sexual intercourse between young people can be evaluated (the other two being the somatic and the psychohygienic points of view) is that of sexual ethics. And from this point of view the doctor can never say yes, can never directly recommend sexual intercourse in a given case. For here is drawn the line beyond which advising cannot go. As a counselor it is not the doctor's function to relieve of responsibility the person seeking advice; on the contrary, the doctor's task is to teach him to be responsible. The young person will have to decide himself on his own responsibility. The question of whether a young person who really loves his partner should enter into a sexual relationship cannot be answered by the doctor and counselor; it remains a personal, moral problem for the individual himself. The most the doctor can do is to point out that there is nothing to fear from abstinence—in case an individual should freely decide upon such a course for whatever reason (perhaps because he conceives it as a sacrifice necessary to his love).

Responsibility, when attained, covers not only the partner as an individual. For, particularly if a monogamous relationship is to culminate in marriage, there are social, economic, and eugenic responsibilities to be considered by the young person. As we have already seen in another connection, marriage involves a number of independent areas of existence and thus transcends the psychological field. The psychotherapist, however, is asked to deal only with the problems of the psyche; his concern can only be with the inner capacity for a monogamous relationship, and with ways of promoting this monogamous attitude. In dealing with young men, the psychiatrist must encourage them to accept all the difficulties which youth, being a period of erotic preparation, imposes upon them. The young man must have the courage to fall in love, to fall out of love, to court, to be alone, and so on. Where sexuality threatens to take precedence over eroticism and become dominant, the psychiatrist or the sex educator must raise his warning voice. A large-scale statistical psychological study of the Charlotte Bühler School has shown that serious sexual relationships of very young girls (in whom we may assume no proper erotic relationships have yet developed) led to a distinct shrinking of general interests, a limitation of the mental horizon. Within the structure of a still incomplete personality the sex instinct, holding out the promise of easy pleasure-gains and vehemently demanding gratification, swallowed up, as it were, all other concerns. As a result of this deviant development, inner preparation for the generally esteemed and culturally valuable state of marriage must naturally suffer. For the happiness and duration of marriage are guaranteed only by attainment of the ideal aim of normal development: the maturity for a monogamous relationship, which means successful synthesis and congruence of sexuality and eroticism.

Human existence as a whole is fundamentally grounded in responsibility. The counselor, the psychiatrist, bears an additional responsibility, for he is also responsible for the patient who comes to him seeking advice. His responsibility grows even greater when he is asked to give advice in sexual matters. For this responsibility transcends the present and may well extend to the fate of a future generation.

All those concerned with adolescent sex education must bear in mind the greatness of their responsibility. In carrying out their task, they will have to hold fast to the general principles of adolescent education. The factor of trust is perhaps the most important one in such a relationship. This trust is threefold. First, there is the trust of the young people in the educator, whether he be parent or teacher, youth leader, family physician, or counselor. The adult must make every effort to win and to keep the confidence of the young people. This is especially important when it comes to instructing the young in the "facts of life." On this subject we will say only the following: such sex information should never be given to a group. For if that is done, the revelations will come too soon to some, and only dismay them, while for others they will come too late and only seem ridiculous. To instruct each boy or girl individually is the only sensible way. Here the young person's confidence in the educator is of supreme importance. Having that confidence, a young person troubled by a question about sex will ask the adult whom he trusts at the right time, neither too soon nor too late.

The second kind of trust which must be the aim of adolescent education is the young person's trust in himself, which will keep him from becoming discouraged on the steep road to the mature personality. The third kind of trust must be our own trust in the young person—a trust which is ideally designed to increase his self-confidence and provide a foundation for his trust in us. In trusting him (or her) we aid him in developing independence in thought and action and help him on the way to freedom and responsibility.

B   Special Existential Analysis

In the foregoing chapters we have often had occasion to mention the existential analytical approach and treatment of neurotic cases. Although we have not systematically delineated a theory of the neuroses, we have seen how logotherapy works in the case of so-called Sunday neurosis or various forms of sexual neurosis. While we still do not intend to proceed systematically, we wish to discuss in fuller fashion the special existential analysis of the neuroses and psychoses, with particular emphasis upon case histories. We shall see to what extent the ground for a logotherapy of the neuroses unfolds—a therapy "in spiritual terms," as we formulated the problem at the beginning of this book, where we made the point that consciousness of responsibility is the foundation of human existence and that existential analysis was the method for bringing out that consciousness. By way of introduction, however, we want to present some general psychological and pathogenetic considerations.

We have already pointed out several times that every neurotic symptom has a fourfold root, being grounded in the four basically different layers (or "dimensions") of man's being. Thus neurosis appears in four forms: as the result of something physical, as the expression of something psychic, as a means to an end within the societal field of force, and finally as a mode of existence. The last-named form alone offers a point of approach for existential analysis. For only where neurosis is understood as a product of decision can there be the freedom to which existential analysis attempts to appeal. On the other hand, this freedom disappears in increasing measure as we descend the ladder from man's spirit— the locus of attack for logotherapy or existential analysis—to his body, from the realm of the spirit to the realm of physiology. There is no foothold for man's spiritual, existential freedom in the physiological bases of neurosis. Psychotherapy in the narrower sense of the word can also scarcely reach them, scarcely reshape them. In general the only possible and effective therapy for the physiological base is drug treatment.

Insofar as a neurotic symptom can be interpreted as an "expression" and as a "means," it is primarily a direct expression and only secondarily a means to an end. The so-called purposiveness of a neurotic symptom does not explain the origin of a neurosis; it explains only the fixating of the particular symptom. Knowledge of the purpose the neurosis serves does not, that is, tell us how the patient happened to acquire the neurosis; it tells us at most why he clings to a particular symptom. Here we take a contrary position to the views of individual psychology. According to individual psychology, neurosis is "used" to keep a person from getting on with his life task. According to existential analysis, neurosis does not have this purposive function; nevertheless, existential analysis aims to bring the person to an understanding of his true life task, for with such understanding he will find it all the easier to cast off his neurosis. This "freedom to," the "decision for" the life task, therefore comes before the "freedom from." The more we can from the start link this positive (logotherapeutic) factor with the negative (psychotherapeutic) factor, the more quickly and surely will we reach the goal of our therapy.

1   On the Psychology of Anxiety Neurosis

In the following section we intend to examine, in the light of selected cases, the psychological structure of anxiety neurosis. Our examples will show the extent to which the neurosis is also rooted in layers not actually psychic.

One case is that of a young man who suffered from constant fear of dying of cancer. Nevertheless, it was possible to achieve some beneficial effect by existential analysis. In the course of the existential analysis of this case the patient's continual preoccupation with the future manner of his death turned out to be essentially a disinterest in his present mode of life. For he was oblivious of his obligations, not conscious of his responsibility to life. His fear of death was ultimately the sting of conscience, that fear of death that a person must have when he disdains what life offers him. His existence must necessarily appear meaningless to himself. The disinterest our patient showed for his own most personal potentialities was paralleled by the neurotic counterpart, his lively and exclusive interest in death. By his fear of cancer he punished himself because of his "metaphysical frivolity" (Scheler).

Back of such neurotic anxiety, then, there is an existential anxiety which is made specific, so to speak, in the phobic symptom. The existential anxiety is condensed into a hypochondriacal phobia, the original fear of death (uneasy conscience) concentrating upon a particular fatal disease. In hypochondriacal anxiety, then, we have a condensation or derivative of existential anxiety applied to a single organ. Death, feared because the person has a guilty conscience toward life, is pushed out of the mind—and the fear centers instead upon a particular organ of the body. In fact, every inferiority feeling about a particular organ is probably only a making specific of the primary sense of not having realized one's own value-potentialities. If that is so, the concentration of this feeling upon a single organ or a particular function is a secondary phenomenon.

The condensation of existential anxiety, which is fear of death and simultaneously fear of life as a whole, is something we encounter again and again in neurotic behavior. The original total anxiety apparently seeks some concrete content, some objective representative of "death" or "life," a representative of the "border situation" (Jaspers), a symbolic representation (Erwin Straus). In a case of agoraphobia, for example, this symbolic function is assumed by "the streets," or in a case of stage fright by "the stage." Often the very words in which patients describe their symptoms and complaints—words which they apparently mean only in a figurative sense—can put us on the track of the real, the existential reason for the neurosis. Thus, a patient suffering from fear of open places expressed her anxiety as: "A feeling like hanging in the air." This was in fact an apt description of her whole spiritual situation. In fact, her entire neurosis was ultimately the psychic expression of this spiritual condition. The paroxysms of anxiety and giddiness which attacked our agoraphobic patient when she went out on the street were, shall we say, "vestibular" expressions of her existential situation. Quite similar are the words in which an actress suffering from stage fright once described the sensations she felt when in the grip of her anxiety: "Everything is huge—everything is pursuing me—I am terrified that life is passing."*

---

* Another patient described her agoraphobic experience, quite without any prompting, in these words: "Just as I often see an emptiness before me in my soul, I also see this emptiness in space. . . . I don't know at all where I belong—where I want to go."

Insofar as neurotic anxiety is not only the direct psychic expression of general anxiety about life but is also in individual cases a means to an end, it is such a means only secondarily. Sometimes, but not always, it serves to tyrannize a member of the family or is used to justify oneself to others or to the self—as individual psychology has brought out in countless cases. Antecedent to and coeval with this indirect use of anxiety as a means, before and along with this secondary quality of neurotic anxiety as "arrangement," it always has a primary significance as expression. Freud rightly speaks of "neurotic gain" as a "secondary" motive force of illness. But even in cases where such a secondary motive force is actually present, it is not advisable to put this fact frankly before the patient. No good comes from "throwing it up" to him that he is only using his symptoms in the hope of binding his wife to him or dominating his sister, etc. Or else we are engaging in a kind of blackmail of the patient. We keep at him with arguments to show that his symptom is only a weapon he is employing to terrorize members of his family, until at last he summons up all his remaining reserves of strength and somehow conquers the symptom—solely in order to avoid being morally condemned, to escape our criticism. This kind of psychotherapeutic treatment, though it may be successful, is essentially unfair. Instead of forcing a cure by pressuring the patient into "sacrificing" his symptom, it would seem far more sensible to wait until the psychologically relaxed patient himself realizes that he has been exploiting a symptom as a means for imposing his will to power upon his social environment or his family. The spontaneity of confessions and insights into the self are what bring about true therapeutic effects.

Insofar as existential analysis of a case of anxiety neurosis interprets the neurosis as ultimately a mode of existence, a sort of spiritual attitude, the groundwork has been laid for logotherapy as a specific treatment. Let us take as an example a case of climacteric-anxiety neurosis. Disregarding the glandular imbalance which is the somatogenic substructure of the illness, the real root of the neurosis is to be found in the existential layer. The patient experiences this critical phase of her life as an existential crisis; she feels threatened because she finds a spiritual deficit when she draws up the balance sheet of her life.

The patient in question was a beautiful woman, the darling of society. Now she had to face up to a new period in her life in which her physical charm would no longer count; she had to be able to "bear up" in spite of her vanishing beauty. Erotically this woman was finished. She found herself without aim or purpose in life, without a content for her life; her existence seemed meaningless to her. "I get up in the morning," she said, "and ask myself: What is happening today? Nothing is happening today. . . ." Naturally she grew anxious. And since there was no content to her life, since she had no resources for building up a full life, she had to incorporate her anxiety into the structure of her life. It was necessary for her to seek some content for life, to find the meaning of her life, and thereby to find herself, her self, her inner potentialities. Erotic success and social status no longer counted; she could only reach for moral status. It was necessary to induce this patient to turn away from her anxiety and toward her tasks. This positive aim of existential-analytical logotherapy can be attained even before the negative goal of psychotherapy in the narrower sense of the word is achieved. In fact, the attainment of the positive aim will in some circumstances clear up the neurotic anxiety—since the existential basis of this anxiety will have been withdrawn. As soon as life's fullness of meaning is rediscovered, the neurotic anxiety (to the extent that it is existential anxiety) no longer has anything to fasten on. There is no longer room for it and, as our patient spontaneously remarked, "no time."

What had to be done here was to lead this particular person in her concrete situation to the unique and singular task of her life. It was up to her to become what she was going to be; before her there stood an image of what she ought to be, and as long as she had not become that she could not be at peace. The climacteric crisis had to be reshaped into a spiritual rebirth—that, in this case, was the task of logotherapy. The therapist took the part of a midwife in the Socratic sense. It would have been a distinct blunder, as we shall see, to attempt to impose any particular tasks upon the patient. On the contrary, existential analysis must aim at leading the patient to independent responsibility. And if it is successful, the patient finds "his" life task—as the patient in question did. Having turned wholeheartedly toward new content in her life, devoting herself to the newly acquired meaning of her existence and the experience of fulfilling her own personality, she was reborn as a new person—and at the same time all neurotic symptoms vanished. All the functional cardiac sensations from which the patient had suffered—palpitation, a feeling of uneasiness around the heart—vanished, even though the climacteric basis of them remained. Evidently these neurotic cardiac reactions, this "uneasiness," were ultimately the expression of uneasiness of the spirit. "Restless are our hearts . . ." says Augustine. Our patient's heart was restless, too, as long as it could not rest in the consciousness of her singular and unique task, in the consciousness of responsibility and obligation to perform her own life task.

Like all other neurosis, obsessional neurosis also has a constitutional basis. Wexberg and others, whose interests lie mainly in the fields of psychogenesis or psychotherapy, have assumed that a somatic substructure ultimately underlies obsessional neurosis. A number of clinical pictures had been observed in which post-encephalitic behavior showed striking similarities to obsessional neurotic syndromes. The mistake was made of confusing similarity in form with identity in nature.

An "anankastic syndrome" was considered to be the hereditary element in obsessional neurosis; it was believed to have a special genetic radical which was supposedly dominant. Finally it was proposed that the term "obsessional disease" be used instead of "obsessional neurosis," in order to stress the constitutional quality of the illness.

As far as therapy is concerned, these various views strike us as largely irrelevant. Moreover, to make much of the constitutional factors underlying obsessional neurosis does not relieve psychotherapy of its obligation, nor deprive it of its opportunities. For anankasm consists of nothing more than a mere disposition toward certain characterological peculiarities such as meticulosity, exaggerated love of order, fanatical cleanliness, or overscrupulousness—traits which, in fact, must be recognized as culturally valuable. They do not seriously incommode the person who has them or those around him. They are only the soil in which the actual obsessional neurosis can grow, though it does not necessarily do so. Where such a constitution does give rise to neurosis, human freedom is involved. Revealing the psychogenic nature of the particular neurotic content need not be therapeutically effective, nor is it indeed even indicated. On the contrary, detailed treatment of symptoms in obsessional neurotics would only give encouragement to their compulsion to brood over their symptoms.

We must, however, distinguish carefully between such symptomatic treatment and palliative treatment by logotherapy. The logotherapist is not concerned with treating the individual symptom or the disease as such; rather, he sets out to transform the neurotic's attitude toward his neurosis. For it is this attitude which has built up the basic constitutional disturbance into clinical symptoms of illness. And this attitude, at least in milder cases or in the early stages, is quite subject to correction. Where the attitude itself has not as yet taken on the typical obsessional-neurotic rigidity, where it is not yet infiltrated, so to speak, by the basic disturbance, a change in its direction should still be possible.

Anticipating a logotherapeutic principle to be discussed more elaborately in a later, clinical chapter, we can say that in dealing with obsessional neurosis, even psychotherapy in the narrower sense of the word has the problem of inducing a change in the patient's attitude toward the neurosis as a whole. Therapy of obsessional neuroses should aim at relaxing the patient and relieving the tension in his total attitude toward the neurosis. It is well known that the very tension of the patient's fight against his compulsive ideas only tends to strengthen the "compulsion." Pressure generates counterpressure; the more the patient dashes his head against the wall of his obsessional ideas, the stronger they become and the more unbreakable they appear to him.

There is one prime prerequisite, however, for not fighting

against obsessional ideas. We must assume that the patient is not afraid of his obsessions. But all too frequently patients overestimate their obsessional-neurotic symptoms, considering them harbingers or actual signs of a psychotic illness. In that case they cannot help fearing their obsessions. It is necessary, then, first of all to dispose of this fear of imminent psychosis, which otherwise may mount until it becomes a pronounced psychotophobia. In cases where such a fear of psychosis does occur, it is well to go into the problem quite matter-of-factly. We might call the patient's attention to the works of Pilcz and of Stengel, which suggest a certain antagonism between obsessional neuroses and psychotic illnesses and which indicate that the obsessional neurotic in spite of, or in fact because of, his obsessional fears seems to be all but immune to psychoses.

Another fear of obsessional-neurotic patients is that their suicidal or homicidal impulses may some day be translated into action; consequently, they are engaged in a perpetual struggle with these impulses. In such cases we must instruct them to stop fighting, in order to avert the unfortunate effects of combatting obsessional impulses. When the patient stops fighting them, the impulses may very well cease to obsess him. In no case, however, will they be translated into acts. To be sure, obsessional neurotics do carry out compulsive acts; but these are always so harmless in nature that they offer no grounds whatever for psychotophobic fears in the patient.

In removing from the patient his unfounded fear of psychosis we are achieving a significant relief of the psychic pressures upon him. We bring about a cessation of that counterpressure which in itself was intensifying the pressure of the obsession. If we want to relieve this pressure, which task comes before all further psychotherapy, and logotherapy as well, it is important to bring about a complete change in the patient's attitude toward his illness. That is, insofar as his illness does have some constitutional core, the patient should learn to accept the character structure as fate, in order to avoid building up around the constitutional core additional psychogenic suffering. There is a minimal constitutional basis which in fact cannot be influenced by psychotherapy. The patient must learn to affirm this minimum. The more we train him to a glad acceptance of fate, the more insignificant will be the residues of symptoms which are beyond help.

We recall the case of a patient who suffered for fifteen years from a severe form of obsessional neurosis. In search of treatment he left his home town and came to the big city for a few months' stay. Here he underwent psychoanalysis, which was unsuccessful—if only because of the short time at the analyst's disposal. The patient decided to go home—but only to set his family and business affairs in order. That attended to, he planned to commit suicide—so great was his despair because there seemed no hope that his illness would ever be cured.

A few days before his departure he yielded to the urging of his friends and visited a second psychiatrist. This doctor, since there was so little time in which to work, had to discard any idea of analyzing the symptoms and concentrate on the problem of revising the patient's attitude toward his obsessional illness. He tried, so to speak, to reconcile the patient to his illness, basing his efforts on the fact that the patient was a deeply religious person. The doctor asked the patient to accept his illness as "the will of God," something imposed upon him by destiny against which he must stop contending. Rather, he ought to try to live a life pleasing to God in spite of his illness. The inner change these arguments produced in the patient had so amazing an effect that the doctor himself was surprised. After the second therapeutic session the patient stated that for the first time in ten years he had just spent a full hour free of his obsessional ideas. Thereafter he had to leave, since all the arrangements for his homeward journey had been made. But he reported to the doctor in a letter that his condition was so tremendously alleviated that he could call himself practically cured.

In correcting our patients' misguided efforts to fight desperately and tensely against their obsessions we have to make two points: that on the one hand the patient is not responsible for his obsessional ideas, and on the other hand that he certainly is responsible for his attitude toward these ideas. For it is his attitude which converts the embarrassing ideas into torments when he "gets involved" with them, when he carries them further in his thoughts or, fearing them, fights them back. Here, too, positive logotherapeutic components must come into play in addition to the negative psychotherapeutic (in the narrower sense of the word) components. The patient will finally learn to ignore his obsessional neurosis and lead a meaningful life in spite of it. It is obvious that his turning toward his concrete life task facilitates his turning away from his obsessional thoughts.

In addition to such general logotherapy we may treat obsessional neurosis by a special logotherapy which deals with the obsessional neurotic's characteristic world-view, which we shall shortly discuss. Special existential analysis of obsessional neurosis will help us to understand this world-view. That analysis must start from an unprejudiced phenomenological examination of obsessional-neurotic experience.

What goes on in an obsessional neurotic when, say, he is plagued by doubts? Suppose he reckons: two times two equals four. In every concrete case it can be demonstrated that before the doubts crop up he does know that his reckoning is correct. Nevertheless, he promptly begins to doubt. "I shall have to figure it out again," such a neurotic will say, "though I know I have done the example well." Emotionally, that is, he feels there is a troublesome remainder. The normal person is satisfied with the given results of his acts of thinking and does not question them any further; but the obsessional neurotic lacks that simple feeling of satisfaction which follows the thought, and which in the case of the arithmetic example "two times two equals four" would be followed by: "Of course that's right." The normal person experiences the sense of certainty that comes from obviousness; the obsessional neurotic has no normal sense of obviousness. Even when dealing with far more difficult arithmetic examples or more complicated thought processes in other fields, the normal person disregards that irrational residue which necessarily attaches to all the results of thinking. But the obsessional neurotic cannot get around this irrational residue; his thoughts cannot go past it. Along with his inadequate sense of obviousness, he has an intolerance for that irrational residue. The obsessional neurotic simply does not succeed in disregarding it.

How, then, does the obsessional neurotic react to the irrational residue? By launching out on a fresh process of thought he tries to overcome it, but in the nature of things he can never wholly eliminate it. Therefore he is forced to repeat the process of thought again and again, each time trying to annihilate the irrational residue. At best he can only succeed in diminishing it. The game resembles the functioning of a vacuum pump, which can never create an absolute vacuum; it can remove from a vessel to be emptied of air only a certain percentage of the air each time. The first piston stroke reduces the air content to a tenth, the next to a hundredth part, and so on. Ultimately the piston strokes go on and on in vain repetitions—corresponding to the repetition compulsion in obsessional neurosis. With each revision of the results of his thinking the obsessional neurotic will feel a bit surer, but some residue of uncertainty will still remain and will continue to remain, no matter how often the neurotic obeys his repetition compulsion and tries to eliminate that residue. He continues his efforts until he is exhausted, then pulls himself together to murmur a vague credo, finds temporary absolution in a round sum, and leaves off brooding until the next time.

This disturbance of the sense of obviousness in the sphere of cognition corresponds to a disturbance of instinctive certainty in the sphere of decision. Further phenomenological analysis shows that the obsessional neurotic's instinctive certainty has been shattered—that very certainty of instinct which in the healthy person guides conduct in daily life and relieves him of the burden of trivial decisions. The instinctive certainty of the normal person saves his awareness of responsibility for the crucial moments of life, and even then that responsibility operates in somewhat irrational form: as conscience. The obsessional neurotic, however, must compensate by special alertness and special conscientiousness for the twin thymopsychic defects with which he is cursed: disturbance of the sense of obviousness and of instinctive certainty. Such over-conscientiousness and overconsciousness amount, therefore, to noöpsychic overcompensation (I avail myself here of Stransky's well-known pair of opposites: *noöpsyche—thymopsyche*). The shattering of emotional self-confidence in cognition and decision leads, in obsessional neurotics, to forced, artificial self-scrutiny. It engenders in them, by way of compensation, the desire for absolute certainty in cognition and in decision, and a tendency toward rigid moral decisions. The obsessional neurotic mails a letter or locks his door with the same gravity and care that a normal man might employ in choosing his profession or his wife. It is obvious that such excessive awareness and intensified self-observation must in themselves be disturbing. Because of the overdeveloped awareness that accompanies the obsessional neurotic's acts of cognition or decision, he lacks that "fluent style" in which the healthy person lives, thinks, and acts. A pedestrian will stumble as soon as he focuses his attention too much on the act of walking instead of keeping his eye on the goal. A person may at best initiate some act with excessive awareness, but he cannot carry it out in the same spirit without that awareness being itself a disturbing factor.

The excessive consciousness and excessive conscientiousness of the obsessional neurotic, then, represent two of his typical character traits, the roots of which we can trace to the thymopsychic substructure of the personality. It therefore follows that one task of therapy is to help the obsessional neurotic to find his way back to the buried sources of instinctive certainty and the sense of obviousness, which sources lie in the deep emotional layers of the personality. The method for doing so may be re-education: the person should be trained to trust those remnants of certainty and the sense of obviousness which can still be discerned even in obsessional neurotics.

The obsessional neurotic seeks, as we have said, absolute certainty in cognition and decision. He strives for hundred-per-centness. He always wants the absolute, the totality. The obsessional neurotic suffers profoundly from the limitations of all human thought and the dubiousness of all human decisions.

The obsessional neurotic is characterized by intense impatience. He is troubled not only by intolerance of the irrational residue of thought, but also by intolerance of the tension between what is and what ought to be. Underlying this may be that striving toward "godlikeness" of which Alfred Adler has spoken, which to our mind is the counterpart to admitting creatural imperfection. This admission amounts to recognizing the tension between what is and what ought to be.

From the existential-analytic point of view, then, the ultimate essence of obsessional neurosis is the distortion of a Faustian urge. In his will to absolutism and his striving for hundred-per-centness in all fields, the obsessional neurotic is like a frustrated Faust.

We have seen that in anxiety neurosis metaphysical anxiety is condensed in the phobic symptom. Something similar takes place in obsessional neurosis. Since it is impossible for the neurotic ever to realize his totalitarian demands, he concentrates upon a special area of life. Since he perceives that hundred-per-centness cannot be realized always and in everything, he restricts this insistence to a definite field where it seems more likely to be achievable (for example, cleanliness of the hands: washing-compulsion). Areas in which the obsessional neurotic succeeds in imposing his ideal—at least halfway—are, for example: for the housewife, her household; for the brain worker, the orderliness of his desk; for the man who likes to work things out on paper, careful itemizing of schedules and notations on experiences; for the bureaucratic type, absolute punctuality, and so on. The obsessional neurotic always restricts himself to a definite sector of existence; in this sector, as a "part for the whole," he tries to realize his totalitarian demands. The two processes are similar: in phobia (on the part of people of a more passive type), fear of the universe as a whole is given concrete content and fixed upon a single object; in obsessional neurosis, the will (of people of a more active type) to shape the world after the person's own image is directed toward a single sphere of life. But even in this one sphere the obsessional neurotic can accomplish his purpose only partially, or only fictively, and always at the price of his naturalness, his "creaturalness." Thus all his strivings have an inhuman quality.

Characteristic of both the obsessional and the anxiety neurotic is that their striving for security is "deflected," tortuous, and has a distinctly subjectivistic, if not psychologistic, quality. For a better understanding of this we must start with the normal person's striving for security. The content of that striving in the normal person is security in itself. The neurotic, however, is far from content with any such security; he considers it too vague. For the neurotic person is usually in a state of alarm, and hence there is a forced and artificial quality about his striving for security. There arises in him consequently a desire for absolute security. In the anxiety neurotic this desire is expressed in a need for security from all disasters. But since absolute security of this sort is impossible, the anxiety neurotic is forced to content himself with the mere *feeling* of security. Thereby he takes leave of the world of objects and objective reality and seeks refuge in subjectivity. The anxiety neurotic ceases to live his existence in the ordinary world where the normal person finds a measure of tranquillity because he recognizes that disasters are relatively improbable. Demanding to be insured against any possible disaster, the anxiety neurotic is compelled to make a virtual cult of his security feeling. His flight from the world engenders a guilty conscience. That in turn demands compensation, which he can find only in an inhuman exaggeration of his subjectivistic striving for security.

The obsessional neurotic, on the other hand, seeks a different kind of security—security in cognition and decision. But for him, too, this striving for security does not take account of the approximation and provisionality of human existence. For him, too, the striving for security takes a subjectivistic turn and ends in an obsessive striving for the mere *feeling* of "hundred per cent" security. Tragic futility is the outcome. For if his "Faustian" striving for absolute security is doomed to failure, the striving for a *feeling* of absolute security is all the more doomed. The moment the mind is directed toward this feeling as such (instead of the feeling's arising naturally as a consequence of intentional acts), the feeling is dispelled. Man, therefore, cannot achieve perfect security—not in living, not in knowing, not in making decisions. But least of all can he obtain that *feeling* of absolute security which the obsessional neurotic so desperately pursues. (Man can achieve a true sense of safety only in very different terms; see note on page 270.)

To sum up, we may say that the normal person desires a halfway-secure world, whereas the neurotic seeks absolute security. The normal person desires to surrender himself to the one he loves— while the sexual neurotic strives for orgasm, aims at that in itself, and thereby impairs his sexual potency. The normal person wishes to know a part of the world approximately—while the obsessional neurotic wants a feeling of obviousness, aims at that, and thereby finds himself being carried away on an endless moving belt. The normal person is ready to take existential responsibility for actual existence, while the neurotic with his obsessional scruples would like to have only the feeling (though an absolute one) of a conscience at peace with itself. From the point of view of what men should desire, the obsessional neurotic wants too much; in terms of what men can accomplish, he wants too little.

The obsessive neurotic despises reality, which those who do not suffer from obsessional neurosis use as a springboard to existential freedom. He anticipates solution of his life task in fictive form. Allers says: "Meticulosity is nothing more than the determination to impose the law of one's own personality upon trivialities in the environment." And yet this determination, like the obsessional-neurotic will to orderliness in general, can still be called human in the best sense. "The Eternal's thought comes to fulfillment through order, and through order alone man lives up to his being the image of God" (Werfel).

Obsessional neurosis beautifully exemplifies the counterplay of freedom and constraint within neurosis in general. We do not think the characterological development into pronounced obsessional neurosis unavoidably destined. Instead, we consider a kind of psychic orthopedics perfectly feasible. The importance of introducing the neurotic to those character traits he so badly lacks—humor and calmness—must be stressed. Straus deserves credit for being one of the first to see the existential aspects of obsessional neurosis, but he overlooked the possibility of treating obsessional neurosis in spiritual terms. Obsessional neurosis is not a psychosis; the sick person's attitude toward it is still relatively free. In any given case, "attitude" would mean the spiritual position taken toward the sickness of the psyche. The spiritual attitude of the person to psychic illness provides the starting-point for logotherapy. We have already discussed general logotherapy of obsessional neurosis (changing the person's attitude toward psychic illness) and special existential analysis of obsessional neurosis (interpretation of the neurotic as a caricature of the Faustian man). We will now deal with special logotherapy of obsessional neurosis, with the possibilities for correcting the obsessional-neurotic world-view.

Obsessional neurosis is not a mental disease, let alone a disease of "the spirit"; the position the person takes on the disease is independent of the disease. He remains free to change his attitude. It is imperative for the therapist to make use of this freedom. For obsessional neurosis "seduces" the obsessional neurotic to a particular philosophical position, namely that world-view of hundred-per-centness of which we have spoken above. A case that shows the obsessional-neurotic world-view in its incipient stages is that of a young man in late puberty. Amid the labor pains of adolescence it became plain that an obsessional-neurotic world-view was setting in.

The young man in question was filled with a Faustian urge to know the roots of everything. "I want to get back to the origin of things," were his words. "I want to be able to prove everything; I want to prove everything that is immediately obvious—for example, whether I am living."

We know that the obsessional neurotic's sense of obviousness is defective. However, even the normal sense of obviousness has its limitations. For one thing, it is out of reach of intentionality: if we try, for epistemological reasons, to depend solely upon our sense of obviousness, we fall into an endless logical progression. The psychopathological counterpart of this is the obsessional neurotic's repetition compulsion.

The ultimate—or, if you will, the first—question of radical skepticism is about the meaning of existence. But to ask the meaning of existence is meaningless in that existence precedes meaning. For the existence of meaning is assumed when we question the meaning of existence. Existence is, so to speak, the wall we are backed up against whenever we question it. Our patient, however, wanted to prove intuitive data. He had to be shown that it is impossible to "prove" such data—but that it is also unnecessary, since as intuitive data they are obvious. His objection that he nevertheless doubted was completely pointless. For the logical impossibility of doubting intuitively evident, immediate data of existence is reflected in psychological reality: such doubting represents empty talk. In actuality the most radical skeptic behaves in both thought and action precisely the same as the person who accepts the laws of reality and of thought.

In his book on psychotherapy Arthur Kronfeld has re-marked that skepticism negates itself—a common philosophical view which, however, we see as faulty. For the dictum "I doubt everything" implies always: "everything except this particular dictum." When Socrates said: "I know that I know nothing," he meant: "I know that I know nothing except—that I know nothing."

Like all epistemological skepticism, the obsessional neurotic's seeks to find an Archimedean point, an absolutely solid basis from which to start out and on which to build up, with logical consistency and uncompromising truthfulness, a complete world-view. A radical beginning is being sought. Such an "ultimate philosophy" would ideally take for its first premise a statement which would, epistemologically, be its own justification. The only kind of statement which could meet this requirement would be one affirming the inescapable necessity of employing conceptual thinking in spite of its dubious nature—in other words, an idea that is self-sustaining because its very content is the dependency of thought upon concepts (that is, upon something other than self-evident intuitions).

Any such self-justification of rationalism would be tanta-mount to its self-elimination. Logotherapeutic treatment of our obsessional-neurotic patient therefore had to aim at overthrowing his exaggerated rationalism (which is what underlies all skepticism) by rational means. The rational way is a "golden bridge," which we must build for the skeptic. One such bridge might be the suggestion: "The most reasonable procedure is not to want to be too reasonable."*

Our patient should have remembered Goethe's "Skepticism

---

* Cf. Leo Tolstoy: "The intellect, like an opera glass, should only be turned up to a certain point; if you screw it any farther, you see more hazily."

is that which endeavors incessantly to overcome itself." The logo-therapist therefore had to take this neurotically skeptical world-view and enlarge it to include this form of skepticism. By rational means the patient fought through to a recognition of the ultimately irrational nature of existence. The original complex of problems now appeared to him in a new light. Originally he had been seeking a theoretical axiom to be his new, radical basis of thought. Now he posed the problem differently and looked for its solution in a realm antecedent to all philosophical thought, a realm in which the origins of action and feeling lie: an existential realm. What has to be achieved is what Eucken calls the "axiomatic deed."

Combatting and overcoming typical obsessional-neurotic rationalism by rational means must be followed through by a prag-matical counterpart. For the obsessional neurotic with his hundred-per-centness is seeking absolute certainty in decision as well as in cognition. His overconscientiousness is as much of a handicap to his acting as overconsciousness is to his knowing. The other half of his theoretical skepticism is an ethical skepticism; along with his doubts of the logical validity of his thinking run doubts of the moral validity of his actions. From this stems the obsessional neu-rotic's indecisiveness. An obsessional-neurotic woman, for example, was tormented by continual doubts as to what she ought to do. These doubts mounted to such proportions that finally she did nothing at all. She could never decide on a single thing; even in the most commonplace matters she did not know what choice to make. For example, she could not make up her mind whether to go to a concert or go walking in the park, and so she stayed home—having spent in interior debates the entire time in which she might have been doing either. Such indecisiveness is character-istic of the obsessional neurotic when facing the most trivial as well as the most important decisions. But by special logotherapy even this obsessional-neurotic overconscientiousness can be made to eliminate itself, just as exaggerated rationalism can be. Although Goethe has said: "Conscience is for the man who reflects, never for the man who acts," this maxim was never intended for our type of overscrupulous obsessional neurotic. For him we must build our golden bridge. We need only supplement the Goethean maxim with a little common sense: It may be unconscionable to act in this way or that, but it would be outrageous not to act at all. The man who can decide on nothing, can make up his mind about nothing at all, is undoubtedly making the most unscrupulous of decisions.

II From Psychoanalysis
to Existential Analysis

Endogenous psychoses are also susceptible to treatment by logotherapy: not the constitutional components themselves, of course, but the psychogenetic components resulting from them. We have already said that man is free to take a position on his psychological destiny, that here is a "pathoplastic" factor involved— meaning that he can shape his destiny and decide how he will react to the constitutional disease. In this connection we cited an organic depression which might have been treated pharmacologically, psychotherapeutically, or logotherapeutically. And we have said that the latter type of treatment aimed to change the patient's attitude toward her disease as well as toward her life as a task.

It is clear that the "pathoplastic" factor already contains an attitude toward the psychotic disease—even before logotherapy has brought about any change of attitude. To this extent, then, the psychotic patient's manifest behavior is already something more than the mere direct consequence of the fated, "creatural" affliction; it is also the expression of his spiritual attitude. This attitude is free. Understood in this light, even psychosis is at bottom a kind of test of a human being, of the humanity of a psychotic patient. The residue of freedom which is still present even in psychosis, in the patient's free attitude toward it, gives the patient the opportunity to realize attitudinal values. Even in and in spite of psychosis, logotherapy makes the patient see chances for the realization of values, though these may be only attitudinal values.

In the following section we will attempt to understand melancholia—that is, psychotic or endogenous depression—in existential analytical terms, as a mode of existence. Special existential analysis of melancholia deals first of all with the most prominent of melancholic symptoms: anxiety. From the somatic point of view, melancholia represents a vital low—no less, but also no more. For the fact that the melancholiac's organism is in a vital low by no means explains the whole complex of melancholic symptoms. It does not explain melancholic anxiety. This anxiety is primarily fear of death and of the stings of conscience. We can only understand the melancholic sense of anxiety and guilt if we consider it a mode of human existence, an aspect of being human. Something beyond illness itself is required to produce the melancholic experience; the human element is what transforms the mere disease, what takes the primary vital low and makes of it the melancholic mode of experiencing, which is nothing less than a mode of human existence. The underlying disease in melancholia leads only to symptoms such as psychomotor or secretory inhibitions; but the melancholic experience itself comes about as the result of the interplay between the human and the morbid elements in the human being. Thus, we could easily understand how some kind of depression state might occur in an animal on the basis of an organic low. But true human melancholia with its characteristic guilt feelings, self-reproaches, and self-accusations would be inconceivable in an animal. The "symptom" of conscientious anxiety in the melancholiac is not the product of melancholia as a physical illness, but represents an "accomplishment" of the human being as a spiritual person. Conscientious anxiety can be understood only in human terms, without recourse to physiological explanations. *It is understandable only as the anxiety of a human being as such: as existential anxiety.*

What the vital low, the physiological basis of melancholia,

produces is solely a feeling of insufficiency. But more than the physiological illness has come into play when this insufficiency is experienced as a feeling of inadequacy in the face of a task. An animal, too, can have anxiety, but only a human being can have conscientious anxiety or guilt feelings. For only the human being is faced with obligations that arise out of the responsibility of his being. Human psychoses are inconceivable in an animal: hence the element of humanity, of existentiality, must be crucial to these psychoses. The organic condition underlying psychosis is always transposed into the properly human sphere before it becomes the psychotic experience.

In the case of melancholia, psychophysical insufficiency is experienced in uniquely human fashion as tension between what the person is and what he ought to be. The melancholiac exaggerates the degree to which he as a person falls short of his ideal. The vital low aggravates that existential tension, which is part of human existence as such. In melancholia the insufficiency feeling magnifies the gap between what is and what ought to be. For the melancholiac that gap becomes a gaping abyss. In the depths of this abyss we cannot help seeing what lies at the bottom of all humanness insofar as it is responsibleness: conscience. It becomes clear that the melancholiac's anxiety of conscience arises out of an intrinsically human experience: that of heightened tension between the need and the possibility of fulfillment.

This melancholic experience of radical insufficiency, of being unable to cope with a task, appears in various forms. In the melancholic delusory fear of impoverishment typical of the premorbid middle-class person the insufficiency feeling is directed toward the task of earning money. In terms of Schopenhauer's distinction of "what one is, what one has, and what one seems," the conscientious anxiety and the guilt feeling of this type of person, when he becomes a sufferer from melancholia, revolve about the question of "what one has"; that is, the morbid condition brings out fears which were present in the premorbid condition. The premorbidly insecure person who fears death is applying the melancholiac feeling of insufficiency to the task of preserving life; and in the conscientious anxiety of the premorbidly guilty or over-scrupulous person the sense of inadequacy is focused on the question of moral righteousness.

When the underlying vital disturbance of melancholia increases the existential tension to an extreme degree, the person's life goal seems to him unattainable. Thus, he loses his sense of aim and end, his sense of future. "I lived my life backwards," a melancholiac woman remarked. "The present was done for—I lost myself in living backwards." This loss of a sense of the future, this experience of "futurelessness," is accompanied by a feeling that life is over with, that time has run out. "I looked at everything with different eyes," another patient said. "I no longer saw people as they are today or were yesterday; rather, I saw every single person on the day of his death—no matter whether he were an old man or a child. I saw far ahead, to the end of life, and I myself no longer lived in the present." In such cases of melancholia we may call the underlying mood a "Judgment Day" mood. Kronfeld has characterized existential experience in schizophrenia as the experience of "anticipated death." Similarly, we may say of melancholia that it is the experience of a "permanent Judgment Day."

(The affect of grief in the melancholiac is paralleled by the affect of joy in the maniac. The experience of melancholic anxiety is paralleled by the experience of manic high spirits. While the melancholic person experiences his abilities as insufficient to cope with his obligations, the manic person experiences his abilities as far surpassing his obligations. Thus, the manic delusion of power is the correlative of the melancholic feeling of guilt. And just as melancholic anxiety is, above all, fear of the future [fear of disasters, of a catastrophic future], so the manic person actually lives in the future; he makes plans, draws up programs, is always anticipating the future and assuming that its possibilities are realities.)

Steeped as he is in a feeling of his own insufficiency, the melancholiac becomes blind to the values inherent in his own being. This valuational blindness is later extended to the world around him as well. That is, while at first blindness may be called central, affecting only his own ego, it can progress centrifugally and lead to the blotting out of the valuational shadings of the whole of reality. But as long as the person's ego alone is affected, the melancholiac feels a drastic drop in his own value compared to that of the world. This explains the violent inferiority feeling of the melancholiac. The melancholiac feels himself as worthless and his own life as meaningless—hence the tendency toward suicide.

There is a further development in the nihilistic delusions of melancholia. Along with the values are prestidigitated away the things themselves, the carriers of values; the very substratum of possible valuation is negated. Here, too, the person's ego itself is first affected; depersonalization results. "I am not a human being at all," a patient confessed. She added: "I am nobody—I am not in the world." Later the world itself comes in for this nihilistic treatment; unreality results. Thus, a patient declared, when the doctor introduced himself: "There are no doctors—there never have been any."

Cotard has described a melancholic syndrome which includes "ideas of damnation, ideas of non-existence and of not being able to die." Melancholic ideas of damnation obviously spring from the nihilistic depersonalization mentioned above. The delusion of immortality is also encountered in isolated form in certain types of melancholia. These clinical pictures may be called "Ahasuerian melancholias." How are we to interpret this type of illness in existential analytical terms?

The melancholiac's guilt feeling resulting from his intensified existential tension can swell to such a point that he feels his guilt to be ineradicable. The task which he feels unable to cope with, due to his sense of insufficiency, then appears unfulfillable even if he had all eternity at his disposal. Only in this manner can we understand why patients make such remarks as: "I shall have to live forever in order to make amends for my faults. It is like purgatory." For such melancholiacs the task quality of life assumes colossal dimensions. "I must bear up the whole world," one such patient commented. "The only thing that is still alive in me is conscience. Everything is so oppressive. Everything around me of this world has vanished; I can only see the hereafter now. I am supposed to create the whole world and I cannot. Now I am supposed to replace the oceans and the mountains and everything. But I have no money. I cannot dig out a mine with my fingernails and I cannot replace vanished nations, and yet it has to be. Everything is going to be destroyed now."

The devaluation not only of himself, but of the whole world, engenders in the melancholiac a general misanthropy. He is disgusted by himself and by everyone else also. He can no longer recognize values in anything. As Mephistopheles has it in Goethe's *Faust:* "For all that is deserves to be wholly reduced to nullity." This sentence conveys something of the idea of universal doom in which the melancholiac gives vent to his life-feeling of anxiety. Looked at from an existential analytical point of view, his guilt feeling seems to arise out of his exaggeration of his life task (because of his sense of insufficiency) to superhuman proportions. The wild excessiveness of this guilt feeling can be expressed only in such delusional utterances as: "Everything is going to vanish and I am supposed to create it again—and I know I can't do that. I'm supposed to make everything. Where shall I ever get enough money for it, from eternity to eternity? I cannot create all the foals and all the oxen and cattle that have been since the beginning of the world."

_____

Just as pseudo-movements occur in giddiness, so anxiety (which Kierkegaard has called the giddiness that overcomes us on the peaks of freedom) is characterized by mental pseudo-movements. In the case of melancholia—when the gap between what is and what ought to be is experienced as an abyss—there is the sense of the falling away of the self and the world, of beings and meanings.

4   On the Psychology of Schizophrenia

In discussing the psychology of schizophrenia, and proposing the existential analytic interpretation of that illness, we will start with certain clinical observations. In our dealings with large numbers of schizophrenic patients, a peculiar psychological phenomenon has come up again and again. The patients stated that they sometimes felt as if moving pictures were being taken of them. After suitable exploration it developed, remarkably enough, that this feeling had no hallucinatory basis; the patients did not claim that they heard the turning of a crank or—in cases where they felt they were being still-photographed—the click of a shutter. They averred that the camera had been invisible and the cameraman hidden. Nor were there paranoid ideas from which the photography delusion might have flowed—thus making it a secondary delusion, a carry-through of persecution feelings. There were, to be sure, cases with a delusional substructure; patients would assert, for example, that they had seen themselves in the newsreel. Others maintained that their enemies or persecutors were spying on them by secretly taking pictures. But from the start we excluded such cases with a paranoid basis from our investigations. For in these the sensation of being filmed was not experienced directly, but subsequently constructed and attributed to the past.

Having thus set aside the cases with extraneous causal features, what we were left with might be termed purely descriptively a "film delusion." This film delusion constitutes a genuine "hallucination of knowledge" in Jaspers's sense; but it might also be classed among the "primarily delusional feelings" as defined by Gruhle. When a patient was asked why she thought pictures were being taken of her when she had noticed nothing to suggest that this was happening, she answered characteristically: "I just know—I don't know how."

This delusion may take on various related forms. Some patients are certain that phonograph records of them have been made. Here we have simply the acoustic counterpart to film delusion. Still other patients believe they are being eavesdropped on. Finally, there are cases of patients who insist that they have a definite feeling of being sought for, or an equally irrational certainty that somebody is thinking of them.

What is the common element in all these experiences? We may put it this way: that the person experiences himself as an object—as the object of the lens of a movie camera or still camera, or as the object of a recording-apparatus, or the object of someone's eavesdropping or even seeking and thinking—in sum, then, the object of a variety of intentional acts of other people. All these patients experience themselves as the object of the psychic activity of other persons, for the various types of apparatus involved are simply symbols, the mechanical extensions of others' psyches or a mechanical extension of the intentional acts of seeing and hearing. (Thus, it is understandable that the mechanisms in question retain for the schizophrenics a kind of mythical intentionality.)

In these cases of schizophrenia, then, we are dealing with a primarily delusional feeling which may be called the "experience of pure objectness." All the phenomena that come under the headings of "sense of being influenced" or "observation delusion" or "persecution delusion" can be thought of as special forms of the more general experience of pure objectness. The schizophrenic experiences himself as the object of the observing or persecuting intentions of his fellow men.

This experience of pure objectness we consider to be an aspect of that central disturbance of the ego which Gruhle counts among the "primary symptoms" of schizophrenia. We can reduce the various forms of the experience of pure objectness to a general law of schizophrenic experience: The schizophrenic experiences himself as if he, the subject, were transformed into an object. He experiences psychic acts as if they were being rendered in the passive mood. While the normal person experiences himself thinking, watching, observing, influencing, listening, eavesdropping, seeking, and persecuting, taking still or moving pictures, etc., the schizophrenic experiences all these acts and intentions, these psychic functions, as if they were being rendered in the passive; he "is being" observed, "is being" thought about, etc. In other words, in schizophrenia there takes place an experiential passivizing of the psychic functions. We consider this to be a universal law of the psychology of schizophrenia.

It is interesting to see how the experiential passivity of such patients leads them even in speech to use transitive verb forms in the passive mood where active intransitive verbs would be more appropriate. Thus one schizophrenic woman complained that she did not feel as if she ever awoke, but always that she was being awakened. This passivistic tendency is the explanation for the well-known schizophrenic avoidance of verbs and preference for substantive constructions—since by its nature the verb assumes and expresses an active experience.

The typical language of autistic schizophrenics—that is, those who are wrapped in their own fantasies and thus "inactive" with respect to the outer world—has another characteristic: that of being predominantly expressive rather than representational. That is why we can explain, and in fact even understand, the artificially created languages of a good many schizophrenics who have ceased to respond to normal language, by confining ourselves to the expressive elements of language, by talking to the patient as we "speak" to a dog. The significant thing is intonation rather than words.

Our interpretation of the schizophrenic mode of experience as a passivizing of psychic activity approaches Berze's theory of schizophrenia. Berze speaks of an insufficiency of psychic activity in schizophrenics. He considers the chief symptom of schizophrenia to be "hypotonia of consciousness." If we consider this hypotonia of consciousness along with what we have called experiential passivizing, we arrive at the following existential-analytic interpretation of schizophrenia: in schizophrenia the ego is affected both qua consciousness and qua responsibility. The schizophrenic person is limited in respect to these two existential factors. The schizophrenic person experiences himself as so limited in his full humanity that he can no longer feel himself as really "existent." These are the qualities of the schizophrenic experience which made Kronfeld call schizophrenia "anticipated death."

Berze has drawn a sharp line between the process symptoms and the defect symptoms of schizophrenia, and it is upon the process symptoms alone that all phenomenological-psychological interpretations of schizophrenia are based. The existential-analytic interpretation of the schizophrenic mode of experience also takes the process symptoms as its point of departure. To our mind, a similar cleavage to that between schizophrenic process and defect symptoms exists between two modes of experience in normal persons: the experiences of falling asleep and of dreaming. C. Schneider in his study of the psychology of schizophrenia has wisely taken somnolescent thinking as his model, rather than dream-thinking—the latter being singled out by C. G. Jung, who interprets the schizophrenic as a "dreamer among wakers."

In what way does the normal experience of falling asleep resemble the schizophrenic mode of experience? The thing is that somnolence also exhibits hypotonia of consciousness or, to use Janet's phrase, an *"abaissement mentale."* Löwy has pointed out the "half-done products of thought," and Mayer-Gross speaks of "empty husks of thought." All these phenomena are to be found both in normal somnolescent thought and in schizophrenic thinking. Moreover, the school of Karl Bühler speaks of "thought patterns" and the "blank form quality" of thinking. The research of Löwy, Mayer-Gross, and Bühler agrees strikingly in this respect. We may put it this way: the somnolent person falls asleep over the blank form of thought instead of filling it out.

Dream-thinking differs from somnolescent thinking in that dreams employ figurative language. In the course of falling asleep the consciousness drops to a lower level—what we have referred to as hypotonia of consciousness. Once this process is completed and the bottom, so to speak, of consciousness is reached, dreaming begins immediately. Dreaming, that is, takes place upon this lower level. In accordance with the functional changes that take place during the transition from waking to sleeping, the sleeper "regresses" to the primitive symbolic language of dreams.

For the moment, however, let us put aside the fundamental distinction between process symptoms and defect symptoms in schizophrenia and ask ourselves to what extent other schizophrenic symptoms besides those we have discussed (disturbance of the ego and of thinking) fall into the theory we have presented: a thoroughgoing experiential passivizing of psychic events. In this connection we shall not discuss the extent to which the motor system of the schizophrenic is also subject to this passivizing—although our theory would seem to throw light on catatonic and cataleptic forms of schizophrenia. We shall limit our discussion to the psychological problem of acoustic hallucination in schizophrenia. If we start with the phenomenon of "thinking aloud," the passivizing principle offers the key to the mystery. The normal person's thinking is accompanied by more or less conscious "internal speech." These acoustic elements are experienced in passive form by the schizophrenic; he feels that his thoughts come from outside himself and so "hears voices," experiences his thoughts as if they were perceptions. For what is hallucination if not experiencing something personal and internal as if it were foreign to the personality, as if it were a manifestation of something outside oneself?

Unfortunately, there is no way to use this discovery of experiential passivizing in practical therapy. But practice yields ample empirical confirmation of the theory. For example, a young man came to us with a severe delusion of reference. Cure consisted in training him to pay no attention to the imaginary observers and not to watch his supposed watchers—à la *"persécuteur persécuté."* (The question of whether there were any grounds for his belief that he was surrounded by spies was excluded from discussion right from the start.) His feeling of being under observation disappeared. As soon as he had relaxed his own close watch on his environment, his constant state of alertness to detect the imaginary observers, the miracle happened—the spies took themselves off. As soon as he stopped his own watching, there was a cessation of the corresponding passive experience of feeling that he was being watched. To our mind this can be explained only by the assumption that the underlying disturbance had produced an inversion of the experience of watching, had converted it into the passive mood.

Special existential analysis need not confine itself to cases of severe schizophrenic disturbance. Much may be learned of schizophrenic experience by analysis of borderline cases—such as the above-mentioned young man with his delusion of reference. For this reason we will deal with those forms of schizoid character structure which were formerly comprehended within the term "psychasthenia." The chief characteristic of this illness is what used to be described as *"sentiment de vide";* there is a conspicuous lack of the *"sentiment de réalité."* One of our patients tried to describe his sensations by comparing himself to a "fiddle without a sounding-box, utterly without resonance"; he felt about himself "as if" he were "merely his own shadow." This lack of "resonance" he complained of produced in him a sense of depersonalization.

Haug has written an interesting monograph to prove that a sense of depersonalization can be provoked by exaggerated self-observation. We wish to add a few comments. Knowledge is never only a knowledge about something, but also a knowledge of the knowledge itself—and, furthermore, a knowledge that the knowing proceeds from the ego. "I know something" means all at once: "I know *something*," and "I *know* something," and simultaneously "*I* know something." The psychic act of knowing or thinking gives rise, as it were, to a secondary, reflexive act, the object of which is the primary act and the ego as the starting-point of the primary act. In other words, the act of knowing makes the subject into an object. The primary act reflected by the secondary, reflexive act becomes a psychic datum, is qualified as a psychic act; the experiential quality of "being psychic" therefore arises only in and through the reflection.

Let us try to see these connections in terms of a biological model. Suppose that the primary psychic act corresponds, in our biological parallel, to the pseudopodium of an amœba which reaches out from its cell nucleus toward some object. Then the secondary, reflexive act would correspond to a second, smaller pseudopodium which is "turned back" toward the extended one. We can then very well imagine that this "reflexive" pseudopodium, if it is overstrained, will lose its syncytial connection with the plasma of the amœbal cell and break off. This is somewhat the process by which exaggerated self-observation produces depersonalization. Exaggerated self-observation is over-straining; the connection with the observing ego is snapped and the psychic functions seem to be taking place by themselves. The exaggerated reflexive act of self-observation may be likened to screwing the strings of intentionality too tight—until they snap and there is no longer felt to be a connection with the primary act and the active ego. There necessarily follows from this the loss of the sense of activity and personality; the disturbed ego feels itself depersonalized.

This must be borne in mind: as a result of the concomitant reflection of a psychic act, it is itself present as a bridge between subject and object, and moreover the subject itself is present as the carrier of all psychic activity. In "having something," I have, along with the something, the having itself, and also the ego as the self. The "self," then, is the ego having itself, the ego that has become conscious of itself. For this becoming conscious via self-reflection there is also a biological model, namely the phylogenesis of the prosencephalon: the forebrain is folded around the brain stem, "bent back" as the inhibiting function of consciousness is "reflected" back upon the instinctual reactions of the diencephalic centers.

We have said that in case of depersonalization the "strings of intentionality" are screwed so tight that they may snap, and that this is the reason why exaggerated self-observation makes for a rift in the ego's self-awareness. It is then clear that the hypotonia of consciousness in schizophrenia may lead to the same kind of ego-disturbance as the hypertonia of consciousness in psychasthenia. The difference between schizophrenic ego-disturbance and psychasthenic depersonalization consists only in this: in the former the strings of intentionality are too slack (hypotonia of consciousness), while in the latter they are so tight that they snap (hypertonia of consciousness).

Along with the lower level of consciousness to which a person regresses in sleep there goes non-pathological hypotonia of consciousness. We may therefore expect it to be expressed in a lowering of the tendency toward reflection. We may assume that in the dream the reflexive cilium of the mental act is, as it were, more or less withdrawn. The effect of this withdrawal is that the perceptual elements of "freely emerging images" can weave their hallucinatory patterns unchecked by the operations of the higher faculties.

If in conclusion we survey the findings of special existential analysis concerning the essential differences among the obsessional-neurotic, melancholic, and schizophrenic modes of experience, we may sum up as follows: The obsessional neurotic suffers from hyper-awareness. The schizophrenic suffers from hypotonia of consciousness. The schizophrenic experiences a restriction of the ego both qua consciousness and qua responsibility (experience of pure objectness or principle of passivizing). This is a basic distinction between the schizophrenic and the melancholiac. For the morbidity of the melancholiac could be understood in existential-analytic terms only as a shaping of the disease process by the human person—that is, as a mode of humanness. In the schizophrenic, however, existential analysis has shown that the person's very humanness is also affected, is itself shaped by the disease process. Nevertheless, even for the schizophrenic there remains that residue of freedom toward fate and toward the disease which man always possesses, no matter how ill he may be, in all situations and at every moment of life, to the very last.

III

Logotherapy

as a

Psychotherapeutic

Technique

III   Logotherapy as a Psychotherapeutic Technique

According to Gordon W. Allport, logotherapy is an "existential psychiatry." Among all the schools that have been given this label, however, logotherapy "is a notable exception," as Professor Robert C. Leslie of the Pacific School of Religion, Berkeley, California, has pointed out; for, "although a good deal of attention is being given in the psychotherapeutic world to existentialism as a new movement rivaling Freudian psychoanalysis and Watsonian behaviorism, specific elaborations of an existentialist psychotherapy are difficult to find." Logotherapy, however, is the only existential psychiatry that has succeeded in developing a therapeutic technique, according to a paper read by Godfryd Kaczanowski, Clinical Director of the Ontario Hospital, before the Conference on Existential Psychiatry, Toronto, on May 6, 1962. It is the contention of Aaron J. Ungersma, in his book on logotherapy, that this school is actually the only one, within the vast field of existential psychiatry, which includes what might be justifiably spoken of as a therapeutic technique. In his *Logotherapy and the Christian*

Faith, Professor Donald F. Tweedie observes that because of this logotherapy will be of particular interest to the typical American, whose outlook is traditionally pragmatic.

This special logotherapeutic technique I have called "paradoxical intention." It was first set forth by me in 1946, and in a more systematized manner in 1960.

Paradoxical Intention

To understand what happens when this technique is used, let us take as a starting point a phenomenon that is known to every clinically trained psychiatrist—namely, anticipatory anxiety. It is commonly observed that such anxiety often produces precisely that situation of which the patient is afraid. The erythrophobic individual, for example, who is afraid of blushing when he enters a room and faces a group of people, will actually blush at precisely that moment. A symptom evokes a psychic response in terms of anticipatory anxiety which provokes the symptom to reappear. The recurrence of the symptom in turn reinforces the anticipatory anxiety, and thus a vicious circle is completed. Within this vicious circle, the patient himself is enclosed; he weaves himself in, as in a cocoon.

As far as anxiety is involved as a point of departure, the patients themselves often report an anxiety about being anxious. Apparently, they are in accord with Franklin D. Roosevelt's well-known statement: "The only thing we have to fear is fear itself."

When we investigate this fear of fear more closely, however, we may see that there are three typical reasons for it, as patients suffering from fear of fear typically relate that they are afraid: (1) that an attack of anxiety may eventuate in collapsing or fainting (the technical term reserved by logotherapy for this condition is "collapse phobia"); (2) that it may result in a coronary infarct ("infarct phobia"); (3) that the result may be a brain palsy ("insult phobia").

Thus far we have referred to the motivations of fear of fear. What, now, about the reactions to fear of fear? Generally, it is an avoidance pattern of response, or, as it is called in logotherapy, flight from fear. The patient begins to avoid open places or closed rooms—in other words, to exhibit the agoraphobic or claustrophobic pattern of behavior.

This pattern of flight from fear in anxiety neurosis is paralleled by a pattern in obsessive neurosis—namely, a fight against obsessions. It is motivated in the first place by the obsessive neurotic's fear that his obsessions might form the symptom of an imminent psychosis ("psychotophobia," as it is termed in logotherapy). However, psychotophobia is not the only event that can motivate the patient to fight his obsessions; "criminophobia," as it is called in logotherapy, may just as well be the motivating agent. In fact, those obsessive patients who are crippled by the fear that they may actualize any of their obsessions—for example, that one day they may really jump from an open window, or that they may actually kill a person with a knife lying before them on the table— also fight their obsessions. In such cases, the logotherapist speaks of a "suicide phobia" or "homicide phobia."

Finally, there is a third pattern of response and behavior paralleling flight from and fight against something—namely, fight for something. It is noticeable in sexual neurotics. Many sexual neuroses, at least according to the findings and teachings of logotherapy, may be traced back to the forced intention of attaining the goal of sexual intercourse—be it the male seeking to demonstrate his potency or the female her ability to experience orgasm. As a rule, the patient seeks pleasure intentionally (one might say that he takes the "pleasure principle" literally). However, pleasure belongs to that category of events which cannot be brought about by direct intention; on the contrary, it is a mere side effect or by-product. Therefore, the more one strives for pleasure, the less one is able to attain it.

Thus we see an interesting parallel in which anticipatory anxiety brings about precisely what the patient had feared, while excessive intention, or "hyper-intention," as it is called in logotherapy, prevents the accomplishment of what the patient had desired. It is this twofold fact on which logotherapy bases its technique called paradoxical intention, in which the phobic patient is invited to intend, even if only for a moment, precisely that which he fears.

The following clinical reports will indicate what I mean:

A young physician came to my department in the Polyclinic Hospital suffering from severe hidrophobia. He had for a long time been troubled by disturbances of the autonomic nervous system. One day he happened to meet his chief on the street and, as he extended his hand in greeting, he noticed that he was perspiring more than usual. The next time he was in a similar situation he expected to perspire again, and this anticipatory anxiety precipitated excessive sweating. It was a vicious circle; hyperhidrosis provoked hidrophobia, and hidrophobia, in turn, produced hyperhidrosis. In order to cut this circle we advised our patient, in the event that his anticipatory anxiety should recur, to resolve deliberately to show those whom he was with at the time how much he could really sweat. A week later he returned to report that whenever he met anyone who triggered his anticipatory anxiety, he said to himself: "I sweated out only a quart before, but now I'm going to pour out at least ten quarts!" What was the result of this paradoxical resolution? After suffering from his phobia for four years, he was able, after only one session, to free himself of it for good within one week.*

The reader will note that this treatment consists of a reversal of the patient's attitude, inasmuch as his fear is replaced by a paradoxical wish. In other words, *the wind is taken out of the sails of the phobia.* This brings about a change of attitude toward the phobia. According to logotherapeutic teaching, the pathogenesis in phobias and obsessive-compulsive neuroses is partially due to the increase of anxieties, obsessions, and compulsions that is caused by the attempt to avoid anxieties or fight obsessions and compulsions. A phobic person usually tries to avoid the situation in which his anxiety arises, while the obsessive-compulsive tries to suppress, and thus to fight, his threatening ideas. In either case the result is a strengthening of the symptom. Conversely, if we succeed in bringing the patient to the point where he ceases to flee from or to fight his symptoms, but, on the contrary, even exaggerates them, then we may observe that the symptoms diminish and that the patient is no longer haunted by them.

This procedure, however, must make use of the specifically human capacity for self-detachment inherent in a sense of humor. That is why paradoxical intention is carried out in as humorous a setting as possible. This enables the patient to put himself at a distance from the symptom, to detach himself from his neurosis.

Along with Heidegger's assertion that "sorrowful concern" (*Sorge*) is the essential feature permeating human existence, and Binswanger's subsequent substitution of "loving togetherness" (*lie-*

---

* Wherever in this book short-term therapeutic results are described, it is not to be assumed that either logotherapy in general or paradoxical intention in particular will yield such short-term results in every case. Material regarding them is included here for didactic purposes.

bendes Miteinandersein) as the chief human characteristic, I would venture to say that humor also deserves to be mentioned among the basic human capacities.* After all, no animal is able to laugh.

As a matter of fact, when paradoxical intention is used, the purpose is to enable the patient to develop a sense of detachment toward his neurosis by laughing at it, to put it simply. A statement somewhat consistent with this is found in Gordon Allport's book *The Individual and His Religion*: "The neurotic who learns to laugh at himself may be on the way to self-management, perhaps to cure." Paradoxical intention is the empirical validation and clinical application of Allport's statement.

A few more case reports may serve to develop and clarify this method further:

I once received a letter from a young medical student who had attended my clinical lectures on logotherapy. She reminded me of a case that I had presented of a young doctor who was on the staff of one of the ophthalmological clinics of the University of Vienna and was primarily concerned with eye surgery. He consulted me because, when performing an operation, he began to be afraid that he would tremble whenever the chief of the clinic entered the operating room. Subsequently this fear led to an actual tremor under these circumstances and the expectation became a fact. He was able finally to overcome this anxiety and the consequent trembling only by drinking alcohol immediately prior to an operation! In her letter the medical student said: "I tried to apply the method you had used in the classroom demonstration to myself. I, too, suffered continually from the fear that, while dissecting at the Institute of Anatomy, I would begin to tremble when the

* In addition to being a constituent element in man's existence, humor may well be regarded as an attribute of deity. See Psalms 2:4, 37:13, and 59:8.

anatomy instructor entered the room. Soon this fear actually did cause a tremor. Then, remembering what you had told us in the lecture that dealt with this very situation, I said to myself whenever the instructor entered the dissecting room: 'Oh, here is the instructor! Now I'll show him what a good trembler I am—I'll really show him how nicely I can tremble!' But whenever I deliberately tried to tremble, I was unable to do so!"

Another case, which was treated by one of my associates, Dr. Kurt Kocourek, concerned a woman, Mary B., who had been undergoing various methods of treatment for eleven years, yet her complaints, rather than being alleviated, had increased. She suffered from attacks of palpitation accompanied by marked anxiety and anticipatory fears of a sudden collapse. After the first attack she began to fear that it would recur and, consequently, it did. The patient reported that whenever she had this fear, it was followed by palpitations. Her chief concern was, however, that she might collapse in the street. Dr. Kocourek advised her to tell herself at such a moment: "My heart shall beat still faster! I would just love to collapse right here on the sidewalk!" Furthermore, the patient was advised deliberately to seek out places which she had experienced as disagreeable, or even dangerous, instead of avoiding them. Two weeks later the patient reported: "I am quite well now and feel scarcely any palpitations. The fear has completely disappeared." Some weeks after her discharge she reported: "Occasionally mild palpitations occur, but when they do, I say to myself: 'My heart should beat even faster,' and at that moment the palpitations cease."

Paradoxical intention is intrinsically a nonspecific method. This nonspecificity helps to clarify why the technique is sometimes effective in severe cases. Let us turn to an illustrative case history:

Mrs. Elfriede G., a thirty-five-year-old woman, was a patient in the Neurological Department of the Polyclinic Hospital when

I presented her at one of my clinical lectures. She reported that as a child she was meticulous, and while her friends were playing in the park, she stayed at home scrubbing and cleaning. For three years the patient had been virtually incapacitated by an extreme fear of bacteria; hundreds of times a day she had washed her hands. Fearing contact with germs, she no longer left the house; fearing exposure through outsiders, she excluded all visitors. She would not even allow her husband to touch the children for fear he would transmit germs to them. Finally she wanted a divorce because she felt she had made her family unhappy. She had been institutionalized because of several attempts at suicide. After unsuccessful treatment in various clinics and hospitals, she had finally been taken to the Neurological Department of the Polyclinic Hospital by ambulance, for she had become completely helpless. In the lecture hall of the hospital, in the presence of a class of students, I spoke to the patient for the first time. I asked her: "Are you accustomed to check the door many times before leaving home, or to check whether a letter has really fallen into the mailbox or not, or to check several times whether the gas valve is really closed before going to bed?" "Yes, that is my case," she said anxiously. I then proceeded by pointing out that this meant she belonged to a certain type of character structure which in traditional European psychiatry was conceived of as "anankastic," and that this meant immunity to psychoses. A sigh of relief was her response, relief after long years of suffering from the fear of becoming psychotic. Because of her fear that the obsessions had been psychotic symptoms, the patient had fought them. By this very counterpressure, however, she had increased the pressure within herself. I then remarked: "You have no reason for such a fear. Any normal person can become psychotic, with the single exception of people who are anankastic character types. I cannot help but tell you this and destroy all your illusions in this respect. Therefore you need not fight your obsessive ideas. You may as well joke with them."

Then I started paradoxical intention. I invited the patient to imitate what I did. I scrubbed the floor of the lecture hall with my hands and said: "After all, for the sake of a change, now, instead of fearing infection, let's invite it." Stooping and rubbing my hands on the floor, I continued: "See, I cannot get dirty enough; I can't find enough bacteria!" Under my encouragement, the patient followed my example. And so she began the treatment which, in five days, removed ninety per cent of her symptoms. Regular therapeutic treatments with my associate speeded the recovery. Thus an incapacitating pattern of three years' standing was broken up in a matter of a few weeks. She spoke jokingly of all her former symptoms. She asked her fellow patients whether any of them could provide her with "some more bacteria." She cleaned post-operative patients in the Laryngological Department. She was in steady contact with bloody things. She washed her hands only three times a day although she frequently handled putrid material. She wanted "to make as much acquaintance with germs as possible." She spontaneously declared: "I want to let the poor beings live and not wash them away." On the sixth day she left the hospital to buy wool to knit a pullover for her youngest child, to knit it "here in an environment full of bacteria." "On each loop of the sweater," she said humorously, she wanted "one bacterium sitting." She was beaming with joy and felt completely healthy. When she went home for Christmas her behavior was, for the first time, as normal as it had been before the onset of her neurosis three years before. There was no longer any need to apply paradoxical intention. The patient embraced the children, caressed them without the slightest fear of infecting them. She resolved deliberately: "Now I will transfer the bacteria onto my children." The washing compulsion had disappeared. "I am the happiest person on earth," she declared. She was able to do everything in the normal routine including tasks that formerly she had not been able to finish. She did all of the housework and devoted herself to her children as she had not been able to do since her neurosis became full-fledged. She was able to devote herself to her youngest child for the first time in his life! Some time later I asked her about the washing compulsion. She replied: "I have to laugh at that now. It seems quite unreal to me that I ever had to suffer from anything like that. Now at ten o'clock in the morning my housework is finished. Before, I got up at three o'clock in the morning and even by night my housework was not completed."

I do not wish to convey the impression that paradoxical intention is a panacea. On the other hand, however, I feel obliged to state that the percentage of cures, or of cases improved to a degree that has made further treatment unnecessary, is—according to the follow-ups by Kurt Kocourek, Eva Niebauer, and Paul Polak—somewhat higher than the figures reported in the literature. Recently Dr. Hans O. Gerz, Clinical Director of the Connecticut Valley Hospital, reported on this point at the Symposium on Logotherapy at the Sixth International Congress of Psychotherapy (London, 1964). In his introductory paper, "Six Years of Clinical Experience with the Logotherapeutic Technique of Paradoxical Intention in the Treatment of Phobic and Obsessive-Compulsive Patients," he said: "Since the first presentation of our experiences with paradoxical intention at Harvard in 1961 and our subsequent publications in English and German, we have successfully continued to use paradoxical intention in hospitalized patients and in private practice. I would like to present brief statistics and follow-up. During the past six years we have treated 41 patients.

88.2% of all patients recovered or made considerable improvement. Most of these cases suffered from their illness up to 24 years and had received all forms of therapy except paradoxical intention and Wolpe's 'deconditioning therapy.'" Dr. Gerz concluded by saying that "paradoxical intention lends itself in the acute cases to short-term therapy. Chronic patients may need up to one or two years of treatment. Psychoanalysis often requires many years, with questionable results to say the least."

The remarkable results obtained by some who have practiced paradoxical intention should not tempt us to assume that it is a miracle method. Logotherapy cannot be applied with equal success to all patients. Nor is every doctor capable of handling it with equal skill. For these reasons, if for no other, it is justifiable to combine logotherapy with other methods, as has been suggested by, among others, Dr. Lederman (hypnosis), Professor Bazzi (relaxation training after Schultz), Kvilhaug (behavior therapy after Wolpe), and Dr. Kratochvil of the Psychiatric Clinic of the University of Brno (activation training after Bojanovský and Chloupková).

The following will demonstrate that even instances of severe obsessive-compulsive character neurosis may be appropriately and beneficially treated by means of paradoxical intention.

Mrs. Anna H. is forty years of age. A washing compulsion was noticed when she was only five years old. Later, during her school days, she often stayed up until 5 a.m. because of chronic perfectionism regarding her assigned homework. She also had a severe *délire de toucher*. She received many treatments, including periods of hospitalization, with no therapeutic effect. Her handicap of compulsive repetition became so severe that at the time of her application for admission to our clinic, she had to start toileting at 4 a.m., in order to arrive at the clinic at noon. My associate Eva Niebauer had daily therapeutic sessions with the patient in which

she learned to wish that everything would be "as dirty as possible."
(One interesting statement taken from the case notes: "The patient
'wishes' to jump head first into the mud.") By the eighth day the
patient required only a half hour for washing and dressing. After
two weeks she went home for a few hours without washing there
at all. On the twenty-fifth day, during a visit home, she did some
cooking, a task which had not been possible for years! (Before
leaving the clinic that day she had mentioned that she would not
be able to do any cooking, which, perhaps, demonstrates that the
results of paradoxical intention should not be considered simply
effects of suggestion.) Before she had terminated her month-long
hospitalization, she was able to help the nurses in their cleaning
work. At the time of her discharge she was practically symptom-
free. Six months later she reported that she needed less than an
hour to get dressed and that she had fully resumed her professional
work, from which she had been incapacitated for a long period
prior to admission to the hospital.

It may be of interest to cite a case of speech disturbance
treated by a young German psychiatrist, Manfred Eisenmann, of
Freiburg im Breisgau. The stuttering problem of seventeen-year-old
Horst S. began four years previously during a recitation in class.
His schoolmates laughed at him, and their derision became for him
a very traumatic experience indeed. Subsequently, his speech difficulty occurred with increasing frequency. Finally he refused to
attempt oral recitation altogether. A year before he was referred
to Dr. Eisenmann, he was treated by a psychiatrist who employed
"autogenous training" (relaxation exercises, after J. H. Schultz of
Berlin), but there were no beneficial results. Dr. Eisenmann explained to the patient how the mechanism of anticipatory anxiety
was involved in the pathogenesis of the trouble, and pointed out the
false attitude he had adopted toward it. Though the patient was
very pessimistic, Dr. Eisenmann succeeded in getting him to say to

himself, whenever the stuttering anxiety gripped him: "Oh, I'm afraid that I'll stutter on a 'b' or a 'p'! Well, today I think I'll stutter through the whole alphabet for a change!" At first Horst merely laughed at the instructions, but later discovered that this laughter was the heart of the matter. When he could be ironic about his fears and thus could put himself at a distance from them, he was actually detaching himself from his painful problem. Though he could not bring himself to actually try paradoxical intention until after the fifth interview, he finally succeeded, and after only two more psychotherapeutic sessions was able to resume classroom recitation free of any speech difficulty.

Paradoxical intention is particularly useful in short-term therapy, especially in cases of phobia with an underlying anticipatory anxiety mechanism. A statement made by Dr. Hans O. Gerz, in his article "The Treatment of the Phobic and the Obsessive-Compulsive Patient with Viktor E. Frankl's Paradoxical Intention" (published in the *Journal of Neuropsychiatry* in 1962), seems to me to be particularly noteworthy: "The number of therapy sessions depends largely on how long the patient has been sick. Most acute cases who are sick for a few weeks or months respond to this therapy within about 4 to 12 sessions. Those who have been sick for several years, even as long as twenty or more (in my experience I had six such cases, although more have been reported in the literature), need up to 12 months of biweekly sessions to bring about recovery. . . . The therapist must never tire of encouraging the patient to continue to use paradoxical intention over and over—just as his neurosis produces the symptoms over and over. . . . Finally, paradoxical intention strangles them."

The following is a remarkable instance of short-term therapy through the application of paradoxical intention.

In 1960 a man came to the Neurological Department of the Polyclinic Hospital who had suffered severe anxiety attacks and in recent months was unable to go on the street unless his wife accompanied him. He would not venture to ride a streetcar and was continually haunted by the fear that he would collapse and die. When Dr. Kurt Kocourek saw him, he was caught in an overpowering fear, with intense excitement and copious perspiring. So severe was his condition that he was scheduled for admission to the ward of the Polyclinic Hospital; yet after two ten-minute sessions in which he was treated by paradoxical intention, he was able to travel by streetcar, and he felt incomparably better than before. In his third visit to the Polyclinic Hospital he saw me and said: "On the doctor's advice I started telling myself: 'Now I shall go out on the street and try to collapse.' After two psychotherapeutic sessions, I was sitting in a crowded coffeehouse. First I felt again some anxiety (*Angst*), but I said to myself: 'Now let's collapse,' inviting myself to do so. After this, I was quite free from fear. I am very happy to have confided in Dr. Kocourek." Ten days later, during his fifth interview (about three weeks after the first meeting) the patient reported that he had succeeded in going to his child's school for a "parent-teacher conference"—in spite of the fact that the school was overcrowded. It was precisely what he most dreaded, until now. Before leaving his home, he jokingly told himself: "Now I am going to the school building to die. What a beautiful funeral it will be." On the same day the patient went to his mutual savings club. Usually he went there with great anxiety, but this time he went in order that he "should faint away from a heat stroke in the stuffy room," and "for the sake of getting asphyxiated by the fumes of the stove." However, this time there were absolutely no symptoms. Now, when he speaks of paradoxical intention, he laughs heartily and says: "This is fun—it really worked." He now forgets to apply paradoxical intention, for he does not need it any more.

The following case, taken from Dr. Gerz's article, is another illustration of short-term treatment by applying paradoxical intention.

W.S., aged thirty-five, developed the phobia that he would die of a heart attack, particularly after intercourse, as well as a phobic fear of not being able to go to sleep. When Dr. Gerz asked the patient in his office to "try as hard as possible" to make his heart beat fast and die of a heart attack "right on the spot," he laughed and replied: "Doc, I'm trying hard, but I can't do it." Following my technique, Dr. Gerz instructed him "to go ahead and try to die from a heart attack" each time his anticipatory anxiety troubled him. When the patient began laughing about his neurotic symptoms, humor entered in and helped him to put distance between himself and his neurosis. He left the office relieved, with instructions to "die at least three times a day of a heart attack"; and instead of "trying hard to go to sleep," he should "try to remain awake." This patient was seen three days later—symptom-free. He had succeeded in using paradoxical intention effectively. He visited Dr. Gerz three times in all, and four weeks later reported that he felt well.

Some cases of successful treatment with paradoxical intention were presented by Dr. Godfryd Kaczanowski, the Clinical Director of the Ontario Hospital, in Toronto, Canada, at the Conference on Existential Psychiatry. A good-looking, well-groomed career woman had been suffering for fifteen years from constant tension, anxiety, periodical depression, feelings of inadequacy, and attacks of panic. She complained that her life was most miserable in spite of the external appearance of success. She had a more than normal growth of soft, slightly dark hair on her arms and legs. At the beginning of her treatment she claimed that her greatest trouble was a horrifying thought that hair might start growing on her face. This fear never left her. She became so frightened that she was unable to look into a mirror except from a considerable distance. She said that she would die the moment she saw hair growing on her face. The underlying psychodynamics were very interesting in this case—just as they usually are. There was narcissistic immaturity, repressed hostility toward her domineering mother, contempt for her deceased father, the unconscious wish to be a man, and, at the same time, the unacceptable strong desire to be possessed by a hairy he-man. The patient gained quite good insight into her emotional situation, she became more relaxed and hopeful, but her fear of hair growing on her face did not abate a bit. She was so scared that she was unable to pronounce the word "hair," except under prodding and then shaking and breaking out in tears. After a considerable number of psychotherapeutic sessions, Dr. Kaczanowski decided to use paradoxical intention. He told her to wish that one hair would grow on her cheek. The woman nearly fainted. She looked at him as if she were seeing a monster. Ten minutes later he was able to lead her to a wall mirror. For the first time in years she looked closely in the mirror and she chose the place on her cheek where she wished one hair to grow. During the next session she chose a place on the other cheek for the second hair to grow. For a long time she could not see any humor in this situation but she had courage. Finally her fear that hair would cover her face was greatly alleviated. Other symptoms were dealt with gradually and the patient regained her ability to enjoy life.

Another patient, a young lady of twenty-five, with many psychoneurotic complaints, came to her psychotherapeutic sessions wearing dark glasses. Dr. Kaczanowski patiently waited for an explanation. During the third session she was able to tell him that her greatest trouble was an irresistible compulsion to look at the genital region of any man she met. For the past three years she always had worn dark glasses outside her own bedroom in order to conceal the movement of her eyes. At the next session she was encouraged to take off her glasses and to have the strong intention to look impudently at the genital region of every man she saw. For a moment the patient looked as though she were paralyzed. Then she slowly took off her glasses and broke into a smile. She claimed that she felt more relaxed than she ever remembered. Over the next few days she not only learned to apply paradoxical intention but actually started to enjoy using this method. It made her somewhat euphoric. In two weeks she reported that her compulsion had disappeared completely.

Although, in many psychotherapeutic circles, it is held that short-term therapy necessarily brings short-lived results, many psychiatrists do not agree. E. A. Gutheil, for example, has called this idea—that "the durability of results corresponds to the length of therapy"—one of "the more common illusions of Freudian orthodoxy." J. H. Schultz maintains that "the frequently expressed misgiving, that cases of symptom removal must necessarily be followed by substitute symptoms or some other internal defection, is, in general, a completely baseless assertion." Ian Stevenson goes beyond this; he believes that "it can no longer be maintained that derepression of past painful experiences is a requirement of recovery, although this may under certain circumstances contribute to it. Nor can spontaneous recoveries be generally attributed only to the operations of suggestions from other persons, an interpretation which seems often to be implied in the use of the concept of 'transference cure.'"

Hans O. Gerz, in his pertinent article, asserts that "one can expect psychoanalysts will claim this type of non-analytic treatment is 'only' symptomatic, and nothing but suggestion, that these patients must develop other symptoms or relapse. . . . Leading psychiatrists have been able to prove that this is not the case. . . . If one needs, however, to apply psychoanalytic theory to explain why paradoxical intention is successful, one could again—only in theory —assume that if phobias can be understood as displaced hostile impulses, the therapist in telling the patient to proceed to do just that which he fears gives the patient permission to act out symbolically his hostile impulses."

Edith Weisskopf-Joelson, an American psychoanalyst and professor at Purdue University, explains the success of paradoxical intention as follows: "By adopting the attitude of paradoxical intention the ego attempts to cheat the punitive superego; the latter uses the symptom as a tool of punishment; the ego discourages such punishment, as it were, by saying to the superego: 'Look, you might as well stop this, since you don't punish me this way. I like my symptom and I experience it as reward rather than as punishment.' In some cases success might be due to still another factor: the obsessive-compulsive neurotic is taught to fight his symptoms by employing a mechanism well suited to his personality and in the use of which he has had much experience. It is the same mechanism which he uses habitually to fight and ridicule the demands of his parents and of society, namely exaggeration to such a degree that the demands become absurd. Thus, the neurosis is fought with its own weapons. . . . Psychoanalytically oriented therapists might argue no real improvement can be achieved with methods such as logotherapy, since the pathology in 'deeper' layers remains untouched, while the therapist limits himself to the strengthening or erecting of defenses. Such conclusions are not free of danger. They may keep us from the awareness of major sources of mental health because these sources do not fit into a specific theoretical framework. We must not forget that such concepts as 'defenses,' 'deeper layers,' and 'adequate functioning on a superficial level with underlying pathology' are theoretical concepts rather than empirical observations."

Dr. Glenn G. Golloway, consultant at the Ypsilanti State

Hospital, contends that paradoxical intention is aimed at manipulating the defenses and not at resolving the "underlying conflict." This, he says, is a perfectly honorable strategy and excellent psychotherapy. "It is no insult to surgery that it does not cure the diseased gall bladder it removes. The patient is better off." Similarly, he thinks that the various explanations of why paradoxical intention works "do not detract from paradoxical intention as a successful technique."

Hans O. Gerz has pointed out: "One often hears the argument that it is 'suggestion' that gets the patients better. Some of my colleagues have attributed the results to my 'authoritarian' approach. Frankl has been accused of having made paradoxical intention successful because he is the great authority, the professor, and helps his patients with 'massive authoritative suggestion.' The fact is, however, that many other psychiatrists have been using Frankl's technique successfully. Cases have been reported as remaining symptom-free for even decades." Our patients often set out to use paradoxical intention with a strong conviction that it simply cannot work—and yet finally succeed. In brief, they succeed not because of, but in spite of, suggestion.

This leads to another question—namely, whether or not paradoxical intention belongs to the persuasive methods. As a matter of fact, paradoxical intention is the exact opposite of persuasion, since it is not suggested that the patient simply suppress his fears (by the rational conviction that they are groundless) but, rather, that he overcome them by exaggerating them! The essential dissimilarity of paradoxical intention and suggestive techniques has been brought to our attention by Polak.

One can cite Donald F. Tweedie's statement (in his book on logotherapy) that "paradoxical intention is not a persuasion method in the traditional sense of the term at all, in spite of the fact that it has been so (mis-)understood. One misses the point in such a criticism, for in many respects paradoxical intention is the exact opposite of therapeutic persuasion. Whereas persuasive techniques would try to convince the patient that 'it can't happen to me,' paradoxical intention instructs the patient to wish, paradoxically, that 'it shall happen to me.'"

To be sure, sometimes persuasion is needed as a technique which must precede the application of the paradoxical intention method. This holds true, for instance, for cases of blasphemous obsessions as they are so often to be met in priests and ministers. My procedure in such cases is as follows: I tell them: "This is obviously a full-fledged case of obsessive neurosis. Do you agree?" When they answer "Yes," I go on to ask: "Are you convinced that my diagnosis is right?" When they say they are, I then ask: "Then what about God? Will not his diagnostic skills infinitely exceed my own?" "Of course," they answer. So I go on: "Now, if God knows that all these blasphemous ideas are of an obsessive-neurotic nature, he certainly will not make you accountable or hold you responsible for these ideas. By the same token, however, there is no need to fight them; on the contrary, your fighting them would rather be the only real blasphemy you run the risk ot committing, inasmuch as thereby you would implicitly declare that God cannot differentiate between what is only an obsession and, on the other hand, a real blasphemy. So stop fighting your obsession if you don't want to offend God." From this moment on the priest or minister can apply paradoxical intention. So we see that sometimes a certain preliminary stage of persuasion is needed before using paradoxical intention. Even before doing so, however, the obsessions often disappear as soon as the patient stops fighting them.

Paradoxical intention is not as superficial as it may at first appear. Something is certainly happening at a deeper level whenever it is applied. Just as a phobic symptom originates beneath the surface of consciousness, so paradoxical intention also appears to affect the deeper level. The humoristic formulations of its method* are based on a restoration of basic trust in being (or, as I have called it in German, *Urvertrauen zum Dasein*). What transpires is essentially more than a change of behavior patterns; rather, it is an existential reorientation (*existentielle Umstellung*).

It is in this respect that paradoxical intention represents a truly "logo"-therapeutic procedure in the truest sense of the word. Jorge Marcelo David, a logotherapist from Argentina, has pointed out that its use is based on what is called in logotherapeutic terms psychonoëtic antagonism (or, sometimes, *die Trotzmacht des Geistes*), by which is meant the specifically human capacity to detach oneself, not only from the world but also from oneself. Paradoxical intention mobilizes this basic human potentiality for the therapeutic purpose of combating neuroses.

Hans O. Gerz has found that "this logotherapeutic technique can also be fully successful in very chronic cases of phobic neurosis." The following case, cited from Dr. Gerz's clinical report in the *Journal of Neuropsychiatry,* will demonstrate this.

---

* A. J. Ungersma, in his book on logotherapy, mentions the following formulations: "A patient who has neurotic fears of heart attacks is urged to talk to his symptom thus: 'Well, I must go out on the street and have a heart attack. Yesterday I had two attacks; let's better the record today and make it three!'" Or a patient may fear that he may kill someone. The therapist may prompt the patient to tell himself: "Let's pick up the knife and go out to kill someone. Yesterday I killed several, today I will kill even more!" A patient with an acute phobic reaction was instructed by Hans O. Gerz (as reported in his remarkable article in the *Journal of Neuropsychiatry*) "not to forget to die at least three times a day of a heart attack." To evoke humor in the patient, he always exaggerates by saying, for instance: "Come on; let's have it; let's pass out all over the place. Show me what a wonderful 'passer-out' you are."

A.V., aged forty-five, married and the mother of a sixteen-year-old son, had a twenty-four-year history of phobic neurosis consisting of severe claustrophobia, such as fear of riding in cars or elevators, of heights, and of crossing bridges. She also had a fear of collapsing, of leaving the house, of open spaces, of being alone, and of becoming paralyzed. She was treated for this condition over the past twenty-four years by various psychiatrists and received, repeatedly, long-term "psychoanalytically-oriented psychotherapy." In addition, she was hospitalized several times and received electro-shock therapy on a number of occasions. Finally lobotomy was suggested. She spent the last four years in a state hospital, where she remained continuously in a disturbed ward. Again she received electro-shock therapy and intensive drug therapy, with barbiturates, phenothiazines, MAO inhibitors, and amphetamine compounds; all to no avail. She had become so "paralyzed" by her numerous phobias that she was unable to leave a narrow area around her bed. She was constantly in acute distress in spite of receiving large amounts of tranquilizers. While in the hospital, she was treated for a year and a half by an experienced clinical psychologist with "intensive analytically-oriented psychotherapy." On March 1, 1959, Dr. Gerz began treatment with paradoxical intention. She was removed from the disturbed ward and was instructed to "try to pass out and become as panicky as possible." After a few weeks of struggle, the patient was able to remain in a ward on the third floor and "unsuccessfully" tried hard to pass out and become paralyzed. She was instructed to walk into the elevator and ride up with the strong intention of passing out and showing Dr. Gerz "how wonderfully she can become panicky and paralyzed." She laughed and said: "I am trying so hard—I can't do it—I don't know what is the matter with me—I can't be afraid any more. I guess I'm trying hard enough to be afraid." From then on she used paradoxical intention "any time I needed it." Then, for the first time in many years, she walked outside alone around the hospital without fear but "constantly trying hard to become panicky and paralyzed." After five months of this therapy she was symptom-free. She returned home and enjoyed her visit, free from phobias for the first time in twenty-four years. Shortly thereafter she was released from the hospital. Since then she has seen Dr. Gerz every two or three months for a check-up "because of gratefulness." She has been living a happy and full life with her family for two and a half years.

D.F., aged forty-one, was referred to Dr. Gerz for the treatment of his phobic condition. In his job as an engineer his phobic neurotic symptoms, such as the trembling of his hand when writing in front of people, interfered greatly with his ability to perform detailed mechanical work in the presence of others. For a long time he had not been able to sign checks when anyone was nearby, and had been greatly anxiety-ridden to the point of becoming panicky when he had to give a report at business meetings. On social occasions he had found himself unable to lift a cup or a glass without fear of trembling and spilling the contents. At all costs he avoided lighting another person's cigarette. The patient was instructed to "jump right into" the phobic situations rather than avoid them as he had been doing. He was asked to seek every possible opportunity to demonstrate before groups "what a wonderful shaker" he was. He was to show others "how nervous he could get and how he could spill his coffee all over the place." Having suffered so long from these crippling neurotic symptoms, he gladly followed Dr. Gerz's advice. As a result, after three sessions the patient reported: "I cannot shake. I cannot tremble. I cannot get panicky any more. No matter how hard I try." Subsequently, in the course of logotherapy, Dr. Gerz was able to help the patient to actualize his latent spiritual potentials and thus to find a new meaning to his existence. He recovered from his noögenic neurosis.

To illustrate the treatment of the obsessive-compulsive patient, I should like to quote another of Dr. Gerz's cases. P.K., who had been diagnosed as suffering from schizophrenia, was treated over the years with psychoanalytically-oriented therapy. He also received from various psychiatrists both intensive drug therapy and electro-shock therapy. None of these treatments brought him measurable relief. When he first came to Dr. Gerz, he was in a tense and agitated state and quite tearfully related that for many years he had suffered various neurotic symptoms. "For more than twenty years I have gone through a life of hell! I keep it all a secret, but my wife knows. I am only relieved when I am asleep!" His greatest fear, he said, was that he might, when sitting in a barber's chair, or driving a car, or sitting at a counter, "grab somebody's penis." This would result in fear of losing his job and disgracing himself in public. He feared he might even confess to a sex crime that he had not committed. Further, he complained of an inability to concentrate, of restlessness, and of a fear that his heart might stop beating. He also feared he might scream out loud. He would hold his hands tightly to his body in order not to lose control and not "disgrace" himself. Jealousy of his wife was the latest obsession he had developed. He constantly wondered whether he loved his wife, whether he would disgrace himself or become insane. He felt compelled to look at certain objects and places. He had never been able to go on vacations with his family because of his severe neurosis. Twice a week over a period of six months he was given logotherapeutic treatments. As in previous cases, symptom after symptom was removed. His obsessive doubts about his love for his wife disappeared once he adopted the attitude of: "Who wants to love his wife?" When he was instructed to seek every possible opportunity on the street, in restaurants, in the car, at work, to grab a man's penis, he started to laugh at his obsessions and they completely disappeared. During the treatment he went by plane, for the first time in his life, to Florida on a vacation. When he returned, he reported he had tried very hard to be as panicky as possible on the plane and to go around "grabbing everybody"; instead, he experienced no anxiety and enjoyed his vacation. He sees Dr. Gerz twice a year at most and is presently enjoying a normal and full life with his family and is completely symptom-free.

Undoubtedly the reader has noticed that most of the cases presented here were treated by logotherapists other than the author. This presentation has been deliberate, for it serves to indicate that what works is the method rather than the personality of its creator (though the personal factor must never be neglected).

To illustrate the application of paradoxical intention, Dr. Gerz included the following two case histories in the introductory paper that he presented to the Symposium on Logotherapy at the Sixth International Congress of Psychotherapy (London, 1964):

A twenty-nine-year-old mother of three children had a ten-year history of phobic neurosis for which she had been treated by various psychiatrists. She was hospitalized five and a half years ago in a private sanitarium, where she received electro-convulsive therapy; for two years prior to seeing Dr. Gerz she was treated by means of psychoanalysis. She gained insight into the underlying dynamics of her neurosis, but her symptoms persisted. When she consulted Dr. Gerz, she suffered from multiple phobias: fear of heights, of being alone, of eating in restaurants because she was afraid of vomiting and becoming panicky; fear of going into supermarkets, subways, large crowds, of driving alone, of waiting at stop lights; and fear of screaming and swearing aloud in church during Mass. Paradoxical intention was explained and discussed in detail. She was instructed to wish for whatever she was afraid would happen to her. She was told to dine out with her husband and friends, and vomit into people's faces and create the greatest possible mess. Two weeks later her husband complained that now she was going out *too* much. She began to drive her car to stores, hairdressers, banks, "trying to get as panicky as possible," and proudly reported: "I went there all alone." Six weeks later she said: "My social life is killing me." She had gained seven pounds. Shortly thereafter she drove by herself to Dr. Gerz's office, about fifty miles round trip. "I have been driving all over the place." Four months after the beginning of treatment, she traveled with her husband to New York City, across the George Washington Bridge, through the Lincoln Tunnel, and even attended a bon voyage party on a lower deck of an ocean liner. She went on a "delicious" bus and subway ride through New York City. Finally she went into an elevator in the Empire State Building and rode all the way to the top. Later she remarked to Dr. Gerz: "We had a wonderful time." Within seven months the patient had gained twenty pounds; and her husband said: "My wife is a different person. She looks like a woman now, and she even gets pleasure out of sexual intercourse." Meanwhile she gave birth to their fourth child without any difficulty, and now lives a normal life with her family. Treatment was combined with Diazepam, 15 mg. daily. She has remained free of symptoms for the past two years.

Another of Dr. Gerz's case histories concerned a fifty-six-year-old lawyer, who was married and the father of an eighteen-year-old son. His neurosis began seventeen years ago, when he was still in private practice. "All of a sudden, out of a clear blue sky, an awful obsession came into my mind that I had defrauded the government by underestimating my income tax by some three hundred dollars, even though I made it out as honestly as I knew how. I began to worry that it might be several hundred dollars more. Try as I might, I could not get these ideas out of my head." The patient imagined himself being prosecuted for fraud, going to jail, receiving newspaper publicity, and finally losing his job. He was hospitalized at a private sanitarium, receiving psychotherapy and twenty-five treatments with electro-convulsive therapy, without improvement. Meanwhile he had to give up his law practice. He went back to his job as a court clerk and continued to fight his obsessions, suffering many sleepless nights. Further obsessions developed. They shifted from day to day, and week to week. "I would get rid of one in a day or two, and it would be replaced by another." He developed the habit of checking and rechecking things, such as the wheels of his car and things he did at his office. He became obsessed about his insurance policies, fearing that perhaps one had expired or that one did not include the protection he wanted. It was at this time that he bought special insurance from Lloyds of London, because he feared he might make a mistake in court and be sued. He felt compelled to check and recheck just about everything, including his various insurance policies, which he had locked in a special steel box in a safe at home. The policies themselves were in envelopes secured by a number of strings. His fear of being sued was so great that off and on he had to go through the involved procedure of taking out his policies and making sure he was insured properly; and when he finally had put them back into the steel box in the safe, he wondered whether he had really checked everything. He had to repeat this process over and over until he finally "felt certain" that he was "safe." In court he became so completely incapacitated that he needed to be hospitalized. It was at this time that Dr. Gerz began treating him with paradoxical intention. He was in logotherapy for four months three times weekly, and was instructed to use the following "paradoxical intentions": "I don't give a damn any more. Hell, who wants to be a perfectionist? I hope I get sued very soon, the sooner the better." Dr. Gerz instructed him to try "to get sued three times a day and get his money's worth from Lloyds of London!" He was told to wish that he would make many, many mistakes, really mess up his work, and show his secretaries that he was the greatest "mistake maker" in the world. No doubt, Dr. Gerz's complete lack of anxiety could be adopted by the patient, as a humorous situation was created and as Dr. Gerz kept telling the patient on each visit: "For heaven's sake, are you still around! I've been looking through the newspapers hoping to read about the big scandalous lawsuit." At these comments the patient would burst into laughter, and he finally adopted the attitude of: "To hell with everything. I don't care if I make mistakes; I don't give a damn what happens. Let 'em sue me." He would laugh and say: "My insurance companies will go bankrupt." About a year after therapy began, he said: "This formula has worked a miracle for me. Dr. Gerz has made a new person out of me in four months. I occasionally get a worry, but now I am able to cope with it. I know how to handle it."

The following patient was treated by means of paradoxical intention by one of Dr. Gerz's assistants. A.A., aged thirty-one, married, suffered for nine years from a phobic neurosis with fear of insomnia, claustrophobia, and psychotophobia. She complained of an inability to remain in church or at work, or to stay at home alone, and forced her husband to be with her constantly. She developed a fear of crowds and water, and finally completely confined herself to her home. She had been treated off and on in state hospitals and also in the outpatient clinic of a medical school. During her treatment she received psychoanalytically-oriented therapy, electro-shock therapy, and large amounts of various tranquilizers. Psychological testing indicated that "individual psychotherapy would probably be extremely difficult." This patient was treated successfully within six weeks. She has remained completely symptom-free since her release from the hospital more than three years ago.

Now let us turn to another case from Dr. Gerz's report:

S.H., aged thirty-one, suffered for more than twelve years from a phobic neurosis with the same symptomatology as the last-reported case. Though hospitalized many times and given all types of therapy, the patient still retained her symptoms. A lobotomy was performed, but her condition remained unimproved. Treated with paradoxical intention, she recovered within six weeks. She has remained symptom-free since her discharge from the hospital three and a half years ago.

Dr. Gerz feels that paradoxical intention is a specific and effective treatment for phobic and obsessive-compulsive conditions. "The patient suffering from obsessive-compulsive neurosis can, with this technique, recover or at least be greatly relieved." At times Dr. Gerz has found it helpful to supplement logotherapy with small doses of Librium and Tofranil combined, particularly in the early phase of treatment. "Anti-depressive and anti-anxiety medication will make it easier for the patient to have the courage to apply paradoxical intention. As soon as the treatment shows results, medication is discontinued, and the patient, having become convinced that it works, continues quite readily to use the technique of paradoxical intention."

Such a combination of paradoxical intention and drug treatment is justified not only from the theoretical viewpoint but also from my experience in clinical practice. The following case is a good example:

Anton R. was seized by anxiety attacks five years ago. He was working on his father's farm and suddenly became anxious that he might hurt either himself or the horses that were in his care. Because of additional suicidal obsessions, he tried to avoid sharp objects. The condition ultimately became so severe that he was no longer able to use a knife when he ate because he was afraid he would kill himself with it. Walking on a bridge or seeing an open window aroused the fear that he might jump down without willing or wishing it. In addition, he felt a compulsion to repeat everything. Finally he scarcely was able to perform his daily work. He received some treatment at various periods, including electro-shock therapy when he was institutionalized, but there were no beneficial effects. In the Neurological Department of the Polyclinic Hospital he first was given Chlorpromazin, later Tofranil, and finally new tranquilizing drugs as well as so-called energizers. Not until he was given Marplan was Dr. Kocourek successful in inviting the patient to apply paradoxical intention. In addition to Marplan he also received Mellaril. The field had thus been plowed. When leaving Dr. Kocourek's office and going downstairs to his own room, the patient said to himself: "Oh, I am afraid of jumping down the stairwell. To be sure, yesterday I did so sixty times. Now let's do it a hundred and sixty times." For the first time the patient was observed laughing. On the second day of treatment by paradoxical intention, the patient said to himself during a meal: "Oh, yesterday I ran the fork into my stomach ten times. Today I will enjoy doing it some more." From then on he daily applied paradoxical intention and began to be a most helpful person, always ready to be of assistance to his roommates. He went home for the Christmas holidays, and after about two weeks he was readmitted in excellent condition. His father, who came in with him, reported joyously that the whole family was extremely surprised and overjoyed at how much he had improved. Nothing pathological was noticeable in his behavior any longer, the father said. The patient could use a fork when eating, like a normal person. He himself reported that he was using paradoxical intention again and again, each time with success. Astonishingly he even succeeded in smoking a cigarette in the courtyard of the farm, which he had not been able to do before because of his obsession that he might kindle the hay and burn down the whole farm. Now, however, he simply told himself: "Didn't I kindle the hay a hundred times yesterday? So I'll do it again today, one hundred and one times. Why not burn the whole farm down?" Eventually the obsessive ideas did not occur. Finally he was dismissed completely free of any obsessions or compulsions and in a very optimistic mood. For five years he has been living a normal life.

Such therapy utilizes either tranquilizers in order to smooth the symptoms from which the patient has to detach himself, or energizers in order to strengthen the patient's capacity for self-detachment (as used in paradoxical intention).

The case of Otto G., a customs official with a compulsion to repeat and check everything, may show that there are also patients who can best be helped by simultaneous logotherapy and pharmacotherapy using Tofranil. Otto G., aged twenty-six, had been meticulous and scrupulous, in the pattern of his father, as long as he could remember. When he was a schoolboy this compulsion took so much time that he did not have enough left for his studies. When he was an apprentice it made him too slow, and in his work as a country policeman it interfered with his professional duties. In his work as a customs official his meticulousness was rather welcomed by his superiors, but he wanted to be relieved of it. He was depressed and feared that he would become psychotic. His condition did not improve during a month of hospitalization two years ago. Last year a short-term logotherapy by my associate Dr. Eva Niebauer relieved his condition for the first time, but recently his compulsion returned and he was readmitted to the Polyclinic Hospital. My present associate there, Dr. Kurt Kocourek, encouraged him to deal with the compulsion in an ironical way, to take the wind out of the obsession by "deliberately intending to become the most disorderly patient in the ward." For example, he should try to disrupt the order on his bedside table. However, the patient resisted, declaring that all his compulsions were tied up with his *Weltanschauung*. It was only after he was given Tofranil that he was able to respond to paradoxical intention. For several weeks a number of tranquilizers and energizers had been tried without success, but with the administration of Tofranil the condition changed. The patient reported joyously that he had succeeded in applying paradoxical intention by "intending disorder." He described how he could get along without striving for 100 per cent perfection, the pattern with which he had lived as a *Weltanschauung*. It is to be noted that there is no indication that any suggestive factors were present during the drug treatment, since several different ones had been tried prior to Tofranil. The patient left the hospital after about five weeks, hopeful about starting a new life. In a non-specific way Tofranil had made him available for logotherapy by loosening the typical rigidity of the obsessive-compulsive neurotic personality. It was as if a kick had been given which mobilized the human capacity for self-detachment, so that, with the help of the sense of humor which is inherent in paradoxical intention, the patient could put himself at a distance from his neurosis.

This instance demonstrates that in exceptional cases drug therapy proves to be an indispensable adjunct to the logotherapeutic treatment.* Generally, however, logotherapy can be applied without the assistance of drugs, as a matter of course.

In recent years there have been increasing reports of the use

---

* Dr. Gerz treated sixteen pseudoneurotic schizophrenics with either phobic or obsessive-compulsive symptoms masking a schizophrenic process, making use of combined intensive phenothiazine therapy and paradoxical intention. He had eleven recoveries, one improvement, two failures; two patients discontinued the therapy prematurely.

of paradoxical intention. Authors from various countries, as well as those collaborating in the work of the Neurological Department of the Polyclinic Hospital, have published results of the clinical application of this technique. In addition to David (Buenos Aires), mention may be made of the associates of Ernst Kretschmer (Psychiatric University-Clinic of Tübingen), Langen and Volhard, Prill (Gynecological University-Clinic of Würzburg), and Rehder (Hamburg). At the Fourth International Congress for Psychotherapy, held in Barcelona in 1958, Ledermann (London) declared: "The results (of logotherapy) are not to be denied. I have found the method helpful in cases of obsessional neurosis." Frick (Bolzano, Italy) goes still further by stating that there are cases of severe obsessive-compulsive neurosis in which a logotherapeutic procedure is the "only therapeutic way," and refers to some cases in which electro-shock therapy had failed and logotherapy alone proved successful. Lopez-Ibor (University of Madrid) makes a similar statement. In addition to my associates, Kocourek and Niebauer, who have published papers about paradoxical intention, N. Toll reports that she has been using it successfully for over six years. Bazzi (University of Rome) has even worked out special indicators to enable the psychiatrist to distinguish between those cases in which paradoxical intention should be applied and those in which the autogenous training method of Schultz is indicated.

De-reflection

In cases which display anticipatory anxiety, the fear of some pathological event (which thus, ironically, precipitates that event), one may frequently observe an analogous phenomenon. This is the compulsion to self-observation or, as it is called in logotherapy, hyper-reflection. In the etiology of a neurosis one often finds an excess of attention as well as intention. This is especially true in cases of insomnia in which the forced intention to sleep is accompanied by the forced attention to observe whether the intention is becoming effective or not.

Insomniac patients often report that they become especially aware of the problem of falling asleep when they go to bed. Of course, this very attention inhibits the sleeping process and helps to perpetuate the waking state. Paradoxical intention can also be applied in such cases. The fear of sleeplessness results in a hyper-intention to sleep which incapacitates the patient to do so since sleep presupposes the utmost of relaxation. Dubois, the famous French psychiatrist, once compared sleep to a dove which has landed near one's hand and stays there as long as one does not pay any attention to it; if one attempts to grab it, it quickly flies away. But how can one remove the anticipatory anxiety which is the pathological basis of hyper-intention and brings about a vicious circle that increases the disturbance? The hyper-intention to fall asleep must be replaced by the paradoxical intention to stay awake.

In order to take the wind out of the sails of his fearful expectation, we advise the patient not to try to force sleep, since his body will automatically obtain the necessary amount of sleep. Therefore, he can safely try to do just the opposite, to stay awake as long as possible. In other words, the hyper-intention to fall asleep, arising from the anticipatory anxiety of not being able to fall asleep, should be replaced by the paradoxical intention not to fall asleep, which soon will be followed by sleep.

It is noteworthy that this procedure, in cases of insomnia, has subsequently been applied by two other workers in the field. One advises his patients to keep their eyes open as long as possible, while the other recommends to doctors who work with hospitalized patients that they let the patients punch a timeclock every quarter hour. He reports that after a very few fifteen-minute intervals they succumb to increasing fatigue and sleepiness.

However, there are patients whose sleep is disturbed so that they are awakened early in the morning by a noisy neighborhood, for instance, and cannot sleep further because of anger at their neighbors and their hyper-intention to fall asleep again. I advise such patients simply to imagine that they are urged to leave their bed to do something disagreeable—for example, shoveling snow or coal at five o'clock in the morning. If they yield to this fantasy, they suddenly feel so tired that they fall asleep again.

I have said that a sleepless patient must not think of sleep or sleeplessness. Of course, this advice should not be given in a negative way such as this, but rather positively, for otherwise the patient's attention would be centered on the problem all the more. Instead, we have him focus his attention on something positive. We invite him to face his everyday problems. With respect to sleep, he is to try to remain sleepless for the very purpose of dwelling upon such matters.

Forcing the patient to divert his attention in negative terms would have much the same result as the advice given to a man who, once upon a time, sought to make pure gold. He was told to mix together ten ounces of copper, five ounces of mercury, two ounces of onions, and eight ounces of pepper. This mixture was to be heated slowly over a medium gas flame for ten minutes. He was told that he would obtain pure gold from this mixture if, during these ten minutes, he did not think of a chameleon. Never in his life had the man thought of a chameleon until then, when he was forbidden to do so. During these ten minutes, in spite of himself, he continually thought of a chameleon! And that is why he could not obtain pure gold.

This is tantamount to what really happened to Immanuel Kant. He once caught Lampe, his servant, in an act of thievery and felt obliged to discharge him. It hurt Kant to the depth of his heart that after living together for so long he had to discharge him. So he put a large sign above his desk: "Lampe must be forgotten." Of course, as long as the sign remained he was reminded of Lampe.

This pattern holds true not only for insomnia, but also for neurosis in general. Again and again we may notice that, in addition to anticipatory anxiety, which is so commonly observed in the anamnesis of neuroses, the neurotic condition is further reinforced by crippling hyper-reflection. This is illustrated in the story of the centipede who ran very well until he decided one day to observe just how he ran. The more he became conscious of the process, the more difficult it was to function, and finally he could only lie in a ditch in despair.

In reference to hyper-reflection, logotherapy makes use of a therapeutic device which I call "de-reflection." Just as paradoxical intention is designed to counteract anticipatory anxiety, de-reflection is intended to counteract this compulsive inclination to self-observation. Through paradoxical intention the patient tries to ridicule his symptoms, while he learns to "ignore" them through de-reflection. The following accounts will show this technique in a clinical setting:

Miss B. compulsively observed the act of swallowing; having become uncertain, she anxiously expected that the food would "go down the wrong way," or that she would choke. Anticipatory anxiety and compulsive self-observation disturbed her eating to the extent that she became very thin. She was taught to trust her organism and its automatically regulated functioning. The patient was therapeutically de-reflected by the formula: "I don't need to watch my swallowing, because I don't really need to swallow, for actually I don't swallow, but rather *it* does." And thus she was able to leave to the *it*, the unconscious, the unconscious and unintentional act of swallowing.

Gerhardt B., nineteen years old, suffered since he was six from a speech disturbance which began during a storm in which a bolt of lightning struck near him. For eight days he could not speak at all. He was given psychoanalytic treatment for five months, and took speech and breathing exercises for four additional months. We attempted to make one thing clear to him: that he would have to give up any ambition of becoming a good orator. We further explained that to the degree to which he became resigned to being a poor speaker, he would, as a matter of fact, improve his speech. For then he would pay less attention to the "how" and more to the "what" of his speech.

I should like to quote from the paper that Dr. Godfryd Kaczanowski, Clinical Director of the Ontario Hospital, presented at the Conference on Existential Psychiatry in Toronto, Canada. He said that "de-reflection is less specific and more difficult than paradoxical intention," yet it is also "a still more logotherapeutic procedure." He then briefly summarized one of his own cases.

256

An unmarried professional man of thirty-eight had stopped work ing eight years before he came to see Dr. Kaczanowski. Each year he paid his dues to his professional organization, so he remained "in good standing," but for the past two years his name was not listed in the yearly register of his profession. He was living alone in a comfortable small apartment and had a moderate income from investments. For ten years he had been troubled with sudden, unexpected bouts of diarrhea. At times he soiled his pants; on two different occasions it happened while he was at a dance. He avoided all company and stayed at home almost all the time. He ventured out to a store or a restaurant only if he could be sure that he could reach the washroom in a matter of seconds. He had been treated by a number of good physicians, among them two psychiatrists, and had undergone two abdominal operations in which sections of intestine were removed. He became desperate. During his first interview with Dr. Kaczanowski, he made an eye-opening statement: "Doctor, I don't justify my existence." Dr. Kaczanowski agreed with him. He even offered him some proof by pointing out that he had not reacted to the omission of his name from the professional register. He almost did not exist, not only as a professional man but as a man, as a human being with freedom and responsibility. He had submitted completely to his bowels. They were his master; they dictated to him what he should and what he should not do. For the next few weeks Dr. Kaczanowski was worried that he might commit suicide. Finally the patient started to see that he had potentialities, that he could try to rebel against his tyrannical bowels. In a little more than a year he was free again and was able to make decisions. It was a great day for him, and for Dr. Kaczanowski, when he started to work again. The washroom is, of course, close to his office, but his bowels don't give him more trouble than most normal people's. Dr. Kaczanowski sees him now once every few months and, if he would not ask him about his bowels, he would forget to mention them.

As we see, de-reflection can only be attained to the degree to which the patient's awareness is directed toward positive aspects. The patient must be de-reflected *from* his disturbance *to* the task at hand or the partner involved. He must be reoriented toward his specific vocation and mission in life. In other words, he must be confronted with the logos of his existence! It is not the neurotic's *self-concern*, whether pity or contempt, which breaks the vicious circle; the cue to cure is *self-commitment*.

This conviction is supported by Gordon Allport, who once said: "As the focus of striving shifts from the conflict to selfless goals the life as a whole becomes sounder even though the neurosis may never completely disappear."

Sigmund Freud once used de-reflection. Bruno Walter had complained of pains in his arms, but when questioned by Freud, he admitted that the pains disappeared as soon as he committed himself wholeheartedly to his work at the Vienna Opera House. Freud advised him to go to Sicily and visit the art treasures there. What was needed was not analysis but de-reflection from his troubles—de-reflection, however, with an artistic content.

Let us, in conclusion, review the indications of paradoxical intention and de-reflection from the perspective of what logotherapy presents as the four characteristic patterns of response to neurotic problems:

I. *Wrong Passivity*: By this is meant the behavioral pattern that may be observed in cases of anxiety neurosis or phobic conditions or both—namely, the withdrawal from those situations in which the patient, because of his anticipatory anxiety, expects his fears to recur. Here we are dealing with the pattern in which he "flees from fear."

II. *Wrong Activity*: This behavioral pattern is characteristic, first of all, of obsessive-compulsive neurosis. (1) The individual, rather than trying to avoid conflict situations, *fights* against his obsessive ideas and neurotic compulsions and thus reinforces them. This struggle is motivated by two basic fears: (a) that the obsessive ideas indicate an imminent, or actual, psychotic condition and (b) that the compulsion will someday result in an attempt at homicide or suicide. However, fighting against obsessions and compulsions increases their strength and their power to plague the obsessive-compulsive patient in the same manner as flight from fear (arising from fright of fear) increases fear in anxiety neurosis, since counter-pressure increases the pressure. (2) Another aspect of "wrong activity" may be observed in sexual neurosis, namely, a struggle *for* something, rather than *against* something: a striving for orgasm and potency. This very "pursuit of happiness," however, again is foredoomed to fail.

In contrast to these negative, neurotic, "wrong" behavioral patterns, there are two positive ones that are effective therapeutic counter-measures to neurotic behavior:

III. *Right Passivity*: This pattern is illustrated by the patient who, through paradoxical intention, ridicules his symptoms rather than trying either to run away from them (phobias) or to fight them (obsessive compulsions).

IV. *Right Activity*: Through de-reflection the patient is enabled to "ignore" his neurosis by focusing his attention away from himself. This is possible, however, only to the extent to which he becomes reoriented to the unique meaning of his life. And to enable him to find that meaning is precisely the task of existential analysis.

In cases of psychosis logotherapy is applied in a different way than it is with neuroses. In psychoses the therapist must bring about a detachment of the patient's personality from the psychotic process with which he is afflicted. Such self-detachment, however, is based on that psycho-noëtic antagonism which is an inherent capacity in a human being—that is, man's faculty as a spiritual being to freely take a stand toward inner as well as outer conditions. This means that in psychoses logotherapy is essentially a therapy directed to the aspect of personality that remains healthy, for the aspect that has become diseased is open only to other treatments, such as drug and shock therapy.

ENDOGENOUS DEPRESSION

First some general remarks about endogenous depression. In conjunction with drug treatment and shock therapy, logotherapy must support the patient by making him aware again and again of his extremely good prognosis so that he may believe that his suffering will pass. The patient must be prevented from making value judgments while in a state of depression. Instead, he should say to himself: "Whatever I see is gray. But though the sky may be cloudy momentarily, the sun still exists. Likewise, I cannot see the meaning of my life during the depressive phase, yet the meaning exists." The patient must stop fighting his depression, for he will never succeed in such a struggle and his tendency to self-reproach will be strengthened by his failure. I frequently have the patient put in a hospital just to demonstrate to him that he is really ill and not, as is so often assumed by the patients themselves (because of their tendency to depreciate themselves), that he is "merely lacking will power."

In a neurosis, the patient's sense of responsibility should be challenged; a patient suffering from endogenous depression, however, must be relieved of his monstrous burden of guilt feelings. To analyze these pathological feelings psychologically, even in an existential analysis, may be extremely dangerous, inasmuch as it could serve to increase the patient's pathological tendency toward self-reproach. Might this not result in a suicide attempt?

Perhaps a special comment should be made in reference to

the application of paradoxical intention to situations involving suicidal ideas and impulses. It cannot be too strongly stressed that it is to be used only when suicide is the content of a true obsession, which is being *resisted* (and being reinforced by this resistance) by the patient. In a situation where the patient is prone to *identify* himself with the suicidal impulse (as may be the case in endogenous depression), paradoxical intention would serve to increase the danger and is, therefore, absolutely contraindicated. This should forcefully remind us that there can be no differential therapy unless it is based on a thorough and solid differential diagnosis.

In order to disclose the danger of suicide even where it might be concealed I have developed a simple diagnostic method. This procedure will enable the psychiatrist to determine quickly the presence or absence of suicidal intentions. The patient is asked two questions, the first of which is: Are you planning to commit suicide? The answer is invariably in the negative, for if the patient truly has no such intention, he will say so, and if he is merely dissimulating his real intention, he will also deny that he plans to commit suicide. The second question is designed to catch the dissimulating patient off guard and so identify him: Why not? The patient who has answered the first question truthfully will have a ready answer for the second. He may assert his responsibility to himself, to his family, to his vocation, or, perhaps, to his religious convictions. On the other hand, the patient who is trying to deceive, in order to avoid having his plans thwarted, or perhaps to obtain a discharge from the hospital, will have no such ready answer. Moreover, he will display a typical behavior pattern in which he stirs restlessly in his chair and is unable to give any plausible answer to this unexpected question, any substantial argument in favor of continued living, as the depressed person feels completely hopeless and, indeed, believes that he has nothing to live for.

Let me summarize: Paradoxical intention should not be applied in psychotic depressions, but only in cases in which the individual is haunted by the obsessive idea that he might attempt suicide. The obsessive individual doesn't wish to commit suicide, but rather fears to do so. That is the type of patient whom you may encourage, ironically of course, to attempt suicide.

Now I should like to offer another stratagem, designed to assist the psychiatrist not in the diagnosis but in the therapy of suicide-proneness. It consists of using one of the typical tendencies in endogenous-depressive patients as a weapon against the other—that is, the tendency toward scrupulosity is utilized against the tendency toward suicide. The psychiatrist addresses himself to the patient as follows: If you commit suicide while in my care in our hospital's outpatient ward, my associate as well as I will get into serious trouble. We could be fired and even lose our licenses as doctors because we let you stay out of an institution. Thus the scrupulosity acts as a counterweight in combating the suicidal tendency. It goes without saying that one cannot make use of this stratagem in severe cases, only in marginal ones—that is, when there is some doubt about the necessity of institutionalization in a given case.

Now let us turn to schizophrenic cases. Here logotherapy is far from yielding a causal treatment. As a psychotherapeutic adjunct, however, the logotherapeutic technique of de-reflection is recommended for such patients too. The forthcoming volume *Modern Psychotherapeutic Practice: Advances in Treatment,* edited by Arthur Burton (Science and Behavior Books, Palo Alto, California), includes some tape-recorded sessions with schizophrenic patients which demonstrate the way in which de-reflection is applied.

However, at least in some instances, paradoxical intention seems to be effective. For example, a patient at the Polyclinic Hospital reported to one of my doctors in the first interview that she had read about paradoxical intention and had applied it successfully with reference to the "voices" that she was hearing. She had taken her acoustic hallucinations for a neurosis.

But de-reflection can serve only to support other forms of therapy in schizophrenic cases. At all events, one should not lean too heavily on psychodynamics in such cases, for this might well force the patient into a dangerous self-centeredness, whereas reorienting him to a potential meaning to his existence and the task of actualizing such meaning allows for a maximum of de-reflection. It is in such cases that we become most aware of the fact that the psychotherapeutic process consists of a continuous chain of im provisations. The psychotherapist is faced with the twofold task of always considering the uniqueness of each person as well as the uniqueness of the life situation with which this person has to cope. What is demanded of him is to show the patient that he can attain a purposeful life, to help him look upon even his plight in terms of purpose, and to enhance his sense of identity not by reflecting upon the underlying psychodynamics by which he is entangled, but by pointing out the potential meaning which is waiting to be fulfilled by him despite his mental disease and its effects.

Concluding Remarks

It has frequently been asked to what extent psychotherapy can be taught and learned. The choice of an appropriate method to be applied in any particular case depends not only upon the uniqueness of the patient involved, but also upon the uniqueness of the situation involved. After all, individualization and improvisation too can be taught and learned, at least to some degree. To be sure, this can be accomplished only by attending clinical lectures that include case demonstrations and by attending therapeutic sessions in both individual and group settings, preferably in a hospital. This, I think, is in fact the chief source of therapeutic knowledge. A training analysis certainly is of advantage, but one should not overlook or forget the fact that, in a sense, it acquaints the trainee with only one case—his own. And perhaps his own is not a really instructive case.

Every good doctor has been unconsciously a logotherapist all along. But if logotherapy had nothing more to offer than making conscious, explicit, and methodological what had formerly been achieved by intuition and improvisation, that in itself would be a worthwhile achievement, for by that very fact it would have become teachable and learnable.

IV

From

Secular Confession

to

Medical Ministry

IV From Secular Confession to Medical Ministry

In the first chapter we endeavored to show that psychotherapy was in need of supplementing, that therapy should be extended to take in the spiritual sphere. The following section is concerned with the "possibility" of achieving such a supplement.

Paracelsus opined: "It is a lame creature who calleth himself a physician and he be void of philosophy and know her not." We have now to ask ourselves whether a physician who does feel himself something of a philosopher is entitled to bring his philosophical views to bear on treatment.

In our first chapter we laid down the guiding principles of logotherapy, which centers its gaze upon human responsibility, and pointed out the need for existential analysis as an analysis of existence in terms of responsibleness. Existential analysis lays weight on the all-inclusive task quality of existence. It makes for feeling existence profoundly as responsibleness, and in so doing starts an inward process whose therapeutic value we have already discussed.

The road from logotherapy to existential analysis lies behind us. At a certain point logotherapy passed over into existential analysis. The question now arises whether the psychotherapist should or may go beyond this point.

The aim of psychotherapy, especially psychoanalysis, has been secular confession; the aim of logotherapy, especially existential analysis, is medical ministry.

This statement must not be misunderstood. Medical ministry is not intended to be a substitute for religion, nor even for psychotherapy as it has hitherto been known. Rather, as we have already said, it is to be a supplement. We have nothing to say, would have nothing to offer, to the religious person who finds security* in the

---

* Perhaps religion may be said to be ultimately man's experience of his own fragmentariness and relativity against a background which must properly be called "the Absolute"—although it is somewhat arrogant to do so, so *absolutely* must the Absolute be conceived. Perhaps we may at most speak of something which is non-fragmentary, non-relative. But then what is this experience of fragmentariness and relativity in its relation to something "irrelatable"? It is simple: the sense of being sheltered, safe. The religious person feels his shelter and safety to lie in the realm of transcendence. But for the seeker there is always what he has sought. And so this "what he has sought" is nevertheless "given" to the seeker—given not in its "whatness" (as something found would be) but in its pure "thatness." Thus intentionality breaks through immanence, and nevertheless comes to a halt when confronted with transcendence. (After all, that was phenomenology's final conclusion; it came to a halt before the intentional act as an ultimate—just as existential philosophy does in the case of existential decision.) Therefore, for the religious person also, God is always transcendent —but also always intended. For the religious person God is forever silent—but also forever invoked. And for the religious person God is the inexpressible—but is always addressed (see note on page 62).

270

mystery of his metaphysics. But a special problem is involved when the distinctly non-religious person turns to his physician because he is yearning for an answer to questions that profoundly stir him.

If, then, it should be construed that medical ministry is being offered as a surrogate for religion, we can only say that nothing could be further from our intention. When we practice logotherapy or existential analysis, we are medical men and wish to remain so. We have no thought of competing with the clergy. But we do want to extend the sphere of medical activity and avail ourselves of the full possibilities of medical treatment. What we must now show is that opportunities of this sort do exist, and how they can be used.

The psychotherapeutic significance of the confessional has been the subject of many studies. In general counseling as well as psychiatric treatment, it has been abundantly proved that the mere act of talking out the personal problem affords genuine therapeutic relief to the patient. What we have said in the preceding sections, in connection with the therapy of anxiety and obsessional neurosis, about the benefit to the patient of objectifying his symptoms and achieving perspective on them, holds also for talking things out in general, for talking out psychological conflicts. To share one's troubles is literally to share them, to divide them in half.

Psychoanalysts speak of a "confession compulsion," implying that the desire to speak is in itself a kind of symptom. From the one-sided psychoanalytic outlook, the confession compulsion necessarily appears to be a symptom rather than—to employ Oswald Schwarz's antithesis—an "achievement." But the urge to confess need not necessarily be attributed to neurosis; it can also be a moral achievement, as the following case shows.

A patient was sent to a psychiatrist because she was troubled by an intense fear of syphilis. It developed that she was suffering from a general neurotic hypochondria. She misinterpreted neuralgic pains as signs of a luetic infection. In terms of what we have said about neurotic hypochondria, syphilidophobia can be considered the specific expression of a guilty conscience about sexual matters. But in this particular case the patient did not have these sexual guilts. It was true that she had been the victim of a rape, but she was sensible enough to have no guilt feelings about that isolated sexual experience. Her guilt feeling had reference to another aspect of the matter entirely: that she had not told her husband about the incident. Here she was again being sensible; she deeply loved her husband and had wanted to spare his feelings, since she knew him to be a distinctly suspicious person. Her confession compulsion was not a symptom at all. It therefore was not susceptible to the ordinary interpretations of psychotherapy; what was required was the logotherapeutic methods of matter-of-fact discussions, of taking the moral issues at face value. In fact the confession compulsion promptly vanished the moment the patient realized that in the concrete case her continued silence was an obligation she owed to her love. She perceived that there was no need to make any confession since only guilt can be confessed, and she felt herself to be free of any real guilt. Moreover—here we have an analogy to a case mentioned in another connection—she would only have conveyed quite the wrong impression to her suspicious husband and would have been deceiving him with the truth. This patient, then, could only be reassured when her conscience was reassured. And her conscience was not troubled over the sexual incident, but only in regard to the dubious moral obligation to confess.

In progressing from logotherapy through existential analysis to medical ministry, we must deal increasingly with those existential and spiritual problems which psychotherapy can never entirely escape. As soon as logotherapy ventures upon a "psychotherapy in spiritual terms," it touches upon questions of values and enters into a borderland of medicine.

Conventional psychotherapy is content with making people "free from" psychological and physical inhibitions or difficulties and with extending the sphere of the ego as against that of the id. Both logotherapy and existential analysis seek to make people free in another and more basic sense: "free to" take their responsibility upon themselves. Consequently, it moves along that great divide which separates not psyche from soma, but psyche from spirit. There necessarily arises the problem and danger of overstepping the boundaries.

For in point of fact every doctor, and not the psychiatrist alone, evaluates. In all medical practice the value of maintaining or regaining health is assumed. As we have said earlier, the valuational problems of medical practice become acute only in connection with euthanasia or interceding in a suicide or undertaking particularly risky operations—where human existence is wholly at stake. But there can be no medical practice untouched by values or ethical assumptions.

That branch of medicine which we call psychotherapy has always in practice engaged in logotherapy and consequently has exercised a form of medical ministry.

But, practice aside, we must be prepared to answer the question "by what authority and in whose name" (Prinzhorn) we are undertaking to plunge into philosophy, into the spiritual problems, into the realm of values. The problem is one of philosophical fairness. For a doctor trained to think in terms of the problems of method it will be clear that the cause of medical ministry stands or falls upon our answer to this question.

IV From Secular Confession   273
to Medical Ministry

Hippocrates says that the doctor who is also a philosopher is like unto the gods. But in our efforts to introduce questions of philosophy, where these are relevant, into medical practice, we have no wish to vie with the clergy. We simply want to exploit the potentialities of medicine to the utmost, to explore the field of medicine to its very limits. The risk must be taken that our enterprise will be branded a Promethean venture. At every step the doctor in his consulting-room will be confronted with value-judgments. We cannot quietly circumvent these; we are forced again and again to take a position.

The question arises: is the doctor as a doctor authorized to take such a position, and is it perhaps even incumbent upon him to do so? Or is it the better part of wisdom, indeed the better part of duty, for him to avoid taking a stand? Is it permissible for him to interfere with a patient's decisions? Does that not involve interfering in a private, personal area of the human spirit? Will not such interference lead to his thoughtlessly or arbitrarily imposing his own personal outlook on the patient? Although Hippocrates says: "One must bring philosophy to medicine and medicine to philosophy," are we not compelled to ask nevertheless: doesn't this mean that the doctor is introducing into medical treatment something quite foreign to its function? Is he not exceeding his powers when he discusses philosophical questions with the patient who is entrusted to him and who trusts him?

This problem does not arise for the minister, priest, or rabbi, whose function it is to discuss questions of belief and outlook and who is authorized to hand down guiding doctrines. The task becomes equally easy for the doctor who happens to unite within himself the qualities of physician and religious person, and who discusses questions of belief or value with patients of his own faith. The same is true for the doctor whose values are those defined by his mandate from the state and whose role is to further the welfare of that state. But every other physician is confronted with a dilemma, especially the psychotherapist, who on the one hand cannot proceed without making value-judgments and on the other hand must guard against imposing his own outlook upon the dissimilar personality of the patient.

There is a solution to this dilemma, though but a single one. Let us go back to the primary fact of human existence with which we started: to be human, we said, is to be conscious and responsible. Existential analysis aims at nothing more and nothing less than leading men to consciousness of their responsibility. It endeavors to help people experience this element of responsibility in their existences. But to lead a person further than this point, at which he profoundly understands his existence as responsibility, is neither possible nor necessary.

Responsibility is a formal ethical concept, in itself comprising no particular directives on conduct. Furthermore, responsibility is an ethically neutral concept, existing on an ethical borderline, for in itself it makes no statement about responsibility to what or for what. In this sense existential analysis also remains noncommittal on the question of "to what" a person should feel responsible —whether to his God or his conscience or his society or whatever higher power. And existential analysis equally forbears to say what a person should feel responsible for—for the realization of which values, for the fulfillment of which personal tasks, for which particular meaning to life.* On the contrary, the task of existential

---

* It is the business of existential analysis to furnish and to adorn as far as possible the chamber of immanence—while being careful not to block the door to transcendence. It aims to do no more than the former; that it do more than the latter cannot be asked of it. It practices, then, if we may use the term, an "open-door policy."

analysis consists precisely in bringing the individual to the point where he can of his own accord discern his own proper tasks, out of the consciousness of his own responsibility, and can find the clear, no longer indeterminate, unique and singular meaning of his own life. As soon as a person has been brought to that point, he will give a concrete and creative response to the question of the meaning of existence. For then he will have come to the point where "response is called upon to be responsibility" (Dürck).

Existential analysis, then, does not interfere in the ranking of values; it rests content when the individual begins to evaluate; what values he elects is and remains the patient's own affair. Existential analysis must not be concerned with what the patient decides for, what goals he sets himself, but only that he decides at all. But although consciousness of responsibility is ethically neutral, it is by no means lacking in imperativeness: once that consciousness has been awakened in an individual, he will spontaneously and automatically seek, find, and traverse the way to his particular goal. Existential analysis, along with all forms of medical ministry, is content and must be content with leading the patient to an experience in depth of his own responsibility. Continuation of the treatment beyond that point, so that it intrudes into the personal sphere of particular decisions, must be termed impermissible. The physician should never be allowed to take over the patient's responsibility; he must never permit that responsibility to be shifted to himself; he must never anticipate decisions or impose them upon the patient. His job is to make it possible for the patient

---

Through this door which is left ajar the religious person can go out unhindered. Conversely, the spirit of true religious feeling has free entrance. For the spirit of true religious feeling requires spontaneity.

to reach decisions; he must endow the patient with the capacity for deciding.*

But since values are incommensurable and decisions are made solely upon the basis of preference (Scheler), it is in some circumstances necessary to assist a person to determine his preference. The following case will illustrate the necessity for such aid and the means by which it is best given.

A young man came to his doctor to ask advice about a decision he was facing. His fiancée's girl friend had virtually invited him to go to bed with her just once. Now the young man was wondering how he ought to decide, what he ought to do. Should he betray his fiancée, whom he loved and respected, or should he ignore this opportunity and keep the faith which he felt he owed her?

The doctor refused on principle to make the decision for him. However, he quite rightly tried to clarify for the patient where his true wishes lay and what he thought he was going to accomplish in either case. On the one hand the young man had a single opportunity for a single pleasure; on the other hand he also had a single opportunity for morally commendable behavior—namely, renunciation for love's sake, which could constitute an "achievement" for his own conscience (not for his fiancée, who presumably would never know anything about the whole affair). The young man had flirted with this opportunity for sexual pleasure because, as he expressed it, he "did not want to miss anything." But the pleasure being offered to him would quite probably have

---

* Medical ministry is not ultimately concerned with the "soul's salvation." This could not and should not be its business. Rather, it is concerned with the health of man's soul. And man's soul is healthy so long as he remains what he intrinsically is: namely, a being conscious of his responsibility—in fact, the very vessel of consciousness and responsibility.

turned out to be a very dubious pleasure indeed, since the doctor had treated this patient for disturbances of potency. The doctor could therefore assume that the patient's guilty conscience would cross him up by producing temporary impotence if he tried the experiment. For obvious reasons the doctor kept this pragmatic consideration to himself. But he tried to make the patient understand his situation—which resembled that of "Buridan's ass," the donkey of scholastic theory who would necessarily starve if placed at equal distances from two equally large portions of oats because it would be unable to decide between them. What the doctor tried to do was to reduce the two possibilities to a common denominator, so to speak. Both possibilities were "singular opportunities"; in both cases the patient would have "missed something" if he made a choice. In the one case he would have had a dubious pleasure (probably an indubitable displeasure), and in the other case would have been able to confirm to himself the profound gratitude he felt toward his fiancée, which, he said, he could never fully express. His silent renunciation of this little sexual fling could be the expression of his gratitude.

From his conversation with the doctor, then, the young man learned that in both cases he would have to miss something, but also that in the one case he would miss comparatively little, in the other incomparably much. Without the necessity of the doctor's pointing the way, the patient then knew what course he ought to choose. He made his decision, made it independently. It was independent not in spite of, but actually because of this clarifying conversation.

This technique of bringing to light a common denominator can be used to good purpose where comparison of "goods" rather than preference of values is required. For example, a relatively young man paralyzed on one side after a cerebral embolism expressed to his doctor his terrible despair over this physical handicap, for which there was no hope of significant improvement. The doctor, however, helped the patient to draw up a balance sheet. Against the evil of his illness there were a sizable number of goods which could give meaning to his life, including a happy marriage and a healthy child. His handicap was not plunging him into economic ruin, since he had been granted a pension. He came to realize that his kind of paralysis would at most have ruined the career of a professional boxer—and even for such a man need not necessarily have destroyed the whole meaning of his life. The patient ultimately achieved philosophical perspective, stoic tranquillity, and a wise serenity in the following manner. The doctor had recommended that he practice reading aloud in order to improve his speech, which had been impaired by the stroke. The book which the patient used for his practice reading was Seneca's *On the Happy Life*.

We must not overlook the very large incidence of cases and situations in which it would be dangerous, if not fatal, for the psychotherapist to leave the decision entirely to the patient. No doctor is going to abandon a person in great despair or sacrifice a human life to a principle. The doctor cannot let his patient fall. He must model his conduct on the leading mountain-climber, who keeps the rope slack for the man below because otherwise his companion would be spared the effort of climbing independently. But if there is any danger of a fall, he will not hesitate to tug on the rope in order to pull the endangered man up to him. Such aid is certainly indicated at times, both in logotherapy and medical ministry—for example, in a case of potential suicide. But such exceptional cases only confirm the rule that in general the doctor must treat questions of valuation with the utmost circumspection. In principle he must observe the limits we have drawn.

We have been trying to find in existential analysis a solution for the spiritual and axiological problems of logotherapy and thereby to establish a foundation for a kind of medical ministry. We are now aware of the special requirements of a psychotherapy committed to questions of value. But what are the special requirements of the doctor who enters this kind of psychotherapy? Is medical ministry—or, for that matter, psychotherapy in general—learnable? Is it teachable?

All psychotherapy is ultimately something of an art. There is always an irrational element in psychotherapy. The doctor's artistic intuition and sensitivity is of considerable importance. The patient, too, brings an irrational element into the relationship: his individuality. Beard, the originator of the concept of neurasthenia, long ago remarked: if a doctor treats two cases of neurasthenia by the same technique, he will unquestionably be treating one case wrongly. That is to say, it is questionable whether there can ever be "the" correct psychotherapy. Is there not rather "a" correct psychotherapy practiced by a particular doctor upon a particular patient? At any rate, psychotherapy resembles an equation with two unknowns—corresponding to the twin irrational factors.

Psychoanalysis has long been considered as a specific and causal therapy. But the "complexes" and "traumas" which it considers to be pathogenic are probably universal, and therefore cannot be pathogenic. Nevertheless, psychoanalysis has helped a great many people—and must therefore have been all along an unspecific therapy.

To say that a thing is "psychogenic" is not equivalent to saying "psychotherapy is indicated." Contrariwise, psychotherapy can be indicated even when it is not causal therapy. In other words, it can be the therapy that solves the problem, even when it is not specific therapy. The case of logotherapy is similar. Logotherapy can be an entirely suitable therapy even though it is neither causal nor specific. Under certain circumstances it will be wise to begin at the top layer of the pyramidal structure to which we compared man; to provide the patient with a spiritual anchorage, even though the genesis of his particular trouble may lie in the lower layers, in the psyche or the body.

But, after all, medical ministry is not primarily concerned with the treatment of neuroses. Medical ministry belongs in the work of every physician. The surgeon should have recourse to it as much and as often as the neurologist or psychiatrist. It is only that the goal of medical ministry is different and goes deeper than that of the surgeon. When the surgeon has completed an amputation, he takes off his rubber gloves and appears to have done his duty as a physician. But if the patient then commits suicide because he cannot bear living as a cripple—of what use has the surgical therapy been? Is it not also part of the physician's work to do something about the patient's attitude toward the pain of surgery or the handicap that results from it? Is it not the physician's right and duty to treat the patient's attitude toward his illness—an attitude which constitutes a philosophy of life, though this may not be formulated in so many words? Where actual surgery comes to an end, the work of medical ministry begins. For something must follow after the surgeon has laid aside his scalpel, or where surgical work is ruled out—as, for example, in an inoperable case.*

---

* Existential analysis had to take the heretical and revolutionary step of making its aim not only man's capacity for achievement or enjoyment, but, beyond that, his capacity for suffering as a

Merely slapping the patient on the shoulder or offering a few facile, conventional encouragements is not enough. What counts is the right word at the right time. That right word should not be mere phrasemaking, nor should it "degenerate" into full-fledged philosophical debates. But it must strike to the heart of the patient's problem.

A prominent attorney had to have his leg amputated for arteriosclerotic gangrene. When he left his bed for the first time after the operation to try to walk on one leg, he burst into tears. Whereupon his doctor asked him whether he hoped to run a four-minute mile—because only if that were his aim did he have any cause for despair. This question instantly conjured up a smile amid the tears. The patient had promptly grasped the obvious fact that the meaning of life did not consist in walking jauntily—not even for a distance runner—and that human life is not so poor a thing that the loss of a limb would make it meaningless. (Comparisons useful for clarifying our patients' philosophical attitudes may well be taken from the world of sports for the reason we have already mentioned: patients can learn to be "good sports"; they can learn that difficulties only make life more meaningful, never meaningless. The typical athlete seeks and makes difficulties for himself—consider obstacle races or handicap races. The greater the handicap he can give, the greater honor the athlete has.)

---

possible and necessary task. Thereby it has become a tool for every physician—and not only for neurologists or psychiatrists. Above all, it becomes the concern of internists, surgeons, orthopedists, and dermatologists, and more so for them than for their colleagues in neurology or psychiatry. For the internist is frequently dealing with the chronically ill and with incurable invalids, the surgeon with inoperable cases, the orthopedist with permanent cripples, and the dermatologist with persons disfigured for life. That is to say, physicians in these fields are dealing with people suffering from a destiny which they can no longer shape, but can only master by enduring.

The night before her leg was to be amputated for tuberculosis of the bone, another patient wrote a letter to a friend hinting at thoughts of suicide. The letter was intercepted and fell into the hands of a doctor in the surgical ward where this patient lay. The doctor lost no time, but found a pretext for a talk with the woman. In a few appropriate words he too pointed out to the patient that human life would be a very poor thing indeed if the loss of a leg actually involved depriving it of all meaning. Such a loss could at most make the life of an ant purposeless since it would no longer be able to achieve the goal set for it by the ant community—namely, running around on all six legs and being useful. For a human being it must be different. The young doctor's chat with the woman, couched rather in the style of a Socratic dialogue, did not fail to take effect. His senior surgeon, who undertook the amputation next morning, does not know to this day that in spite of the successful operation this patient almost ended up on his autopsy table.

Medical ministry is indicated wherever inevitable, "fated" conditions exist in the life of the patient, where he is crippled or faced with an incurable disease or chronic invalidism. It is also useful where persons are in a really inescapable predicament, faced with unalterable difficulties imposed from outside themselves. We will recall in this connection our earlier chapters on the possibility and necessity for medical ministry with persons helpless in the grip of social evils (the psychic conflicts of the unemployed, etc.). Medical ministry helps the patient to shape his suffering into inner achievement and so to realize attitudinal values.

The area we have entered with our logotherapy, and, above all, with existential analysis, is a borderland between medicine and philosophy. Medical ministry operates along a great divide—the dividing line between medicine and religion. Anyone who walks along the frontier between two countries must remember that he is under surveillance from two sides. Medical ministry must therefore expect wary glances; it must take them into the bargain.

Medical ministry lies between two realms. It therefore is a border area, and as such a no-man's-land. And yet—what a land of promise!

V

Psychotherapy
on Its
Way to
Rehumanization

V   Psychotherapy
on Its Way to Rehumanization

I personally met both Sigmund Freud and Alfred Adler, and further was invited by both to contribute an article to their international journals of psychoanalysis and individual psychology, respectively.[1] Why this historical digression? Because the Freudian and Adlerian views on psychotherapy were diametrically opposed to one another. But this is not unusual, for wherever you open the book of the history of psychotherapy, you are confronted with two pages, a left page and a right page, and both pages show pictures—pictures of man, that is—that not only differ from one another, but even contradict one another. Let us symbolize such mutual contradictions by a square on one page and a circle on the facing page (fig. 1). And now remember what you know from mathematics, namely, the fact that the age-old problem of squaring the circle has

---

This chapter was one of four addresses given at the invitation of Professor Joseph Wolpe at the symposium "Four Viewpoints of Psychotherapy" in Philadelphia on March 28, 1980.

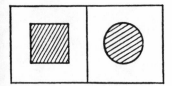

Figure 1

been proven to be insoluble. But what if we turn the left page to a perpendicular position (fig. 2)? All of a sudden you can imagine that the square and the circle are but the (two-dimensional) projections of a (three-dimensional) cylinder, inasmuch as they represent its profile view and its ground-plan, respectively (fig. 3). And then

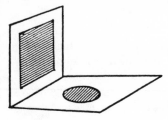

Figure 2

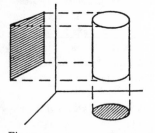

Figure 3

we notice that the contradictions between the pictures need no longer contradict the oneness of what they depict.

Incidentally, there is another contradiction that disappears as soon as we conceive of the pictures as mere projections. If we assume that the cylinder is not a solid but rather an open vessel—say, an empty cup—this openness, too, disappears in the lower dimensions: both the square and the circle are closed figures (fig. 4). But once we view them as mere projections, their closedness no longer contradicts the openness of the cylinder.

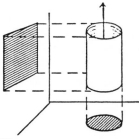

Figure 4

How shall we now apply all this to our concept, our theory, of man, to our anthropological theory as it—explicitly or implicitly —underlies our psychotherapeutic practice? By the same analogy, the contradictions between the disparate pictures of man as they are propounded by the different psychotherapeutic schools cannot be overcome and surpassed unless we proceed into a higher dimension. That is to say, as long as we remain in those lower dimensions into which we have projected man in the first place, there is no hope for a unified concept. Only if we open up the higher dimension which is the human dimension, the dimension of specifically human phenomena; only if we follow man into this dimension is it possible to catch the oneness as well as the humanness of man. And if for no other reason, entering the human dimension becomes mandatory if we are to tap and muster those resources which are available solely in the human dimension, in order to incorporate them in our therapeutic arsenal.

And among these resources, there are two which are most relevant for psychotherapy: man's capacity for self-detachment and his capacity for self-transcendence. The first could be defined as the capacity to detach oneself from outward situations, to take a stand toward them; but man is not only capable of detaching himself from the world but also from himself. And it is this very capacity which is mobilized in the logotherapeutic technique of paradoxical intention. I started practicing it as early as 1929 at the Psychiatric Hospital of the University of Vienna Medical School, published it the first time in 1939 in a Swiss neuropsychiatric journal,[2] and coined the term "paradoxical intention" in 1947 in a book that I published in German.[3]

I would like to quote a passage from this book in order to show you on what theoretical grounds the practice of paradoxical intention had been based. (In addition, the quotation may build a bridge of mutual understanding between logotherapists and behavior therapists.) "All psychoanalytically oriented psychotherapies," I said in 1947, "are mainly concerned with uncovering the primary conditions of the 'conditioned reflex' by which neurosis may well be understood, namely, the situation—outer or inner—in which a given neurotic symptom emerged the first time. It is this author's contention, however, that the full-fledged neurosis is caused not only by the primary conditions but also by secondary conditioning. This reinforcement, in turn, is caused by the feedback mechanism called anticipatory anxiety. Therefore, if we wish to recondition a conditioned reflex, we must undo the vicious circle formed by anticipatory anxiety, and this is the very job done by our paradoxical intention technique."

This technique lends itself to the treatment of phobic and obsessive-compulsive conditions. I usually explain its therapeutic effectiveness to my students by starting with the mechanism called anticipatory anxiety. A given symptom evokes on the part of the patient a phobia in the form of the fearful expectation of its recurrence; this phobia causes the symptom actually to recur; and the recurrence of the symptom reinforces the phobia (fig. 5).

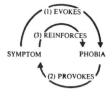

Figure 5

There are cases in which the object of the "fearful expectation" is—fear itself. Our patients spontaneously speak of a "fear of fear." Upon closer interrogation it turns out that they are afraid of the consequences of their fear: fainting, coronaries, or strokes. As I pointed out in 1953[4] they react to their "fear of fear" by a "flight from fear"—what you would call an avoidance pattern of behavior. In 1960 I had arrived at the conviction that "phobias are partially due to the endeavour to avoid the situation in which anxiety arises."[5] Since that time, this contention has been confirmed by behavior therapists on many occasions.

Along with the phobic pattern that we may characterize as a "flight from fear," there is another pattern, the obsessive-compulsive one, which is characterized by what one may call a "fight against obsessions and compulsions." The patients are afraid that they might commit suicide or homicide or that the strange ideas haunting them might be the precursors, if not already the symptoms, of a psychosis. In other words, they are afraid not of fear itself, but rather of themselves.

Again, a circle formation is established. The more the patient fights his obsessions and compulsions, the stronger they become. Pressure induces counterpressure, and counterpressure, in turn, increases pressure (fig. 6).

Figure 6

In order to undo all the vicious circles discussed, the first thing to do is to take the wind out of the anticipatory anxieties underlying them, and this is precisely the business of paradoxical intention. Paradoxical intention may be defined as a procedure in whose framework the patients are encouraged to do, or wish to happen, the very things they fear—albeit with tongue in cheek. In fact, "an integral element in paradoxical intention is the deliberate evocation of humor," as A. A. Lazarus justifiedly points out.[6] After all, the sense of humor is one of the various aspects of the specifically human capacity of self-detachment. No other animal is capable of laughing.

In paradoxical intention, therefore, the patients are invited to exaggerate their fears and anxieties, and to do so with as humorous formulations as possible.

Hand et al.,[7] who had treated chronic agoraphobia patients in groups, observed that they spontaneously used humor as an impressive coping device: "when the whole group was frightened, somebody would break the ice with a joke, which would be greeted with the laughter of relief." They reinvented paradoxical intention, one might say.

Paradoxical intention may be effective even in severe cases. Y. Lamontagne,[8] just to invoke a few instances, cured a case of incapacitating erythrophobia that had been present for twelve years, within four sessions. E. Niebauer[9] successfully treated a 65-year-old woman who had suffered from a hand-washing compulsion for sixty years. And M. Jacobs[10] cites the case of Mrs. K., who for fifteen years had suffered from severe claustrophobia and was cured by him within a week. His treatment was a combination of paradoxical intention, relaxation, and desensitization, a fact that should demonstrate that paradoxical intention, or for that matter logotherapy, in no way invalidates other, previous, psychotherapies, but rather presents a means to maximize their effectiveness. In the same vein, L. M. Ascher[11] points out that "most therapeutic approaches have specific techniques," and that "these techniques are not especially useful for, nor relevant to, alternative therapeutic systems." But there is "one notable exception in this observation," namely, paradoxical intention. "It is an exception because many professionals representing a wide variety of disparate approaches to psychotherapy have incorporated this intervention into their systems both practically and theoretically." In fact, "in the past two decades, paradoxical intention has become popular with a variety of therapists" who had been "impressed by the effectiveness of the technique." Even more important, "behavioral techniques have been developed which appear to be translations of paradoxical intention into learning terms."[12]

Incidentally, L. M. Ascher and R. M. Turner[13] were the first to come up with a "controlled experimental validation of the clinical effectiveness" of paradoxical intention in comparison with other behavioral strategies. But also Solyom et al.[14] proved experimentally that paradoxical intention works and published thereon in *Comprehensive Psychiatry*.

But now let us turn to the second human capacity, that of self-transcendence.[15] It denotes the fact that human existence always points, and is directed, toward something other than oneself; or rather, toward something or someone other than oneself, namely, toward meanings to fulfill, or toward other human beings to encounter lovingly. And only to the extent to which a human being lives out his self-transcendence is he really becoming human and actualizing himself. This always reminds me of the fact that the eye's visual capacity to perceive the surrounding world, ironically, is contingent on its incapacity to perceive itself, to see anything of itself. Whenever the eye sees anything of itself its function is impaired. When does the eye see anything of itself? If I am affected by a cataract, I see something like a cloud—then my eye sees its own cataract. Or if I am affected by a glaucoma, I see rainbow halos around the lights—then my eye perceives, as it were, the heightened tension that causes the glaucoma. The normally functioning eye does not see itself, it is rather overlooking itself; likewise man is human to the extent that he overlooks and forgets himself by giving himself to a cause to serve or another person to love. By being immersed in work or in love, we are transcending ourselves and, thereby, actualizing ourselves.

Why has the self-transcendent quality of the human reality been so completely ignored and neglected by psychology? As I see it, this has something to do with the Heisenberg law, which I would restate a bit freely, as follows: The observation of a process unavoidably and automatically influences the process. Well, something similar holds for the strictly scientifically (rather than phenomenologically) oriented observation of human behavior in that it cannot avoid making a subject into an object. But alas, it is the inalienable property of a subject, I would say, that it has objects of its own. (According to the terminology of Brentanoian-Husserlian-Schelerian phenomenology, they are called intentional objects or intentional referents.) Understandably, at the moment the subject is made into an object, its own objects disappear. And inasmuch as the "intentional referents" form "the world in" which a human being "is," as a "being-in-the-world," to use the more-often-than-not-misused Heideggerian phraseology, the world is shut out as soon as man is seen no longer as a being, so to speak, acting into the world, but rather as a being reacting to stimuli (the behavioristic model) or abreacting drives and instincts (the psychodynamic model). In either case, the human being is dealt with as a world-less monad or a closed system, and now we remember what was said at the outset, namely that the openness of a vessel projected into lower dimensions disappears.

To repeat, human behavior is really human to the extent that it means "acting into the world." This, in turn, implies being motivated by the world. In fact, the world toward which a human being transcends himself is a world replete with meanings that constitute the reasons to act—and other human beings who constitute the persons to love. As soon as we project human beings into the dimension of a psychology conceived strictly scientifically, we cut them off from the world of potential reasons. What is left instead of reasons are causes. The difference? Reasons motivate me to act in the way I choose. Causes determine my behavior unwillingly and unwittingly, whether I know it or not. When I cut onions I weep. My tears have a cause. But I have no reason to weep. When a loved one dies I have a reason to weep.

And what are the causes that are left to the psychologist with a blind spot for self-transcendence, and consequently for meanings and reasons? If he is a psychoanalyst, he will replace motives with drives and instincts as that which causes human behavior. If he is a behaviorist, he will see in human behavior the mere effect of conditioning and learning processes. If there are no meanings, no reasons, no choices, determinants have to be hypothesized, one way or another, to replace them. To be sure, the humanness of human behavior is done away with, under the circumstances. And if psychology, or for that matter psychotherapy, is to be rehumanized it has to remain cognizant of self-transcendence rather than be blind to it.

One of the two aspects of self-transcendence is what is called in logotherapy, the will to meaning. If man can find and fulfill a meaning in his life he becomes happy but also able and capable of coping with suffering. If he can see a meaning he is even prepared to give his life. On the other hand, if he cannot see a meaning he is equally inclined to take his life even in the midst, and in spite, of all the welfare and affluence surrounding him. Just consider the escalating suicide figures in welfare states such as Sweden and Austria. To deliberately quote a behaviorist, L. Bachelis,[16] director of the Behavioral Therapy Center in New York, "many undergoing therapy at the center tell [him] they have a good job, they're successful but they want to kill themselves, because they find life meaningless." I do not intend to say that most of the suicides are undertaken out of a feeling of meaninglessness; but I am convinced that people would have overcome the impulse to kill themselves if they had seen a meaning in their lives. Meanwhile, people have the means to live but no meaning to live for. As you see, logotherapy squarely faces the situation confronting us "in a post-petroleum society" and even "has special relevance during this critical transition," to quote A. G. Wirth.[17]

Happiness is not only the result of fulfilling a meaning but also more generally the unintended side effect of self-transcendence. It therefore cannot be "pursued" but rather must ensue. The more one aims at it the more one misses the aim This is most conspicuous with sexual pleasure and it is the characteristic of the third pattern to be discussed, the sexually neurotic pattern, in which people directly strive for sexual performance or experience, male patients trying to demonstrate their potency or female patients their capacity for orgasm. In logotherapy, we are used to speaking of "hyperintention" in this context. Since hyperintention is often accompanied by what we call in logotherapy "hyperreflection," i. e., too much self-observation, both hyperintention and hyperreflection join to form another, the third, circle formation (fig. 7).

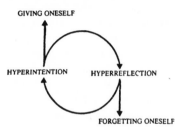

Figure 7

In order to break it up, centrifugal forces must be brought into play. Hyperreflection can be counteracted by the logotherapeutic technique called "dereflection," that is to say, the patients, instead of watching themselves, should forget themselves. But they cannot forget themselves unless they give themselves.

Again and again, it turns out that the hyperintention of sexual performance and experience is due to the patient's sexual achievement orientation and tendency to attach to sexual intercourse a "demand quality." To remove it is the very purpose of a logotherapeutic strategy that, in addition to the dereflection technique, I described in English for the first time in 1952[18] and more elaborately in *The Unheard Cry for Meaning* [19] W S. and B. J Sahakian[20] were the first to point out what later on was confirmed by L 'M Ascher[21] and finally by R P Bulka,[22] who sees in dereflection a clear anticipation of the approach of Masters and Johnson "

The feeling of meaninglessness not only underlies the mass neurotic triad of today i e, depression-addiction-aggression, but also may eventuate in what we logotherapists call a 'noogenic neurosis " Thus far, ten researchers have, independent of one another, estimated that about twenty percent of neuroses are noögenic.[23] In such cases, logotherapy is a specific procedure devised to assist and help the patient in finding meaning As such, logotherapy is based on a logotheory and the logotheory in turn is empirically based The logotherapist never prescribes meaning but he may well describe how the process of meaning perception is enacted by the 'man or woman in the street," more specifically, by virtue of their prereflective ontological self-understanding," as I usually call it In other words, logotherapists neither preach meaning nor teach it, but learn it from people who have discovered and fulfilled it for themselves [24] And a phenomenological analysis reveals that there are three main avenues by which one arrives at meaning in life The first is finding it by creating a work or by doing a deed It is unbelievable how inventive the "man or woman in the street" may become when it comes to squeezing out meaning from a life that seems to lack it

Several years ago a garbage collector received the order of merit from the German government. This man did his job to everyone's satisfaction, but the special effort that gained him the award was this: He looks in the garbage cans for discarded toys, spends his evening hours repairing them, and gives them to poor children as presents Talented as a fix-it man he adds magnificent meaning to his clean-up job [25]

In addition to the meaning potential inherent and dormant in creating and doing, a second avenue to meaning in life is available in experiencing something or encountering someone·· in other words, meaning can be found not only in work but also in love E Weisskopf-Joelson[26] observes in this context that the logotherapeutic "notion that experiencing can be as valuable as achieving is therapeutic because it compensates for our onesided emphasis on the external world of achievement at the expense of the internal world of experience "

Most important, however, is a third avenue to meaning in life: it finally turns out that even the helpless victim of a hopeless situation, facing a fate he *cannot change,* may rise above himself, may grow beyond himself, and by so doing *change himself* He may turn a personal tragedy into a triumph Again to quote a pertinent example

A few years after World War II a doctor examined a Jewish woman who wore a bracelet made of baby teeth mounted in gold. "A beautiful bracelet," the doctor remarked. "Yes," the woman answered, "this tooth here belonged to Miriam, this one to Esther, and this one to Samuel . . " She mentioned the names of her daughters and sons according to age. "Nine children," she added, "and all of them were taken to the gas chambers " Shocked, the doctor asked: "How can you live with such a bracelet?" Quietly, the Jewish woman replied· "I am now in charge of an orphanage in Israel."[27]

V Psychotherapy on Its Way
to Rehumanization

For a quarter of a century I was running the neurological department of a general hospital and bear witness to my patients' capacity to turn their predicament into a human achievement.[28] Who tells the story of the young men who yesterday were skiing in the Austrian Alps or riding a Yamaha and today are paralyzed from the neck down? Or of the girls who yesterday were dancing in a disco and today are confronted with the diagnosis of a brain tumor? Let me just invoke what P L Starck, a nurse working in Alabama, reported to me:

> I have a twenty-two-year-old female client who was injured at age eighteen by a gunshot as she walked to the grocery store She can only accomplish tasks by use of a mouthstick She feels the purpose of her life is quite clear She watches the newspapers and television for stories of people in trouble and writes to them (typing with her mouthstick) to give them words of comfort and encouragement.

By virtue of the fact that meaning may be "squeezed out" even from suffering, life proves to be potentially meaningful literally up to its last moment, up to one's last breath But let me make it perfectly clear that in no way is suffering *necessary* to find meaning I only insist that meaning is possible even in spite of suffering. Provided, to be sure, that we are dealing with unavoidable suffering—if it were avoidable, the meaningful thing to do would be to remove its cause, be it psychological, biological, or political To suffer unnecessarily is certainly masochism rather than heroism. But if you really cannot change a situation that causes you suffering, what you still can choose is your attitude. And I won't forget an interview I once heard on Austria's TV given by a Polish cardiologist who, during World War II, had organized the Warsaw ghetto upheaval. "What a heroic deed," exclaimed the reporter.

"Listen," calmly replied the doctor, "to take a gun and shoot is no great thing; but if the SS leads you to a gas chamber or to a mass grave to execute you on the spot, and you can't do anything about it, except for keeping your head high and going your way with dignity, you see, this is what I would call heroism." He should know.[29]

So life is potentially meaningful under any conditions, be they pleasurable or miserable, and precisely this cornerstone of logotherapeutic teachings (which had been based solely on the intuitions of a teenager named Viktor E. Frankl) has lately been corroborated on strictly empirical grounds, through tests and statistics applied to ten thousands of subjects. The overall result (of research conducted by Brown, Casciani, Crumbaugh, Dansart, Durlak, Kratochvil, Lukas, Lunceford, Mason, Meier, Murphy, Planova, Popielski, Richmond, Roberts, Ruch, Sallee, Smith, Yarnell, and Young) was that meaning is in principal available to each and every person irrespective of sex, age, IQ, educational background, character structure, and environment and, last but not least, irrespective of whether one is religious or not, and if religious, irrespective of the denomination to which one belongs.

Those suffering from obsessive-compulsive and phobic conditions who can be aided by paradoxical intention are but a minority. The majority, however, is not a silent one. To those who know how to listen, it is rather a crying majority—crying for meaning! For too long the cry has remained unheard. But a psychotherapy that sets out "on its way to rehumanization" should listen to the unheard cry for meaning.

NOTES

1. V. E. Frankl, "Zur mimischen Bejahung und Verneinung," *Internationale Zeitschrift für Psychoanalyse* 10 (1924): 437–438; "Psy-

chotherapie und Weltanschauung," *Internationale Zeitschrift für Individual-psychologie* 3 (1925): 250–252.

2. V. E. Frankl, "Zur medikamentösen Unterstützung der Psychotherapie bei Neurosen," *Schweizer Archiv für Neurologie und Psychiatrie* 43 (1939): 26–31.

3. V. E. Frankl, *Die Psychotherapie in der Praxis* (Vienna: Deuticke, 1947).

4. V. E. Frankl, "Angst und Zwang." *Acta Psychoterapeutica* 1 (1953): 111–120.

5. V. E. Frankl, "Paradoxical Intention : A Logotherapeutic Technique." *American Journal of Psychotherapy* 14 (1960) 520–535.

6. A. A. Lazarus, *Behavior Therapy and Beyond* (New York: McGraw Hill, 1971).

7. I. Hand, Y. Lamontagne, and I. M. Marks, "Group Exposure (Flooding) in vivo for Agoraphobics." *British Journal of Psychiatry* 14 (1974): 588–602.

8. Y. Lamontagne, "Treatment of Erythrophobia by Paradoxical Intention." *Journal of Nervous and Mental Disease* 166, no. 4 (1978): 304–306.

9. K. Kocourek, E. Niebauer, and P. Polak, "Ergebnisse der klinischen Anwendung der Logotherapie." In V. E. Frankl, V. E. von Gebsattel, and J. H. Schultz, eds, *Handbuch der Neurosenlehre und Psychotherapie* (Munich: Urban und Schwarzenberg, 1959).

10. M. Jacobs, "An Holistic Approach to Behavior Therapy." In A. A. Lazarus, ed., *Clinical Behavior Therapy* (New York: Brunner-Mazel, 1972).

11. L. M. Ascher, "Paradoxical Intention." In A. Goldstein and E. B. Foa, eds., *Handbook of Behavioral Interventions* (New York: Wiley, 1980).

12. I. D. Yalom, too, holds that paradoxical intention is an "effective" technique which "anticipated the similar technique of symptom prescription and paradox employed by the school of Milton Erickson, Jay Haley, Don Jackson, and Paul Watzlawick." I. D. Yalom, *Existential Psychotherapy* (New York: Basic Books, 1980).

13. L. M. Ascher, and R. M. Turner, "Controlled Comparison of Progressive Relaxation, Stimulus Control, and Paradoxical Intention

Therapies for Insomnia," *Journal of Consulting and Clinical Psychology* 47, no. 3 (1979): 500–508.

14· L. Solyom, J· Garza-Perez, B. L. Ledwidge, and C. Solyom, "Paradoxical Intention in the Treatment of Obsessive Thoughts: A Pilot Study," *Comprehensive Psychiatry* 13, no. 3 (1972): 291–297.

15. Inasmuch as self-detachment and self-transcendence equally derive from logotherapy's concept of man, both paradoxical intention and the business of finding meaning in life belong to one another· It is true that paradoxical intention is not "specifically related to life meaning" (Yalom, *Existential Psychotherapy*)· Yet I cannot subscribe to the statement made by E. Weisskopf-Joelson to the effect that "paradoxical intention is not closely related to the Logotherapeutic position in ways other than owing its origin to Frankl·" (E. Weisskopf-Joelson, "Six Representative Approaches to Existential Therapy· A· Viktor E· Frankl." In R· S. Valle and M· King, eds·, *Existential-Phenomenological Alternatives for Psychology* [New York: Oxford, 1978]. I rather think that the effectiveness of the technique, in the final analysis, is due to some sort of basic trust in *Dasein*, ultimately, to some sort of faith which is reinstalled and reinstated by the technique· As far as fear is concerned, however, faith proves to be the very antagonist· In fact, there is an old saying that reads· "Fear knocked at the door· Faith answered, and no one was there."

16. L. Bachelis, "Depression and Disillusionment," *APA Monitor*, May 1976

17. A. G. Wirth, "Logotherapy and Education in a Post-Petroleum Society." *International Forum for Logotherapy* 1, no 3 (1980)

18. V. E. Frankl, "The Pleasure Principle and Sexual Neurosis," *International Journal of Sexology* 5 (1952)· 128–130.

19. V. E. Frankl, *The Unheard Cry for Meaning* (New York: Simon & Schuster, 1978)

20 W S Sahakian, and B. J Sahakian, "Logotherapy as a Personality Theory," *Israel Annals of Psychiatry* 10 (1972)· 230–244.

21 L. M Ascher, "Paradoxical Intention Viewed by a Behavior Therapist," *International Forum for Logotherapy* 1, no. 3 (1980)· 13–16

22. R. P Bulka, *The Quest for Ultimate Meaning: Principles and Applications of Logotherapy* (New York Philosophical Library, 1979)

V Psychotherapy on Its Way   *303*
to Rehumanization

23. Cf. E. Klinger, *Meaning and Void* (Minneapolis: University of Minnesota Press, 1977).
24. To quote C. Bühler, "All we can do is study the lives of people who seem to have found their answers to the questions of what ultimately a life was about." "Basic Theoretical Concepts of Humanistic Psychology." *American Psychologist* 26 (1971) · 378·
25 G. Moser, *Wie finde ich den Sinn des Lebens?* (Freiburg· Herder, 1978).
26. E. Weisskopf-Joelson, "The Place of Logotherapy in the World Today," *International Forum for Logotherapy* 1, no 3 (1980) · 3–7
27 Moser, *Wie finde ich den Sinn des Lebens?*
28. J. Thomas and E Weiner reported that patients who were critically ill had higher Purpose in Life Test (PIL) scores than had patients with a minor ailment or nonpatients. See "Psychological Differences Among Groups of Critically Ill Hospitalized Patients, Noncritically Ill Hospitalized Patients and Well Controls," *Journal of Consulting and Clinical Psychology* 42, no 2 (1974): 274–279.
29. An empirical study recently conducted by Austrian public opinion pollsters indicated that those who are held in highest esteem by most of the people interviewed were neither the great artists nor the great scientists, neither the great statesmen nor the great sports figures, but those who master a hard lot with dignity

Selected Bibliography

1. Books

Bulka, Reuven P. *The Quest for Ultimate Meaning: Principles and Applications of Logotherapy.* Foreword by Viktor E. Frankl. New York: Philosophical Library, 1979.

Crumbaugh, James C. *Everything to Gain: A Guide to Self-fulfillment Through Logoanalysis.* Chicago: Nelson-Hall, 1973.

Crumbaugh, James C., William M. Wood and W. Chadwick Wood. *Logotherapy: New Help for Problem Drinkers.* Foreword by Viktor E. Frankl. Chicago: Nelson-Hall, 1980.

Fabry, Joseph B. *The Pursuit of Meaning: Victor Frankl, Logotherapy, and Life.* Preface by Viktor E. Frankl. Boston: Beacon Press, 1968; New York: Harper & Row, 1980.

Fabry, Joseph B., Reuven P. Bulka and William S. Sahakian, eds. *Logotherapy in Action.* Foreword by Viktor E. Frankl. New York: Jason Aronson, Inc., 1979.

Frankl, Victor E. *Man's Search for Meaning: An Introduction to Logotherapy.* Preface by Gordon W. Allport. Boston: Beacon Press, 1959; paperback edition, New York: Pocket Books, 1985.

———. *The Doctor and the Soul: From Psychotherapy to Logotherapy* New

York: Alfred A. Knopf, Inc.; second, expanded edition, 1965; paperback edition, New York: Vintage Books, 1977.

——. *The Will to Meaning: Foundations and Applications of Logotherapy.* New York and Cleveland: The World Publishing Company, 1969; paperback edition, New York: New American Library, 1981.

——. *Der Wille zum Sinn: Ausgewaehlte Vortaege ueber Logotherapie.* Bern: Huber, 1982.

——. *Theorie und Therapie der Neurosen: Einfuehrung in Logotherapie und Existenzanalyse.* Munich: Reinhardt, 1983.

——. *Das Leiden am sinnlosen Leben: Psychotherapie fuer heute.* Frieburg im Breisgau: Herder, 1984.

——. *Der leidende Mensch: Anthropologische Grundlagen der Psychotherapie.* Bern: Huber, 1984.

——. *Psychotherapie fuer den Laien: Rundfunkvortraege ueber Seelenheilkunde.* Freiburg im Breisgau: Herder, 1984.

——. *Der Mensch vor der Frage nach dem Sinn: Eine Auswahl aus dem Gesamtwerk.* Vorwort von Konrad Lorenz. Munich: Piper, 1985.

——. *Psychotherapy and Existentialism: Selected Papers on Logotherapy.* New York: Washington Square Press, 1985.

——. *Die Sinnfrage in der Psychotherapie.* Vorwort von Franz Kreuzer. Munich: Piper, 1985.

——. *The Unconscious God: Psychotherapy and Theology.* New York: Simon and Schuster, 1985.

——. *The Unheard Cry for Meaning: Psychotherapy and Humanism.* New York: Simon and Schuster, 1985.

——. *Die Psychotherapie in der Praxis: Eine kasuistische Einfuehrung fuer Aerzte.* Munich: Piper, 1986.

——. *Synchronization in Buchenwald.* A play, offset. (Available from the Institute of Logotherapy, 2000 Dwight Way, Berkeley, CA 94704.)

Lazar, Edward, Sandra A. Wawrytko and James W. Kidd, eds. *Victor Frankl, People and Meaning: A Commemorative Tribute to the Founder of Logotherapy on His Eightieth Birthday.* San Francisco: Golden Phoenix Press, 1985.

Leslie, Robert C. *Jesus and Logotherapy: The Ministry of Jesus as Interpreted Through the Psychotherapy of Viktor Frankl.* New York and Nashville: Abingdon Press, 1965; paperback edition, 1968.

306

Lukas, Elisabeth. *Meaningful Living: Logotherapeutic Guide to Health.* Foreword by Viktor E. Frankl. Cambridge, Massachusetts: Schenkman Publishing Company, 1984.

Takashima, Hiroshi. *Psychosomatic Medicine and Logotherapy.* Foreword by Viktor E. Frankl. Oceanside, New York: Dabor Science Publications, 1977.

Tweedie, Donald F. *Logotherapy and the Christian Faith: An Evaluation of Frankl's Existential Approach to Psychotherapy.* Preface by Viktor E. Frankl. Grand Rapids: Baker Book House, 1961; paperback edition, 1972.

——. *The Christian and the Couch: An Introduction to Christian Logotherapy.* Grand Rapids: Baker Book House, 1963.

Ungersma, Aaron J. *The Search for Meaning: A New Approach in Psychotherapy and Pastoral Psychology.* Philadelphia: Westminster Press, 1961; paperback edition, Foreword by Viktor E. Frankl, 1968.

Wawrytko, Sandra A., ed. *Analecta Frankliana: The Proceedings of the First World Congress of Logotherapy (1980).* Berkeley: Institute of Logotherapy Press, 1982.

2.   *Chapters in Books*

Ascher, L. Michael. "Paradoxical Intention." In *Handbook of Behavioral Interventions,* edited by A. Goldstein and E. B. Foa. New York: John Wiley, 1980.

Ascher, L. Michael, and C. Alex Pollard. "Paradoxical Intention." In *The Therapeutic Efficacy of the Major Psychotherapeutic Techniques,* edited by Usuf Hariman. Springfield: Charles C. Thomas, 1983.

Ascher, L. Michael, Michael R. Bowers, and David E. Schotte. "A Review of Data from Controlled Case Studies and Experiments Evaluating the Clinical Efficacy of Paradoxical Intention." In *Promoting Change Through Paradoxical Therapy,* edited by Gerald R. Weeks. Homewood, Illinois: Dow Jones-Irwin, 1985, pp. 99–110.

Ascher, L. Michael, and Robert A. DiTomasso. "Paradoxical Intention in Behavior Therapy: A Review of the Experimental Literature." In *Evaluating Behavior Therapy Outcome,* edited by Ralph McMillan Turner and L. Michael Ascher. New York: Springer, 1985.

Frankl, Viktor E. "The Philosophical Foundations of Logotherapy" (paper read before the first Lexington Conference on Phenomenology on April 4, 1963). In *Phenomenology: Pure and Applied*, edited by Erwin Straus. Pittsburgh: Duquesne University Press, 1964.

———. "Reductionism and Nihilism." In *Beyond Reductionism: New Perspectives in the Life Sciences (The Alphach Symposium, 1968)*, edited by Arthur Koestler and J. R. Smythies. New York: Macmillan, 1970.

———. "Man's Search for Ultimate Meaning." In *On the Way to Self-Knowledge*, edited by Jacob Needleman. New York: Alfred A. Knopf, Inc., 1976.

———. "Logotherapy." In *The Psychotherapy Handbook*, edited by Richie Herink. New York: New American Library, 1980.

———. "Opening Address to the First World Congress of Logotherapy: Logotherapy on Its Way to Degurufication." In *Analecta Frankliana: The Proceedings of the First World Congress of Logotherapy (1980)*, edited by Sandra A. Wawrytko. Berkeley: Institute of Logotherapy Press, 1982.

———. "Logotherapy." In *Encyclopedia of Psychology*, edited by Raymond J. Corsini, Volume 2. New York, John Wiley, 1984.

———. "Paradoxical Intention." In *Promoting Change Through Paradoxical Therapy*, edited by Gerald R. Weeks. Homewood, Illinois: Dow Jones-Irwin, 1985.

———. "Logos, Paradox, and the Search for Meaning." In *Cognition and Psychotherapy*, edited by Michael J. Mahoney and Arthur Freeman. New York: Plenum Press, 1985.

Marks, Isaac M. "Paradoxical Intention ('Logotherapy')." In *Fears and Phobias*. New York: Academic Press, 1969.

———. "Paradoxical Intention." In *Behavior Modification*, edited by W. Stewart Agras. Boston: Little, Brown and Company, 1972.

———. "Paradoxical Intention (Logotherapy)." In *Encyclopaedic Handbook of Medical Psychology*, edited by Stephen Krauss. London and Boston: Butterworth, 1976.

Maslow, Abraham H. "Comments on Dr. Frankl's Paper." In *Readings in Humanistic Psychology*, edited by Anthony J. Sutich and Miles A. Vich. New York: The Free Press, 1969.

Sahakian, William S. "Viktor Frankl." In *History of Psychology*. Itasca, Illinois: F. E. Peacock Publishers, Inc., 1968.

Schultz, Duane P. "The Self-Transcendent Person: Frankl's Model." In *Growth Psychology: Models of the Healthy Personality*. New York: Van Nostrand Reinhold, 1977.

————. "Frankl's Model of the Self-Transcendent Person." In *Psychology in Use: An Introduction to Applied Psychology*. New York: Macmillan, 1979.

Spiegelberg, Herbert. "Viktor Frankl: Phenomenology in Logotherapy and Existenzanalyse." In *Phenomenology in Psychology and Psychiatry*. Evanston, Illinois: Northwestern University Press, 1972.

Weeks, Gerald R., and Luciano L'Abate. "Research on Paradoxical Intention." In *Paradoxical Psychotherapy*. New York: Brunner/Mazel, 1982.

Williams, David A., and Joseph Fabry. "The Existential Approach: Logotherapy." In *Basic Approaches to Group Psychotherapy and Group Counseling*, edited by George M. Gazda. Springfield: Charles C. Thomas, 1982.

3. Articles and Miscellaneous

Ansbacher, Rowena R. "The Third Viennese School of Psychotherapy." *Journal of Individual Psychology* 15 (1959): 236–237.

Ascher, L. Michael. "Employing Paradoxical Intention in the Behavioral Treatment of Urinary Retention." *Scandinavian Journal of Behavior Therapy* 6, no. 4 (1977): 28.

————. "Paradoxical Intention: A Review of Preliminary Research." *The International Forum for Logotherapy* 1, no. 1 (Winter 1978–Spring 1979): 18–21.

————. "Paradoxical intention in the treatment of urinary retention." *Behavior Research & Therapy* 17 (1979): 267–270.

————. "Paradoxical Intention Viewed by a Behavior Therapist." *The International Forum for Logotherapy* 2, no. 3 (Spring 1980): 13–16.

————. "Application of Paradoxical Intention by Other Schools of Therapy." *The International Forum for Logotherapy* 4, no. 1 (Spring–Summer 1981): 52–55.

————. "Employing paradoxical intention in the treatment of agoraphobia." *Behavior Research & Therapy* 19 (1981): 533–542.

Ascher, L. Michael, and Jay S. Efran. "Use of Paradoxical Intention in a Behavior Program for Sleep Onset Insomnia." *Journal of Consulting and Clinical Psychology* 46 (1978): 547–550.

Ascher, L. Michael, David E. Scholte, and John B. Grayson. "Enhancing the Effectiveness of Paradoxical Intention in Treating Travel Restriction in Agoraphobia." *Behavior Therapy* 17 (1986): 124–130.

Ascher, L. Michael, and Ralph MacMillan Turner. "A comparison of two methods for the administration of paradoxical intention." *Behavior Research & Therapy* 18 (1980): 121–126.

Ascher, L. Michael, and Ralph MacMillan Turner. "Paradoxical Intention and Insomnia: An Experimental Investigation." *Behavior Research & Therapy* 17 (1979): 408–411.

Boeringa, J. Alexander. "Blushing: A Modified Behavioral Intervention Using Paradoxical Intention." *Psychotherapy: Theory, Research and Practice* 20, no. 4 (Winter 1983): 441–444.

Boeschemeyer, Uwe. "Logogeriatrics." *The International Forum for Logotherapy* 5, no. 1 (Spring–Summer 1982): 9–15.

Cohen, David. "The Frankl Meaning." *Human Behavior* 6, no. 7 (July 1977): 56–62.

Crumbaugh, James C. "The Seeking of Noetic Goals Test (SONG): A Complementary Scale to the Purpose in Life Test (PIL)." *Journal of Clinical Psychology* 33, no. 3 (July 1977): 900–907.

Crumbaugh, James C., and Leonard T. Maholick. "An Experimental Study in Existentialism: The Psychometric Approach to Frankl's Concept of Noögenic Neurosis." *Journal of Clinical Psychology* 20 (1964): 200–207.

Dansart, Bernard. "Development of a Scale to Measure Attitudinal Values as Defined by Viktor Frankl." Ph.D. diss., Northern Illinois University, 1974.

"The Doctor and the Soul: Dr. Viktor Frankl." *Harvard Medical Alumni Bulletin* 36 no. 1 (Fall 1961): 8.

Eisner, Harry R. "Purpose in life as a Function of Locus of Control and Attitudinal Values: a Test of Two of Viktor Frankl's Concepts." Ph.D. diss., Marquette University, 1978.

Eng, Erling. "The Akedah, Oedipus, and Dr. Frankl." *Psychotherapy: Theory, Research and Practice* 16, no. 3 (Fall 1979): 269–271.

Fabry, Joseph. "Some Practical Hints About Paradoxical Intention." *The International Forum for Logotherapy* 5, no. 1 (Spring–Summer 1982): 25–30.

Finck, Willis C. "The Viktor E. Frankl Merit Award." *The International Forum for Logotherapy* 5, no. 2 (Fall–Winter 1982): 73.

Frankl, Viktor E. "Logos and Existence in Psychotherapy." *American Journal of Psychotherapy* 7 (1953): 8–15.

———. "The Concept of Man in Psychotherapy" (paper read before the Royal Society of Medicine, Section of Psychiatry, London, England, June 1954). *Pastoral Psychology* 6 (1955): 16–26.

———. "On Logotherapy and Existential Analysis" (paper read before the Association for the Advancement of Psychoanalysis, New York, April 1957). *American Journal of Psychoanalysis* 18 (1958): 28–37.

———. "The Search for Meaning." *Saturday Review* (13 Sept. 1958).

———. "The Spiritual Dimension in Existential Analysis and Logotherapy" (paper read before the Fourth International Congress of Psychotherapy, Barcelona, Sept. 1958). *Journal of Individual Psychology* 15 (1959): 157–165.

———. "Paradoxical Intention: A Logotherapeutic Technique" (paper read before the American Association for the Advancement of Psychotherapy, New York, Feb. 1960). *American Journal of Psychotherapy* 14 (1960): 520–535.

———. "Logotherapy and Existential Analysis: A Review" (paper read before the Symposium on Logotherapy, 6th International Congress of Psychotherapy, London, August 1964). *American Journal of Psychotherapy* 20 (1966): 252–260.

———. "Logotherapy." The Israel Annals of Psychiatry and Related Disciplines 7 (1967): 142–155.

———. "The Feeling of Meaninglessness: A Challenge to Psychotherapy." *The American Journal of Psychoanalysis* 32, no. 1 (1972): 85–89.

———. "Encounter: The Concept and Its Vulgarization." *The Journal of the American Academy of Psychoanalysis* 1, no. 1 (1973): 73–83.

———. "Endogenous Depression and Noögenic Neurosis." *The International Forum for Logotherapy* 2, no. 2 (Summer–Fall 1979): 38–40.

———. "Psychotherapy on its Way to Rehumanization." *The International Forum for Logotherapy* 3, no. 2 (Fall 1980): 3–9.

———. "The Future of Logotherapy." *The International Forum for Logotherapy* 4, no. 2 (Fall–Winter 1981): 71–78.

———. "The Meaning Crisis in the First World and Hunger in the Third World." *The International Forum for Logotherapy* 7, no. 1 (Spring–Summer 1984): 5–7.

Garfield, Charles A. "A Psychometric and Clinical Investigation of Frankl's Concept of Existential Vacuum and of Anomie." *Psychiatry* 36 (1973): 396–408.

Gerz, Hans O. "The Treatment of the Phobic and the Obsessive-Compulsive Patient Using Paradoxical Intention sec. Viktor E. Frankl." *Journal of Neuropsychiatry* 3, no. 6 (July–Aug. 1962): 375–387.

———. "Experience with the Logotherapeutic Technique of Paradoxical Intention in the Treatment of Phobic and Obsessive-Compulsive Patients" (paper read at the Symposium of Logotherapy at the 6th International Congress of Psychotherapy, London, England, Aug. 1964). *American Journal of Psychiatry* 123, no. 5 (Nov. 1966): 548–553.

Giorgi, Bruno. "The Belfast Test: A New Psychometric Approach to Logotherapy." *The International Forum for Logotherapy* 5, no. 1 (Spring–Summer 1982): 31–37.

Greenberg, R. P., and R. Pies. "Is paradoxical intention risk-free?" *Journal of Clinical Psychiatry* 44 (1983): 66–69.

Hall, Mary Harrington. "A Conversation with Viktor Frankl of Vienna." *Psychology Today* 1, no. 9 (Feb. 1968): 56–63.

Hatcher, Gordon. "A Study of Viktor E. Frankl's and Karl A. Menninger's Concepts of Love." Ph.D. diss., University of the Pacific, 1968.

Havens, Leston L. "Paradoxical Intention." *Psychiatry and Social Science Review* 2 (1968): 16–19.

Holmes, R. M. "Meaning and Responsibility: A Comparative Analysis of the Concept of the Responsible Self in Search of Meaning in the Thought of Viktor Frankl and H. Richard Niebuhr with Certain Implications for the Church's Ministry to the University." Ph.D. diss., Pacific School of Religion, 1965.

Hsu, L. K. George, and Stuart Lieberman. "Paradoxical Intention in the Treatment of Chronic Anorexia Nervosa" *American Journal of Psychiatry* 139 (1982): 650–653

Hutzell, Robert R., and Thomas J. Peterson. "An MMPI Existential Vacuum Scale for Logotherapy Research." *The International Forum for Logotherapy* 8, no. 2 (Fall–Winter 1985): 97–100.

Hyman, William. "Practical Aspects of Logotherapy in Neurosurgery." *Existential Psychiatry* 7 (1969): 99–101.

Kaczanowski, Godfryd. "Frankl's Logotherapy." *American Journal of Psychiatry* 117 (1960): 563.

Kalmar, Stephen S. "The Viktor E. Frankl Scholarship 1983." *The International Forum for Logotherapy* 6, no. 2 (Fall–Winter 1983): 84–85

Klapper, Naomi. "On Being Human: A Comparative Study of Abraham J Heschel and Viktor Frankl." Ph.D. diss., Jewish Theological Seminary of America, 1973.

Kovacs, George. "The Philosophy of Death in Viktor E. Frankl." *Journal of Phenomenological Psychology* 13, no. 2 (Fall 1982): 197–209.

———. "Viktor E. Frankl's Place in Philosophy." *The International Forum for Logotherapy* 8, no. 1 (Spring–Summer 1985): 17–21.

Lamontagne, Ives. "Treatment of Erythrophobia by Paradoxical Intention." *The Journal of Nervous and Mental Disease* 166, no. 4 (1978): 304–306.

Lantz, James E. "Dereflection in Family Therapy with Schizophrenic Clients." *The International Forum for Logotherapy* 5, no 2 (Fall–Winter 1982): 119–122.

Lazar, Edward. "Logotherapeutic Support Groups for Cardiac Patients." *The International Forum for Logotherapy* 7, no. 2 (Fall–Winter 1984): 85–88.

Leslie, Robert C. "Viktor Frankl and C. G. Jung." *Shiggaion* 10, no. 2 (Dec. 1961).

Levinson, Jay Irwin. "A Combination of Paradoxical Intention and Dereflection." *The International Forum for Logotherapy* 2. no. 2 (Summer–Fall 1979): 40–41.

Lukas, Elisabeth S. "New Ways for Dereflection." *The International Forum for Logotherapy* 4, no. 1 (Spring–Summer 1981): 13–28.

———. "Validation of Logotherapy." *The International Forum for Logotherapy* 4, no. 2 (Fall–Winter 1981): 116–125.

———. "The 'Birthmarks' of Paradoxical Intention." *The International Forum for Logotherapy* 5, no. 1 (Spring–Summer 1982): 20–24.

Maslow, A. H. "Comments on Dr. Frankl's Paper." *Journal of Humanistic Psychology* 6 (1966): 107–112.

Mavissakalian, M., L. Michelson, D. Greenwald, S. Kornblith, and M. Greenwald. "Cognitive-behavioral treatment of agoraphobia: Paradoxical intention vs. self-statement training." *Behavior Research and Therapy* 21 (1983): 75–86.

"Meaning in Life." *Time* (2 Feb. 1968): 38–40.

Meier, Augustine. "Frankl's 'Will to Meaning' as Measured by the Purpose-in-Life Test in Relation to Age and Sex Differences." *Journal of Clinical Psychology* 30 (1974): 384–386.

Michelson, L., and M. A. Ascher. "Paradoxical Intention in the treatment of agoraphobia and other anxiety disorders." *J. behav. Ther. exp. Psychiat.* 15 (1984): 215–220.

Milan, M. A., and D. J. Kolko. "Paradoxical intention in the treatment of obsessional flatulence ruminations." *J. Behav. Ther. exp. Psychiat.* 13 (1982): 167–172.

Minton, Gary. "A Comparative Study of the Concept of Conscience in the Writings of Sigmund Freud and Viktor Frankl." Ph.D. diss., New Orleans Baptist Theological Seminary, 1967.

Murphy, Leonard. "Extent of Purpose-in-Life and Four Frankl Proposed Life Objectives." Ph.D. diss., University of Ottawa, 1967.

Nackord, Ernest J., Jr. "A College Test of Logotherapeutic Concepts." *The International Forum for Logotherapy* 6, no. 2 (Fall–Winter 1983): 117–122.

Newton, Joseph R. "Therapeutic Paradoxes, Paradoxical Intentions, and Negative Practice." *American Journal of Psychotherapy* 22 (1968): 68–81.

Noonan, J. Robert. "A Note on an Eastern Counterpart of Frankl's Paradoxical Intention." *Psychologia* 12 (1969): 147–149.

O'Connell, Walter E. "Viktor Frankl, the Adlerian?" *Psychiatric Spectator* 6, no. 11 (1970): 13–14.

Ott, B. D. "The efficacy of paradoxical intention in the treatment of sleep onset insomnia under differential feedback conditions." Ph.D. diss., Hofstra University, 1980.

Ott, B. D., B. A. Levine, and L. M. Ascher. "Manipulating the explicit demand of paradoxical intention instructions." *Behavioral Psychotherapy* 11 (1983): 25–35.

Porter, Jack Nusan. "The Affirmation of Life After the Holocaust: The Con-

tributions of Bettelheim, Lifton and Frankl." *The Association for Humanistic Psychology Newsletter* (August–September 1980) 9–11.

Relinger, Helmut, Philip H. Bornstein, and Dan M. Mungas. "Treatment of Insomnia by Paradoxical Intention: A Time-Series Analysis." *Behavior Therapy* 9 (1978): 955–959.

Sargent, George A. "Combining Paradoxical Intention with Behavior Modification." *The International Forum for Logotherapy* 6, no. 1 (Spring–Summer 1983): 28–30.

Schachter, Stanley J. "Bettelheim and Frankl: Contradicting Views of the Holocaust." *Reconstructionist* 26, no. 20 (10 Feb. 1961): 6–11.

Solyom, L., J. Garza-Perez, B. L. Ledwidge, and C. Solyom. "Paradoxical Intention in the Treatment of Obsessive Thoughts: A Pilot Study." *Comprehensive Psychiatry* 13, no. 3 (May 1972): 291–297.

Timms, M. W. H. "Treatment of chronic blushing by paradoxical intention." *Behavioral Psychotherapy* 8 (1980): 59–61.

Turner, Ralph M., and L. Michael Ascher. "Controlled Comparison of Progressive Relaxation, Stimulus Control, and Paradoxical Intention Therapies for Insomnia." *Journal of Consulting and Clinical Psychology* 47, no. 3 (1979): 500–508.

Victor, Ralph G., and Carolyn M. Krug. "Paradoxical Intention in the Treatment of Compulsive Gambling." *American Journal of Psychotherapy* 21, no. 4 (Oct. 1967): 808–814.

Waugh, Robert J. L. "Paradoxical Intention." *American Journal of Psychiatry* 123, no. 10 (April 1967): 1305–1306.

Yoder, James D. "A Child, Paradoxical Intention, and Consciousness." *The International Forum for Logotherapy* 6, no. 1 (Spring–Summer 1983): 19–21.

4. Films, Records, and Tapes

Frankl, Viktor E. "Frankl and the Search for Meaning." A film produced by Psychological Films, 110 North Wheeler Street, Orange, CA 92669.

———. "The Rehumanization of Psychotherapy: A Workshop Sponsored by the Division of Psychotherapy of the American Psychological Association." A videotape. Address inquiries to Division of Psycho-

therapy, American Psychological Association, 1200 Seventeenth Street, N.W., Washington, DC 20036.

———. "Human Freedom and Meaning in Life" and "Self-Transcendence—Therapeutic Agent in Sexual Neurosis." Videotapes. Copies of the tapes can be ordered for a service fee. Address inquiries to the Manager, Learning Resource Distribution Center, United States International University, San Diego, CA 92131.

———. Two 5-hour lectures, part of the course, Human Behavior 616, "Man in Search of Meaning." (Winter quarter 1976). Copies of the videotapes can be ordered for a service fee. Address inquiries to the Manager, Learning Resource Distribution Center, United States International University, San Diego, CA 92131.

———. "A panel of experts from the fields of medicine, anthropology, psychiatry, religion, social work, philosophy, and clinical psychology, discussing topics of interest with Dr. Frankl at the First World Congress of Logotherapy, San Diego, 1980." A 51-minute videotape ($53.00). Make check payable to the Institute of Logotherapy, 2000 Dwight Way, Berkeley, CA 94704. When ordering, state kind of tape wanted (Beta, VHS, or ¾″ U-matic).

———. "The Meaning of Suffering." A lecture (31 Jan. 1983). Available for rental or purchase from the Department of Audio-Visual Services, Cedars-Sinai Medical Center, 8700 Beverly Boulevard, Los Angeles, CA 90048 (Audiocassette, $15.00; Videocassette, $50.00).

———. "The Will to Meaning." A public lecture recorded at Dallas Brooks Hall, Melbourne (21 July 1985). A Videocassette ($75.00). Address inquiries to the Viktor Frankl Committee, P. O. Box 321, Boronia, 3155, Australia.

———. "Meaninglessness: Today's Dilemma." An audiotape produced by Creative Resources, 4800 West Waco Drive, Waco, TX 76703.

———. "Man's Search for Meaning: An Introduction to Logotherapy." Recording for the Blind, Inc., 215 East 58th Street, New York, NY 10022.

———. "Youth in Search of Meaning." Word Cassette Library (WCL 0205), 4800 West Waco Drive, Waco, TX 76703 ($5.95).

———. "Theory and Therapy of Neurosis: A Series of Lectures Delivered at

the United States International University in San Diego, California."
Eight 90-minute cassettes produced by Creative Resources, 4800 West
Waco Drive, Waco, TX 76703 ($79.95).

———. "Man in Search of Meaning: A Series of Lectures Delivered at the
United States International University in San Diego, California."
Fourteen 90-minute cassettes produced by Creative Resources, 4800
West Waco Drive, Waco, TX 76703 ($139.95).

———. "The Neurotization of Humanity and the Re-Humanization of Psychotherapy." Two cassettes. Argus Communications, 7440 Natchez
Avenue, Niles, IL 60648 ($14.00).

———. "Therapy Through Meaning." Psychotherapy Tape Library (T 656),
Post Graduate Center, 124 East 8th Street, New York, NY 10016
($15.00).

———. "Existential Psychotherapy." Two cassettes. The Center for Cassette
Studies, 8110 Webb Avenue, North Hollywood, VA 91605.

———. "The Defiant Power of the Human Spirit: A Message of Meaning in
a Chaotic World." Address at the Berkeley Community Theater (2
Nov. 1979). A 90-minute cassette tape ($6.00). Available at the
Institute of Logotherapy, 2000 Dwight Way, Berkeley, CA 94704.

———. "The Meaning of Suffering for the Terminally Ill." International
Seminar on Terminal Care, Montreal (8 Oct. 1980). Audio Tran-
scripts, Ltd. (Code 25-107-80 A and B), P. O. Box 487, Times
Square Station, New York, NY 10036.

———. "The Rehumanization of Psychotherapy." Lecture on occasion of
the inauguration of the Logotherapy Counseling Center of Atlanta
and Athens (14 Nov. 1980). An audiocassette (1/404/542-4766). Available from the Center for Continuing Education, University of Georgia,
Athens, GA 30602.

———. "Man in Search of Ultimate Meaning." Oskar Pfister Award Lecture
at the American Psychiatric Association's annual meeting (Dallas
1985). Audiocassette (L 19-186-85) produced by Audio Transcripts,
610 Madison Street, Alexandria, VA 22314 ($10.00).

Frankl, Viktor E., Robin W. Goodenough, Iver Hand, Oliver A. Phillips,
and Edith Weisskopf-Joelson. "Logotherapy: Theory and Practice. A
Symposium Sponsored by the Division of Psychotherapy of the

American Psychological Association." An audiotape. Address inquiries to Division of Psychotherapy, American Psychological Association, 1200 Seventeenth Street, N.W., Washington, DC 20036.

Frankl, Viktor E., and Huston Smith. "Value Dimensions in Teaching." A color television film produced by Hollywood Animators, Inc., for the California Junior College Association. Rental or purchase through Dr. Rex Wignall, Director, Chaffey College, Alta Loma, CA 91701.

"The Humanistic Revolution: Pioneers in Perspective." Interviews with leading humanistic psychologists: Abraham Maslow, Gardner Murphy, Carl Rogers, Rollo May, Paul Tillich, Frederick Perls, Viktor Frankl, and Alan Watts. Psychological Films, 110 North Wheeler Street, Orange, CA 92669 (sale $250; rental $20).

Leslie, Robert C. (moderator), with Joseph Fabry and Mary Ann Finch. "A Conversation with Viktor E. Frankl on Occasion of the Inauguration of the 'Frankl Library and Memorabilia' at the Graduate Theological Union on 12 Feb. 1977," A videotape. Copies may be obtained from Professor Robert C. Leslie, 1798 Scenic Avenue, Berkeley, CA 94709.

5. Braille Editions

Fabry, Joseph B. *The Pursuit of Meaning: Logotherapy Applied to Life.* Available on loan at no cost from Woodside Terrace Kiwanis Braille Project, 850 Longview Road, Hillsborough, CA 94010.

Frankl, Viktor E. *Man's Search for Meaning: An Introduction to Logotherapy.* Available on loan at no cost from Woodside Terrace Kiwanis Braille Project, 850 Longview Road, Hillsborough, CA 94010.

ABOUT THE AUTHOR

VIKTOR E. FRANKL, M.D., Ph.D., is professor of neurology and psychiatry at the University of Vienna Medical School and distinguished professor of logotherapy at the United States International University in San Diego, California. He is the originator of what has come to be called the Third Viennese School of Psychotherapy (after Freud's psychoanalysis and Adler's individual psychology): the school of logotherapy.

Dr. Frankl's first article was published in 1924 in the *International Journal of Psychoanalysis*. Since then he has written twenty-seven books, which have been translated into virtually every major language in the world. The American edition of his book *Man's Search for Meaning* has sold over two million copies to date.

Dr. Frankl has been a visiting professor at Harvard, Southern Methodist, Stanford, and Duquesne universities, and has had honorary doctorate degrees conferred upon him by twelve universities. He is president of the Austrian Medical Society of Psychotherapy and an honorary member of the Austrian Academy of Sciences. In 1985 he was awarded the Oskar Pfister Award by the American Psychiatric Association.

Dr. Frankl's works in English translation include *The Doctor and the Soul: From Psychotherapy to Logotherapy; Man's Search for Meaning: An Introduction to Logotherapy; Psychotherapy and Existentialism: Selected Papers on Logotherapy; The Will to Meaning: Foundations and Applications of Logotherapy; The Unconscious God: Psychotherapy and Theology;* and *The Unheard Cry for Meaning: Psychotherapy and Humanism*. He lives in Vienna.